MOUND BUILDERS

Edgar Cayce's Forgotten Record of Ancient America

by
Gregory L. Little, Ed.D.
John Van Auken,
& Lora H. Little, Ed. D.

Eagle Wing Books, Inc.
Memphis, TN

Published by
Eagle Wing Books, Inc.
P. O. Box 9972
Memphis, TN 38190
web: www.eaglewingbooks.com
Special web site for updates on the Hall of Records:
www.yucatanhallofrecords.com

ISBN: 0-940829-36-3
Retail Price: $16.95
First U.S.A. Printing: August 2001

Table Of Contents

Preface

I value truth, and it really bothers me to see fakes and frauds...
Martin Gardner says that "if a man persists in advancing views that are
contradicted by all available evidence...he will rightfully be dubbed a crank...
Stephen Williams (1991) *Fantastic Archaeology*

This book has been written as an attempt to evaluate the specific claims of the famous psychic Edgar Cayce on the American mound building culture. It is not an academic text, nor do we profess it to be comprehensive. But we do assert that its treatment of Cayce is fair and sincere.

Cayce's health readings have been found to be over 80% accurate, but the apparent "failure" of some of his predictions has led many to believe that *everything* he said was inaccurate or a guess. Cayce did not claim infallibility. In fact, he said that, under some circumstances, a "reading" could be influenced by the intentions and mindset of those asking him questions. This most certainly occurred, but not as often as some people assume.

The scope of the Cayce readings was immense. Cayce is acknowledged as the "father of the holistic health movement" by editorial writers of the American Medical Association. His initial intention in his psychic readings was to provide health suggestions for people who found that the medical treatment they were receiving was ineffective. The success of the health readings brought a degree of fame and notoriety to Cayce. This fame led to Cayce becoming involved in a completely different type of reading. These readings involved reincarnation — an idea that initially disturbed him. But, in the course of these new "life readings," a remarkable outline of ancient history emerged. Cayce described man as being far older than anyone ever suspected and he told of sunken continents — Mu and Atlantis.

The history that emerged from the Cayce readings involved virtually the entire world. His detailed information on Egypt and the Maya civilizations has received the most attention. However, almost completely over-looked in this vast material was what Cayce told us about ancient America. Books and articles on Cayce usually mention that he discussed the American mound builder culture. But not much more information is provided. As such, Cayce's mound builder readings are a "lost" or "forgotten" record.

Since 1997, a remarkable series of discoveries has brought Cayce's mound builder ideas to the forefront. Many of the ideas he professed, simply impossible at the time they were expressed, seem to have been confirmed by the newer research. This book reviews and discusses these ideas. Our conclusion is that Cayce was at least 77% correct in his assertions about ancient America. Only 3% of his ideas appear to be wrong. Another 20% await further evidence.

Academic archaeology portrays Cayce as a "cult archaeologist" and alleges that it has given Cayce a fair hearing. Some archaeology textbooks discuss Cayce and all of them dismiss him rudely. Kenneth Feder's (1990) book, *Frauds, Myths, and Mysteries: Science and Pseudoscience in Archaeology* had this to say about Cayce: "Self-proclaimed psychic Edgar Cayce claimed that knowledge gained from Atlantean texts (Cayce 1968; Noorbergen 1982) enabled him to predict the future and effect cures on terminally ill people."

Stephen Williams's (1991) textbook, *Fantastic Archaeology: The Wild Side of North American Prehistory*, states: "Many gathered at the feet of the late Edgar Cayce..." He then mentions Atlantis and tells us, "in fact, the sunken continent is mentioned in more than 30 percent of Cayce's readings." He

Figure 1
Edgar Cayce late in life. His story has been inaccurately portrayed by many archae-ologists trying to "debunk" him. He has been labelled a "cult archaeologist," a "crank," and a "pseudoscientist." But a careful reading of the arguments against him shows a totally different story.

continues, Cayce had "an extraordinary 'Atlantis Channel'" to which he adds: "most of what he said about Atlantis, for example, sounded like reworked Donnelly or plagiarized Blavatsky." Then he calls Cayce a faith healer and links Cayce to James Churchward (author of several books on Lemuria): "Interestingly names like Churchward pop up in his readings and are duly recorded."

Many other archaeology "debunking books" discuss Cayce. For example, in their (1999) book, *Ancient Mysteries*, Peter James and Nick Thorpe write, "Cayce would place himself in a trance and allow himself to be possessed by 'entities' from their earlier lives."

Those knowledgeable about Cayce will immediately recognize *all* of the academic archaeologists' statements about Cayce to be completely inaccurate. Cayce never claimed to have Atlantean texts or that he could heal the terminally ill. Nor was he a "self-professed psychic." People did not gather at his feet nor was he possessed by entities from past lives. Of all of Cayce's readings, less than 5% mention Atlantis. When *only* the life readings are considered, 28% mention Atlantis, not "more than 30%." Cayce never wrote books, so the idea of him plagiarizing Donnelly or Blavatsky is simply impossible. And Cayce certainly was not a faith healer. Finally, *not a single Cayce reading* ever mentioned the name "Churchward."

In July 2001, the first author of this book contacted two of the authors of these archaeology textbooks to inquire about the inaccurate statements. The discussions revealed that the authors believed that Edgar Evans Cayce,

Figure 2
Williams' text, widely used in academic archaeology, confuses Cayce's son, Edgar Evans Cayce, with the psychic. The book also alleges that Cayce plagiarized Blavatsky and that the name "Churchward" popped up over and over in Cayce's readings. In fact, the name "Churchward" did not appear in a single Cayce reading. Based on the reaction by Williams, he meets his own definitions of a "crank" and a "pseudoscientist."

FANTASTIC ARCHAEOLOGY

THE WILD SIDE
OF
NORTH AMERICAN
PREHISTORY

Stephen Williams

Edgar Cayce's son and the author of several books on Atlantis, *was* Edgar Cayce the psychic. To them, Edgar Evans Cayce's books, apparently, *were* the Edgar Cayce readings. Churchward was mentioned in Edgar Evans Cayce's books — but not in any readings. The other mistakes came from the academics not actually reading the books and garbling various stories and figures.

One of the authors, Williams, refused to believe any of it and insisted that *all of his statements were completely correct and accurate.* He explained repeatedly that a person without advanced archaeological training could not possibly understand his evaluation of Cayce. As "a 40-year teacher of archaeology at Harvard," Williams stated his evaluations of Cayce were completely factual. He refused to consider changing anything in his text and wasn't open to the "idea" that Edgar Evans Cayce and Edgar Cayce the psychic were different people. He ended the discussion by citing a suggested reading list. In his book, Williams professed that it was written because he valued "truth," but that apparently means he values what *he believes* is truth — or what he *wants others to believe* as truth.

In stark contrast to Williams, Dr. Kenneth Feder of Central Connecticut State University handled it as a genuine scientist and professional. He patiently considered all of the contrary evidence given him and rechecked his sources. He sincerely wanted his book to be accurate and he clearly valued the ethics of the situation. After realizing his misunderstandings about Cayce, Feder was apologetic and vowed a revision in his book.

The brief discussion above was provided to illustrate two points. First, Edgar Cayce's statements about ancient history have *not* received a fair or genuine hearing by academics. What is written in the textbooks about him is untrue. Secondly, the diametrically opposed reactions by the two archaeologists (Williams and Feder) appear to be the rule in modern archaeology rather than the exception. Modern archaeology is deeply torn between several factions. Since 1997, the major beliefs in American archaeology have been shattered. Some archaeologists appear willing to do anything to hold onto the past ideology while others are excited about the new information emerging from new technologies. The clashes between these factions will be occasionally mentioned in this book.

The present book, while primarily interested in Cayce's mound builder ideas, also discusses a number of other issues. The scope of Cayce's readings on ancient America was wide, and this necessitated a scope larger than the mounds. But the story that emerged is remarkable. We think you will agree.

Chapter 1

Discovering
The Mysterious
Mound Builders

The most important mysteries may be those in your own back yard. — The authors.

If you are reading this anywhere in the Americas, take a few moments and look outside. Many thousands of years ago people were there. Countless lives were lived and long-forgotten events took place there. Conservative estimates have shown us that, in 1492, when Columbus "discovered" America, at least 57.3 million people lived in the Americas.[1] That's not a misprint. *It is 57.3 million.*

If you live in the eastern half of the United States, chances are there are mounds only a few miles from you. Neither you nor your neighbors may be aware of their existence, but they are there, nonetheless. Within only a few hours driving distance from you there are probably very large mounds and ritual earthworks. Some of these constructions may be miles in length. One set of these ancient complexes in Ohio apparently formed a straight road nearly 60 miles in length and over 100 feet wide connecting Newark with Chillicothe. At the confluence of the Scioto River with the Ohio River another incredible group of mounds and earthworks was constructed around 100 A.D. Three sets of parallel walls forming 160-foot wide walkways extended for over 20 miles connecting three incredible, massive, and drastically different shaped earthworks together. These walkways extended across the Ohio River from one side to the other — and then back. Also in Ohio there remain several enormous circular and octagon-shaped enclosures, many of which perfectly predict lunar movements and eclipses.

Near East St. Louis, Illinois a 100-foot tall earthen, truncated pyramid still exists. Its base is larger than the Great Pyramid at Giza and a maze of other mounds and several "woodhenge" features also remain at this ancient city that once had a population of over 25,000. Just south of Jackson, Tennessee lies a massive mound complex with a circular embankment all aligned to star risings. It forms a massive, 1000-acre medicine wheel. In the states of Iowa and Wisconsin are hundreds of mounds built in the shapes of birds, panthers, bears, and numerous other animal forms. In Georgia a massive eagle mound is formed from piled white quartz. A quarter-mile long serpent mound can still be visited in Ohio. Ancient hilltop forts still exist in many states. Almost every state East of the Rocky Mountains still contains mounds and other ancient structures. In addition, definite evidence now shows that ancient Hebrews were in the Americas along with visitors from many other areas of the world. Ancient America was truly a melting pot of cultures and people.

Artifacts recovered from mounds over the past 200 years have only deepened the mystery. Carved tablets, copper implements, statues, and many anomalous, completely enigmatic finds have been made.

Despite the fact that the majority of mounds from ancient America have already been destroyed, America remains covered in mounds and enshrouded in great mysteries. Ironically, while most Americans remain fascinated with Egypt, Peru, and the Maya, an incredible enigma lies in our own back yard. In this book we hope to help you unravel that enigma and begin to appreciate the genuine mystery that has been patiently awaiting your attention.

Figure 3
Copper falcon from mound excavation at Ohio's Hopewell site.
Photo — National Park Service.

Speculation on the Mounds

When the first European explorers and settlers of historic times pushed into the "New World," they were incredulous as they encountered fantastic earthworks, gigantic mounds, and artifacts of astonishing quality and beauty. Literally tens of thousands of mounds were found and the intricate design and obvious sacred geometry of the ancient works were astounding. Few Europeans believed that the "savage" and primitive native "Indians" then occupying the continent had anything to do with the mounds. A mythical race of advanced "mound builders" was quickly theorized to have built the complexes in the remote past. The settlers, who constantly battled the native Indians as they methodically took their land, found it hard to believe that the mounds were built by the Indians. The natives were looked down upon as primitive and savage and many Whites speculated that the advanced culture of mound builders had been massacred by the native Indians. Some people immediately speculated that Atlanteans, the "Lost Tribes" of ancient Israel, survivors of the sunken continent Mu, or other advanced peoples built the mounds. *The Hope of Israel*, published in 1652 by Menasseh ben Israel, argued that the Native Americans were, in fact, remnants of the fabled Lost Tribes.

Archaeologists fought rampant speculation with quiet fieldwork. In 1848, the first true comprehensive work on America's mounds was published as the Smithsonian's initial publication. That monumental work (*Ancient Monuments of the Mississippi Valley*, Squier & Davis) concluded that the ancestors of the Native Americans constructed the mounds. The Bureau of Ethnology, a branch of the Smithsonian, continued to sponsor field work and publications on mounds. In 1894, Cyrus Thomas' massive 742-page *Report on the Mound Explorations of the Bureau of Ethnology* was issued. It also stated that the mounds were the work of the ancestors of Native Americans. However, with the publication of Ignatius Donnelly's books on Atlantis and James Churchward's later books on Mu, questions about the origins of the mounds have continued to this day.

Fueling these speculations was the fact that the native tribes occupying the eastern portion of the New World often couldn't explain who built the mounds or what their purpose was. It is true that most mounds in the eastern portion of the new world were abandoned by the time the first settlers arrived. However, in the deep south, many mound complexes were still in use — but were soon destined to be abandoned and largely forgotten. The chroniclers of Hernando DeSoto's 1541 march through the southern U.S. left us a written record and even illustrations depicting of the use of mounds by the natives. However, for several hundred years, few people had access to DeSoto's chronicles, and they were written in Spanish. Thus, almost no one realized that some native groups still built mounds and practiced the culture centering on them.

Perhaps the most powerful contributing factor to the natives' lack of knowledge of their own past was revealed in several articles written in the early 1700s. Englishman John Lawson trekked more than 500 miles through the largely "unexplored" Carolina area in 1701. Lawson wrote that less than 1 in 6 Indians had survived the ongoing smallpox epidemic lasting between 1650 and 1700. Entire villages were decimated, to which Lawson added, "without leaving one Indian alive." In 1710, the Etowah Indians were said to have forgotten the old ways: "They keep their festivals and can tell but little of the reasons: Their old men are dead."[2] In his now-classic book, *The Mound Builders*, Robert Silverberg wrote that the Indians, "no longer knew that it was their own great-great-great-grandfathers who built the mounds."

Fascination with the mounds was a near obsession with many in the 1600s and 1700s. Thomas Jefferson and other prominent Americans were deeply involved in some of the earliest excavations into mounds. While Jefferson became convinced that the ancestors of the historic tribes built the mounds, many others were unconvinced and remained believers in a lost race.

Edgar Cayce Enters The Debate

Until recent times, modern archaeology has had little debate about the origin and purposes of the mounds. Recent developments have, however, placed almost all of the preconceived notions about the mounds and America's ancient history in serious question. Beginning in the early 1990s, several new technologies have been brought to bear on some of archaeology's most important issues. The results have been astonishing: just about everything archaeologists have ardently believed about ancient America is wrong. Later chapters will detail these findings, however, it should be pointed out that what is emerging from the new evidence is disturbing to archaeology. Many of the ideas archaeologists have depicted as "cultish," crackpot, and wild are now being confirmed

Often overlooked in this debate are the details provided by Edgar Cayce on ancient America in his psychic readings. Although mainstream archaeology describes Cayce as a "cult archaeologist" and essentially ignores his ideas, the fact is that many of his pronouncements on history have proven to be correct. It is our contention that Cayce's ideas merit a fair review given the current developments in archaeology. From 1924 until his death in 1945, Cayce provided a wealth of information on pre-history in the Americas. Most people have preferred to focus on Cayce's speculations on Atlantis, Egypt, and Central America. This book will focus almost exclusively on Cayce's ideas about America.

Edgar Cayce

The Pennyroyal Museum in downtown Hopkinsville, Kentucky is a unique and fascinating archive primarily depicting the struggle of the tobacco growing south in the post-Civil War era. However, the major attraction of the museum is probably its display on Edgar Cayce, America's most famous and mysterious psychic. The museum does an excellent job of detailing what day-to-day life was like for Cayce from the time he was born near Hopkinsville in 1877 until his death in Virginia Beach in 1945. The museum also houses many of Cayce's personal and family items including the couch upon which he reclined while giving psychic readings. What is most striking about the exhibit is how it humanizes Cayce showing clearly how humble he was and how normal his life was in most respects.

While many aspects of his day-to-day life were normal, Edgar had a series of experiences that made it apparent that he was anything but ordinary. By 1893, Edgar had already gained the reputation of being somewhat "different." He had shown a remarkable ability to memorize the content of books by simply sleeping on them and he was also known for having visions of little people and conversing with deceased relatives.

At the age of 13 he had a visitation from a glowing female angel. He would be granted the ability to heal others, according to the angel, a promise that was to be fulfilled in an unusual manner and to a far greater extent than a young Edgar ever dreamed. As the vast majority of readers already know, Edgar Cayce was indeed able to provide healing to people by diagnosing their physical condition psychically and then suggesting corrective actions. Interestingly, Cayce's first psychic health reading was for himself. At the age of twenty-one, he developed paralysis of the throat muscles which resulted in the loss of his voice. His doctors couldn't determine a cause nor find a treatment. In desperation, he turned to a stage hypnotist who was able to recover his voice while under hypnotic trance. However, when the trance was ended, the voice paralysis returned. Cayce was subsequently hypnotized by Al Layne, a Hopkinsville hypnotist and osteopath who asked the entranced Edgar to diagnose himself and suggest a

Figure 4
A 29 year-old Edgar Cayce;
taken while he working in
Montgomery, Alabama in 1909.
Photo — Courtesy A.R.E.

remedy. The still entranced Edgar instructed Layne to suggest that the blood
flow to Edgar's throat area be increased. When the suggestion was given,
Cayce's throat turned bright red. Then, while still under hypnosis, Cayce
recommended specific medication and manipulative therapy, which eventually aided in restoring his voice completely.

Realizing the potential of Edgar's ability, Layne suggested that Edgar
try the same hypnotic method to help others. Cayce soon established a
typical routine for entering a hypnotic state after going through a brief
routine. He would first loosen his tie and collar and then untie his shoes.
Next, he would recline on his back on his couch and fold his hands over
his solar plexus. After a few moments of deep breathing, his eyelids would
flutter and his breathing would become deep and rhythmical. This was a
signal to the conductor of the session (usually his wife, Gertrude) to make
contact with his subconscious by giving a suggestion. Unless this proce-
dure was timed to synchronize with his breathing, Cayce would move
beyond the trance state and simply fall asleep. However, once the suggestion was made, Cayce would proceed to describe the patient as though he
or she were sitting right next to him.

Layne's own stomach problems were the focus of Edgar's first health reading for others. Following the suggestions outlined in this reading, Layne's decade-long stomach problems disappeared and word of Cayce's ability rapidly spread. Physicians quickly became interested in investigating Cayce, and a 1910 article in *The New York Times* hailed Cayce as the "Sleeping Prophet," thus ensuring both his fame and the unending criticism of skeptics.

By the time he died on January 3, 1945, in Virginia Beach, Cayce had left 14,256 documented stenographic records of the readings he had given for more than 6,000 different people over a period of forty-three years, consisting of 49,135 pages. Over 9,000 of there readings were health related.[3]

Unfortunately, many of Cayce's health readings from his early years were not recorded. For example, it is believed that Edgar gave over 80 readings during 1901, the year he began working with Al Layne. Throughout the years, Edgar also received scattered requests to perform readings to help locate lost or buried treasure. Interestingly, these requests never led to the recovery of treasure. In addition, Edgar performed a long sequence of unsuccessful readings to find oil deposits. However, his health readings yielded successful results eventually inspiring the modern holistic health movement. Many of his treatments are currently receiving both clinical and scientific research attention within the medical community.

Edgar Cayce's fame remains great today and even continues to expand. Amazon.com lists 336 available books on Cayce; however, several hundred others have been published on him or the contents of his readings. A May 2001 search on the popular internet directory Yahoo showed 15,200 web pages devoted to Cayce while the broader Excite search engine showed an astonishing 2,875,740 web pages on him.

Accuracy of Cayce's Health Readings

Edgar Cayce is widely acknowledged as the "father of the holistic health movement."[3, 4] As such, it would be expected that Cayce's health suggestions would be given a great deal of credibility by medical science. Substantial anecdotal reports and follow-up letters from individuals given health readings by Cayce have indicated that the majority of those receiving health readings endorsed his accuracy. In his biography of Cayce, Sidney Kirkpatrick reviewed research that has been done to assess Cayce's health advice.[5] Kirkpatrick reported that, 14 of the 15 physicians who had treated patients who received readings (as surveyed by journalist Sherwood Eddy) gave Cayce a near perfect score. Even the one physician who was cautious had to acknowledge that the psychic's powers were "extraordinary." A 1971 study of Cayce's health readings published by Hugh Lynn Cayce and Edgar Evans Cayce found an overall 86 percent accuracy rate.

Even the most hardened skeptics usually acknowledge the correctness of Cayce's health readings — if only grudgingly. For example, Probe Ministries' website[6] article declaring Cayce as a false prophet states: "Cayce was a very effective healer and helped many people physically." *The Skeptic's Dictionary*, a website devoted to simplistically attacking claims of the paranormal as unsubstantiated, summarily dismisses all of Cayce's health readings as unscientific without any investigation or research or even a brief consideration of the research that has been done. However, it adds, "It is true, however, that many people considered themselves cured by Cayce and that's enough evidence for true believers."

Enter Atlantis & Reincarnation

While the health readings were initially the primary focus of the "work" of Cayce's life, a major development occurred in 1923. It was this development that created not only the fantastic popularity for Cayce's work, but also a barrage of criticism that lasts even to the present.

In 1923, Arthur Lammers, a wealthy Dayton printer and publisher, asked Cayce to come to Dayton and do a short series of readings that would focus on the source of Cayce's information and the underlying meaning of life. At first reluctant, Cayce eventually went to Dayton where a series of readings was held in the Phillips Hotel in August of that year. Little did they realize that Lammers' initial set of philosophical questions would lead to an entirely new way of using Cayce's strange abilities. It was during this line of questioning that the "sleeping" or entranced Cayce first began to talk about reincarnation as though it were as real and natural as the functioning of a physical body. What makes this particularly significant is that, for the most part, Cayce was unaware of the contents of his readings until he was given a report after awakening. When first confronted by these readings he and his family were both shocked and challenged. They were deeply religious people, doing this work to help others because that was what their Christian faith taught. As a child, Cayce began to read the Bible from front to back, eventually doing so for every year of his life. Reincarnation was definitely not part of the Cayce family's reality. Yet, the healings and help continued to come through the work of the readings. So, after much prayer and consideration, the Cayce family continued with the physical readings while cautiously reflecting on this strange philosophical material. Ultimately, the Cayces accepted the ideas, although not as "reincarnation," per se. Edgar Cayce preferred to call it "The Continuity of Life" since he felt that the Bible did contain much evidence that life, the true life in the Spirit, is continual.

These new life readings also gave an astonishing perspective on ancient history as they recounted individual's past lives. The lost continents of Atlantis and Mu were both detailed in Cayce's readings along with an unbelievable history of humanity. Included in Cayce's history was a sequence of cataclysmic events that reshaped the earth as one natural disaster was followed by another, often with assistance from an advanced, and arrogant humankind battling with itself.

Between 1923 and 1944, a total of 700 of Cayce's readings mentioned Atlantis.[7] However, many other readings also mentioned Lemuria (Mu), ancient America, and excursions into the Americas by those fleeing cataclysms in Atlantis, Mu, and elsewhere. The readings also asserted that the mound builder culture of America resulted from a blending of multiple groups. These included descendants of the Atlanteans who had migrated from the ancient Yucatan, survivors from Mu, remnants of the Lost Tribes of Israel, the Norse, and native peoples already present in the lands.

In addition, the readings stated that a portion of southwest America was occupied approximately 10 million years ago, a time when the earth's land surface differed greatly from that of today. However, according to Cayce, these "people" were more like thought forms projected into primitive life than the human beings we know today.

The land of Lemuria, or Mu, was located to the west of the Americas long before the island of Atlantis was occupied. Its destruction occurred sometime around 50,000 B.C. (Cayce's information on Atlantis is far more detailed than that he provided on Mu.) Atlantis, located in the Atlantic Ocean, was first occupied by an advanced race of humans in 210,000 B.C. Then, according to the story Cayce consistently outlined in his many readings, a series of cataclysms occurred resulting in a breaking up of the islands. The first happened in 50,700 B.C., followed by the second in 28,000 B.C. Finally, in 10,014 B.C., the remaining islands of Atlantis sank, as did all but a few small remaining islands of Mu. At each of these critical time periods, groups of people escaped from these sinking lands and fled not only to Egypt, India, and parts of Europe, but also to the Americas. Cayce also stated that the leaders of these ancient advanced civilizations were aware that their lands were doomed. In response, they sent several groups to different locations to preserve records of humanity's history.

Mainstream Archaeology Views Cayce As A "Cult Archaeologist"

The mere mention of Atlantis produces an immediate response of derision and disbelief from the vast majority of academic archaeologists. It is no surprise that few academic textbooks make any mention at all of it, and those that do cloak the reference in ridicule: "Cranks...tend to add new unknown and unknowable factors into their theories: lost continents, men from outer space, planetary collisions, etc."[8] Atlantis theories, as well as virtually all ideas proposing an ancient history involving the Americas before roughly 11,000 B.C., and any migrations into ancient America except over the Ice-Age land bridge called Beringia, have long been cast by mainstream archaeology into a lunatic fringe they term "cult archaeology."[9]

The Departments of Anthropology at the University of Iowa and University of South Dakota maintain a joint web site and course on what they term, "fantastic archaeology," derived from a book by the same title. The course, "Lost Tribes, Sunken Continents and Ancient Astronauts: Cult Archaeology & Creationism," gives the following definitions: "Claims unsupported by scientific evidence, but that claim scientific support, use science terminology, or claim scientific validity can be called *pseudoscientific*. When these relate to the past, they are *fantastic archaeology*, to use Stephen William's term, or *cult archaeology*, if you like John Cole's term better." Edgar Cayce's claims about Atlantis, the Maya, Egypt, the ancient occupation of the Americas, and his history and development of the mound builder era are depicted as aspects of cult archaeology.

Was Cayce A Cult Archaeologist?

When Cayce was becoming aware of the material put forth in the readings, there is substantial evidence that it initially produced consternation. However, he eventually accepted the readings and simply saw them as part of the work he was doing. In addition, a fact that seems completely lost on all critics of Cayce, or at least a fact that they choose to ignore when making their criticisms, is that Cayce made it clear that the readings were not infallible. In one of the Lammers' Dayton readings (3744-1; conducted June, 18, 1923), Cayce was asked, "Is the information always absolutely correct?" His extended reply was that it was *if* there was a harmony between the soul forces involved. In addition, he made it clear that the individual asking him questions or making suggestions could cause a "deflection" of the information as it came to the surface. Therefore, in "reading" the past of an individual or a group of individuals, the readings themselves never claimed infallibility. What emerged through Cayce, the Source explained, could be influenced by the motives of the questioner as well as the balance or "harmony" of the souls involved in a reading.

Prior to his readings with Lammers, Cayce had several discussions with him about reincarnation, karma, and an ancient history that involved Atlantis. Thus, there is the possibility that the discussions and questions posed by Lammers could have "shaded" the information that emerged in response. Shaded was the term reading 3744-1 used to show how the questioner could influence the answer.

In addition, Cayce worked in several bookstores in the early 1900s and, with his ability to memorize books by sleeping on them, it is certainly highly probable that he absorbed an enormous amount of material in that manner. Kirkpatrick's biography of Cayce states that Cayce made good use of his opportunities while working in these bookstores in both reading and sleeping on books[5] (p. 58). And during those time periods, sensationalized books on Atlantis, Lost Tribes, the mound builders, and Egypt were extremely popular and likely to have been available to him. However, knowing that Lammers was interested in Atlantis or that Cayce might have slept on a pile of speculative history books does nothing to either validate or invalidate Cayce's ideas. One interesting fact that makes such speculation all the more interesting is this: Cayce's story of the ancient past doesn't match any of the other "wild" theories on Atlantis or Mu. In short, Cayce's pronouncements about the past are either correct or they aren't.

In answering the question of whether or not Cayce could be considered a cult archaeologist, revisiting the academic's definition is helpful. First of all, it doesn't matter to archaeologists whether or not Cayce professed to be an archaeologist. They define cult archaeology as making claims about the past that are unsupported by scientific evidence, but that claim scientific support, and use science terminology. Cayce's readings did not "claim to be scientific" nor did they use "scientific terminology." Regardless, there is little doubt that the vast majority of academic archaeologists would immediately brand Cayce as a cult archaeologist, in fact, they have already done so — without evaluating his statements. But many of Cayce's assertions could be genuinely verified or discredited. In a sense, this is one reason why this book is needed. Archaeologists point to Atlantis and Mu as impossible to verify, and thereby dismiss everything Cayce stated about ancient American history without even looking at what Cayce's specific statements were. In short, Cayce would truly be a cult archaeologist if *all* of his claims about ancient history were unverifiable and nonspecific. But this is not the case. Cayce did, in fact, make many very specific statements about the ancient past that modern archaeology can answer. The unfortunate fact is that modern archaeologists do not want to attempt to validate or invalidate the archaeological claims of a psychic — no matter how intriguing they may be. They simply dismiss them with ridicule and an air of authority. The reasons for this are discussed in detail later, however, the short answer is fairly simple. The costs in prestige, professional reputation, and even jobs to academic archaeologists in America are too much for them to risk. Thus, we (the authors) feel it wise to state a few caveats at the beginning of this book.

Caveats To Our Readers

First, no matter how well the current archaeological evidence may fit Cayce's history, the vast majority of archaeologists will ignore and continue to ridicule him. This will occur no matter how rigorous the research is that is utilized to evaluate it.

Secondly, the qualifications of those who wrote this book matter little to academic archaeologists nor do they care how convincing its arguments are. Even a respected academic archaeologist investigating Cayce's statements about ancient America, would be rumored to be "going off the deep end" and his or her conclusions would be ridiculed. In truth, many academic archaeologists have had their careers ruined by investigating less sensational claims. Thus, the present authors do not expect this work to sway the opinions of archaeology in America. We do want to note that the subject of this book *was* investigated and written from a skeptical viewpoint — at least initially. However, as the evidence was sifted and compared to what Cayce actually stated, the remarkable accuracy inevitably won out.

Finally, it is important for readers to understand that the vast majority of "facts" recorded in history books about ancient America simply aren't true. Since 1997, almost all of the most sacred "truths" in academic archaeology have been proven false by archaeologists willing to risk their reputation and academic standing. Helping in the effort to break down the barriers to change that academics have long held in place are new technologies that relatively few of the older academics fully understand. For example, the emergence of genetic testing has proven to be of critical importance as has been the ability to test human remains for trace drugs. In addition, archaeoastronomy, the study of how ancient sites are aligned to astronomical patterns, and various forms of satellite imagery have led to major discoveries completely changing how we view these ancient people.

The once sacred, non-assailable beliefs that have now fallen in archaeology are many. We were told for 70 years that the Americas were completely unoccupied until about 11,000 B.C. We have been told that all migrations into the Americas — up until the time of Columbus — came from Siberian Asia via the Bering Straits. We were told that all Native American Indian tribes shared the same genetic lineage. We were told that North American mound builders were not influenced by cultures from Central or South America. We were told that, prior to Columbus, ancient seafarers could not have visited the Americas and that no evidence was in existence that indicated any such visits ever occurred or even could have occurred. The list is much longer, however, readers should keep in mind that, despite the fact that archaeologists are scientifically trained, they are still subject to the same psychological defenses as anyone else. For example, those archaeologists who have spent 20 or 30 years attacking and ridiculing others for asserting that America was occupied 50,000 years ago will not likely stop their attacks regardless of evidence showing that this occupation did occur.

How This Book Came About The Yucatan Hall of Records & America's Mound Builder Culture

In 1999, John Van Auken and Lora Little began work on the book, *The Lost Hall of Records: Edgar Cayce's Forgotten Record of Human History in the Ancient Yucatan*,[10] following a tour to the Yucatan hosted by Van Auken. The book was subsequently published in August 2000 with its release coinciding with the A.R.E.'s annual Egypt and Ancient Mysteries Conference. The book concerns Cayce's story of the establishment of a Hall of Records in the Yucatan by a group of people from Atlantis in approximately 10,000 B.C. According to Cayce, descendants from this group of people migrated north to Ohio sometime afterward, and joined with several other groups of people to become the mound builders. (The A.R.E. is the Virginia Beach, Virginia organization which preserves and researches the Cayce readings.)

During the time period when *The Lost Hall of Records* was being researched and prepared, I (Greg Little) reviewed some of Cayce's statements about the mound builders and ancient American history. As a skeptic of

Cayce's overall outline of history, and being especially skeptical about his statements on the mound builders, I was asked to make a presentation on Cayce and the mound builders at the A.R.E.'s Egypt and Ancient Mysteries Conference. I was also told to present what I found — to present the cards as they fell.

As a psychologist and counselor with a deep interest in how rituals affect brain processes, I have long been interested in Cayce's health readings. However, I had been cynical about Cayce's readings on Atlantis, Mu, ancient America, and his outline of history. As I wrote in my earlier books, when Cayce was following the wish granted him by the angel who apparently visited him (to heal others), his readings seemed accurate. However, when the motives of those asking for readings strayed from that purpose, I felt that the accuracy dropped. The repeated failures via the readings to find buried treasure and hit oil deposits were major cases in point. I also lumped Cayce's past life readings into the same category along with all of the history contained in them. However, since I recognized the importance and validity of the health and spiritual aspects of the work, my wife and I maintained a membership in the A.R.E.

As an off and on academic and an ongoing researcher thoroughly trained in the scientific method, I had been brainwashed by the ridicule

Figure 5
Cover of John Van Auken and Lora Little's book, *The Lost Hall of Records* (2000). It was during the process of researching and writing this book that we realized Cayce's readings on ancient North American history represented a forgotten aspect of the readings.

tactics concealed under the banner of having a "healthy scientific skepticism." When I became fascinated with the so-called "Indian" mounds that seemed to suddenly appear everywhere I looked, I initially investigated them in two ways. The first way was to visit them. And this my wife and I did — often. Since 1982, we have been to thousands of mounds in North America. The goal of these visits was to produce a pictorial encyclopedia of mounds. The second way I investigated mounds was to absorb information from mainstream archaeology. I read hundreds of textbooks, journals, and articles and spoke to many archaeologists. I soon became acquainted with the sarcasm that comes with the expression of ideas that stray outside the boundaries of accepted thinking. This led me to the realization that many archaeologists did not truly utilize the scientific method. Instead of acknowledging the uncertainties and possibilities in their field, they often spoke and wrote in absolutes with an air of scientific superiority. During this long period I gradually became aware that a huge mystery existed in the origins of the mound builder culture and the purposes of the mounds. And it was painfully apparent that mainstream archaeology's simple but absolute answers were not only insufficient, they were a cover for a great void in our knowledge of the past. Nevertheless, I continued to ally my thinking with the academics far more than with what they referred to as the lunatic fringe.

I must confess that Cayce's pronouncements about the mound builders caught me off guard. Surprisingly, many of his statements about the mound builders and ancient American history were very specific and could easily be matched with the current base of knowledge in archaeology. Even more surprising was that there are far more readings on the mound builders and America's history than I had expected. The most compelling thing of all was that most of these matched the updated thinking and findings in post-1997 archaeology.

The Purpose of This Book

Despite the fact that hundreds of books have been published on Cayce, none have focused exclusively on the history of ancient America and the mound builders. Those few that have devoted some attention to the issue have become dated or are limited in scope. These include *Edgar Cayce's Story of the Origin and Destiny of Man* (Lytle Robinson, 1972), *Edgar Cayce on Atlantis* (Edgar Evans Cayce, 1968), *Mysteries of Atlantis Revisited* (Edgar Evans Cayce, Gail Cayce Schwartzer, & Douglas G. Richards, 1997), *The Great Migration: Emergence of the Americas as Indicated in the Readings of Edgar*

Cayce (Vada F. Carlson, 1970), and *The Maya: Based on the Edgar Cayce Readings* (Carolyn Hatt, 1972).

Cayce's history of ancient America is a fantastic, captivating story. We intend to tell this story chronologically as thoroughly as possible. To accomplish this task, we gathered and categorized all of the readings Cayce supplied on ancient American history. These were organized by the era they described, their location, and specificity. Portions of the readings we utilized are located in Appendix A of this book.

Next, we will provide an outline of the history of ancient America that academic archaeology has rigidly maintained up until dramatic changes occurred in the field in 1997. This will include the archaeological explanations of the mound builder culture.

The newest evidence and findings in ancient American archaeology will then be presented. This evidence comes from modern genetics, newer dating techniques, new finds in the field, re-examination of old evidence, and examination of what the native American tribes have themselves said for so long. In the course of these discussions, the evidence will be compared to Cayce's specific claims.

Finally, a synopsis of the remarkable story weaved by the results of this evaluation will emerge. This will be blended with a rich tradition of Native American lore, ritual, wisdom, and some of the most closely guarded secrets of shaman societies.

Chapter 2

Cayce's History of North America — In Brief

The 2500 life readings on file were given for approximately 1600 different people.
…About 700 of these people had incarnations in Atlantis… The amazing thing about
this particular set of readings is their internal consistency. Although given for hundreds
of different people over a period of twenty-one years (1923 to 1944), they may be
pieced together to form a coherent, non-contradictory series of events.

Edgar Evans Cayce (*1968*) *Edgar Cayce on Atlantis*

Many books have provided a review of Cayce's story of ancient history. However, none have exclusively focused on events in America and given a chronological account. A total of 68 Cayce readings were utilized to form this summary. Appendix A contains a listing of these readings by category along with pertinent portions of each reading. It should be noted that, since this book primarily concerns events that directly affected America, the vast majority of Cayce's world history is not included in this discussion. In addition, many of Cayce's readings about the Americas were historical in nature. That is, they told of events that occurred during encounters between the native populations and the settlers entering the New World. These readings were of limited usefulness.

A few of Cayce's readings (especially those describing the Lost Tribes in America) have been interpreted somewhat differently in this book than in earlier books. While such issues are debatable, there is no doubt that Cayce clearly stated that remnants of the Lost Tribes of Israel came to America.

10-12 Million Years B.C.
Mu & the Four Corners Area of America

According to Cayce's chronology, the history of ancient America began over 10 million years ago. At that time, only the western portion of the present United States was above ocean water. The east coast of the mid-Pacific continent of Mu (also known as Lemuria) was located across the ocean west of the four corners area (where Arizona, Utah, New Mexico, and Colorado meet).

While modern American archaeology scoffs at the mere mention of the word Mu, it is taken seriously elsewhere and legitimate evidence of its existence has been found. In 1900, a Taoist Monk named Wang Tao-Shih found a hidden library in a series of caves in China. A famous British archaeologist and geographer, Sir Aurel Stein, subsequently wrote two books detailing these texts: *On Ancient Asian Tracks* and *Ruins of Desert Cathay*. In those books, Stein wrote that the manuscripts speak of an ancient time and a place called the motherland Mu. The texts dated to about 5000 B.C. One manuscript fragment is an ancient map showing parts of a continent located in the ancient Pacific.

The area immediately east of the four corners was also under the Atlantic or Gulf waters (to the Mississippi Valley). The small land area of the western Americas, beginning at the four corners, extended to parts of Nevada and southern California and down to the Andes Mountains in Peru. Cayce referred to these different areas as Og and Oz in his readings. The current polar regions were then tropical and the cooling earth was subject to sudden upheavals and violent change. The entire land surface of the earth, according to Cayce, was obviously quite different than it is today.

The Cayce readings state that humans were in the Americas 10 million years ago, but the earliest forms of "humanity" appeared in Mu 12 million years ago. The first humans in Mu were quite primitive and not truly conscious or mentally developed. Cayce termed these as the "First Root Race." The second wave of humans appearing in 10 million B.C. was, according to Cayce, an improved version of humankind which Cayce called the "Second Root Race." This more advanced form of man gradually began living in small family units and primarily inhabited caves. They produced rudimentary cave drawings and lived in parts of Utah, Nevada, and New Mexico. The early people of Mu and America evolved very slowly, but by 210,000 B.C. they had made some improvements. According to Cayce, the only evidence of the existence of the most ancient of people in America would be cave drawings found in the four corners area.

Figure 6
Cayce's view of North America, Mu, and Atlantis between 210,000 B.C. to 50,722 B.C.
From — *The Great Migration* (1970 by Vada Carlson; courtesy A.R.E. Press.

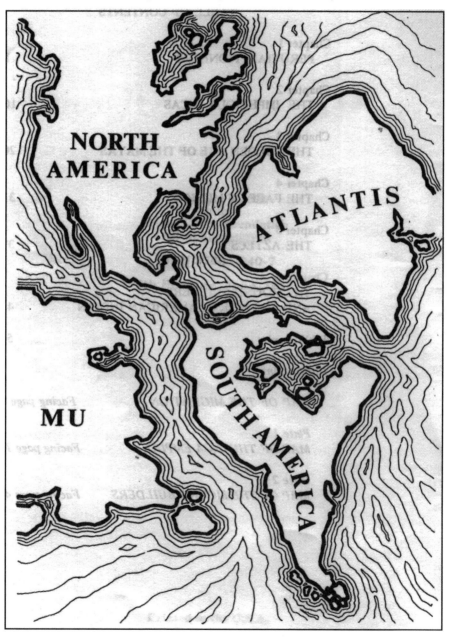

During these ancient times, in the much smaller land areas of Peru and America, groups of brown-skinned people called the Ohlms or Ohums resided. These people were peaceful and spiritual and apparently represented early migrants from Mu. They later became the Incas of Peru as well as eventually migrating throughout all of the Americas.

210,000 B.C. – 50,722 B.C.
Humans Appear in Atlantis

In 210,000 B.C. a somewhat more advanced form of human life appeared in Atlantis. The area of present-day Bimini and the islands now surrounding it in shallow waters had formed mountain peaks of the now-sunken continent.

Cayce provided few details about specific events occurring between the years 210,000 to 50,722 B.C. His life readings covering this vast time period primarily concerned the spiritual plan to assist the souls who had unwittingly become trapped in physical life forms. These souls had lost their awareness of the spiritual plane from which they originated and had become fascinated with aspects of the physical world. However, Cayce stated that a much-improved human form appeared in 106,000 B.C. in Atlantis. These humans were particularly capable and made rapid advances in knowledge developing a number of technological innovations. This new human Cayce called the "Third Root Race."

50,722 B.C. – 28,000 B.C.
Mu Is Destroyed
Survivors Flee to America and Elsewhere

In 50,722 B.C. a conference was held of delegates from all of the world's inhabited areas to try to find a means to cope with the large animals that were then over-running the Earth. Both the Mu lands and Atlantis were represented at this meeting. Plans were made to destroy the animals utilizing chemicals and high explosives.

The Cayce readings reveal that these ancient people were far more technologically advanced than today's science would lead us to believe. They could travel in a type of hot air balloon and developed several ways of obtaining energy and producing weapons. Unfortunately, the energy used in an attempt to destroy the animals was misapplied resulting in violent explosions of underground gas pockets and seismic pressures. These eruptions set off a chain reaction that led to cataclysmic consequences. The entire continent of Mu, except for a few islands, gradually but rapidly sank into the Pacific Ocean. Scattered islands in the South Pacific were all that remained of the southern end of the continent. However, before the entire continent sank in 50,700 B.C., many people from Mu escaped to what is now the west coast of America as well as South and Central America and elsewhere in the world.

50,000 B.C.
Temple to the Sun and Moon Erected
in Santa Barbara, Cal.
People From Mu Migrate to Oregon, Ohio,
and Pennsylvania
People From South Pacific Islands
Establish Pueblo Culture

During the time period when Mu was experiencing its violent end, several specific events are outlined in the Cayce readings. A temple dedicated to the sun and moon was erected near present-day Santa Barbara, California. Some people from Mu journeyed to the coastal area of Oregon and established the custom of totems. Cayce also reveals that women served as the primary rulers during that time. Others went to the areas of Ohio and Pennsylvania while larger groups migrated south to the Yucatan and South America. About the same time, a group of people simply described as from the "South Pacific" came to the southwestern United States and established a "cliff dwelling" culture. It is believed that these people gradually evolved into the "pueblo peoples." In general, the people of Mu were described by Cayce as the "brown race" and as peaceful. They tried to live in harmony with each other as well as with nature. However, there were some disagreements between two opposing religious philosophies. As the people of Mu merged with the Atlanteans, described as Cayce's "red race," increasing disagreements occurred.

50,000 B.C. – 28,000 B.C.
Violent Conflicts Develop Between Two Factions
Human Sacrifice & Sun Worship Arise

About the time Mu sank, more serious problems developed in Atlantis between two groups with vastly opposing views of life. One group believed in the idea of One God. Called the Children of the Law of One by Cayce, this group believed that, ultimately, all souls were one. They taught that humanity should reawaken itself to its spiritual source and try to escape deeper entrapment in the physical world. One tenet of this philosophy was the idea that all actions produce reactions and consequences. Hurting another person would, therefore, create a set of reactions which would inevitably come back to haunt the perpetrator.

The Children of the Law of One believed that the physical world had become a trap for individualized souls. Hedonistic behavior was a part of the trap, and, in order to escape the permanent encasement of the soul in the physical world, treating others as one would treat oneself was critical. This idea was abhorrent to the opposing faction, The Children of Darkness. This group, also called the Sons of Belial, taught survival of the fittest with a self-seeking, self-aggrandizement philosophy. There was no regard for the welfare of others or the consequences of actions. Their philosophy and way of life led to total absorption in the world of physical pleasures and, ultimately, into encasement in physical matter itself. Apparently, the Children of Darkness didn't care whether they became ensnared in the physical world. As a ritual fitting for their philosophy, the Sons of Belial adapted human sacrifice and utilized various forms of sun worship.

In Cayce's history, ancient America is greatly impacted by the ongoing struggle between the Children of the Law of One and the Sons of Belial. Mu also had conflicts between these two groups in their own culture that continued on into the Americas after Mu sank in 50,700 B.C.

As the more advanced Atlanteans migrated into the Americas, the split between the two groups became more violent. The result was a series of battles initiated by the Sons of Belial as they attempted to find and destroy the temples and settlements of the Children of the Law of One. The Children of the Law of One made efforts to live peacefully and in harmony with nature. However, over time they were hunted down and violently opposed by the Sons of Belial who utilized forms of human sacrifice and torture. This conflict continued into historic times.

28,000 B.C. – 10,500 B.C.
Atlanteans Migrate to Nevada & Colorado
Peoples From South Seas Islands Arrive Again
Visitors From China Arrive as do Groups
From "Across the Pacific"

Around 28,000 B.C., Atlantis underwent a series of violent earthquakes causing it to break up into islands. A new wave of migration into the Americas occurred as Atlanteans traveled to the area around Nevada and Colorado to escape the cataclysmic events. In addition, there were individuals and groups banished from Atlantis who migrated to America. These advanced people became highly influential and often became leaders of the people already living there. At the same time, groups of people from the "South Seas Islands," China, and others simply described as coming from "across the Pacific" arrived in America. They were absorbed into the melting pot that ancient America had become.

10,500 B.C. – 3000 B.C.
Atlanteans Establish a Temple in Yucatan
to House Records
More Atlanteans Migrate to Americas
Atlanteans Become Iroquois
Egyptian Priestess Visits Four Corners Area

The last island of Atlantis sunk into the Atlantic Ocean during a violent series of earthquakes in 10,014 B.C. However, in anticipation of the coming destruction, in 10,500 B.C., Atlantean priests began establishing temples at several locations across the Earth to maintain important records of their civilization. The best known of these record locations was at Giza in Egypt. The others were at Bimini and in the Yucatan.

Cayce described a small group of Atlanteans dispatched to the Yucatan where they built a series of temples and merged with the peoples already present. A much larger group of Atlanteans migrated to the northeastern coast of America and gradually became the Iroquois. By historic times, only the Iroquois of "noble blood" had retained their pure Atlantean genetic makeup. Cayce also stated in several readings that Atlanteans migrated to the Iberian Peninsula (Spain and Portugal) at the same time locating themselves mainly in the Pyrenees Mountains. A few others went to the center of an ancient mound-building civilization in the Gobi. In addition, shortly before the sinking of Atlantis, a priestess of the Law of One temple in Poseidia (the last island of the continent to sink) was sent to Egypt to assist in the establishment of a temple there. She was later dispatched from Egypt to the four corners area of America to establish links to the Law of One groups there. Cayce describes a great deal of movement of envoys and others from Egypt to the Gobi to the Americas and back.

In the area of the Yucatan, the Atlanteans who had come to build a temple to house their records rapidly became influential over the peoples already present there. The people of the Yucatan constructed numerous pyramids and temple complexes following the same patterns from Atlantis, Egypt, and a mysterious ancient city located in the area of the Gobi in China. From the Yucatan, these groups slowly began establishing their way of life and customs in other areas of Mexico, especially around the area of Mexico City.

3000 B.C.
Lost Tribes of Israel Arrive In Eastern
and Western America
Lost Tribes Move to Mexico, Then Migrate to Ohio
The Mound Builder Culture Emerges

In 3000 B.C., the date Cayce gives for the events causing the historical Lost Tribes of Israel, a portion of the Lost Tribes arrived by boat at the southernmost portion of the United States. After staying there for a brief time, they moved further south into the area around present-day Mexico City where they added a new dimension to the culture of pyramid and temple building. This was the use of altars and sacrifices. Not long after that time, experiencing pressure from hostile groups, a migration out of the Yucatan occurred. A portion of the Lost Tribes and a group of descendants from the earlier Atlanteans (who had migrated to Yucatan to establish a Hall of Records) moved north into the heart of America. These groups established themselves mainly in Ohio with smaller settlements in Kentucky and Indiana. There, the mound builder era began.

This mound builder culture was originally centered in Ohio. Cayce states that the mounds were built as a replica of the Atlantis, Yucatan, and Gobi experiences. The mound builders, according to Cayce, were a mixture of races and cultures. These included the Atlanteans, the migrants from Mu, and the Lost Tribes. In addition, a slight Norse influence occurred toward the end of the mound building culture as some of the Norse merged with mound builder tribes.

Cayce also describes one other migration into America possibly from ancient Semitic lands. This reading is more difficult to interpret. He describes a small, "lost or strayed tribe" that entered Arizona across Mu. Although this group also went to the Yucatan, this may or may not be the same group described earlier. Since Mu had sunk well before 3000 B.C., it is likely that this group came to America by hopping between islands that had once been part of the Mu continent.

A.D. 900 – 1500s
Norse Establish Vinland in America
Norse Explore Deep Into America Reaching Minnesota, Wisconsin, and Montana

Sometime around A.D. 900-1000, the Norse established a large trading colony on the Atlantic coast. This colony was called Vinland. Vinland, according to Cayce, was the coasts of Rhode Island, Massachusetts, and Connecticut. As to specific locations, he named areas near the present cities of Newport, Salem, and Providence. Some of the Norse traveled inland and settled with the mound builders, however, the Norse made many excursions deep into the Americas via the Great Lakes. They reached Minnesota, Wisconsin, and parts of Montana. They continued these explorations until the 1500s.

Historical Events

Cayce mentions numerous events taking place in America as Europeans were settling it. In fact, one of his own past lives occurred in America during this period. However, one of the most interesting events he relates involves an adopted daughter of the famous Chief Powhatan. In a past life, the daughter was described as having assisted the chiefs of the five great Indian nations as they met to discuss problems they were anticipating with the settlers who would soon be arriving. This meeting, Cayce states, was in an Octagon on the banks of the Ohio River.

Can Cayce's History Be Confirmed?

Prior to the changes that occurred in American archaeology in 1997, virtually everything Cayce stated about ancient America would have been considered ludicrous to academic archaeologists. If archaeologists had been asked the following questions prior to that time, the replies to each would be as follows (in italics):

Could "early man" have existed 10 million years ago? *Certainly not.*

Was there anyone in the Americas before 10,000 B.C.? *Certainly not. (Atlantis and Mu are both fictional stories, because no one migrated to and lived in the Americas before Columbus arrived in 1492 except from Siberia via the exposed Bering Straits.)*

Could people from South Sea Islands, China, or elsewhere across the Pacific visit pre-historic America? *Absolutely not.*

Did people from Central America migrate north to become mound builders? *No.*

Is there even a slight possibility that any ancient Hebrews were in ancient America? *No possibility at all.*

Could the mounds be a representation of something similar in Atlantis, the Yucatan, or an unknown area of China? *Absolutely not.*

Did the Norse really go deep into the Americas and was Vinland located on America's coast? *No, both assertions are wrong. (The Norse never got further than just reaching a coastal area of Canada; all other claims are hoaxes.)*

Thankfully, things have changed on the modern archaeological scene. The earliest date for the appearance of humanity's ancestors has now been pushed back to 6 million years[1] — and chances are that it will be pushed back even further in coming years. New research has emerged showing that an ancient Hebrew presence did, in fact, occur in America. Other evidence shows that the Americas did have many visitors and migrations from across the Pacific, the South Sea Islands, across the Atlantic and elsewhere. The Americas were occupied long before the long-accepted date of 10,000 B.C. with traces now going back to at least 50,000 B.C. In short, many of Cayce's once ludicrous statements about ancient America appear to be true.

Cayce's outline of history provides many statements that can be evaluated with a comparison to the current archaeological record. With that purpose in mind, we have collapsed his most specific statements into 30 basic ideas. In coming chapters we shall touch upon these. For the purposes of this book, the readings used to form each idea have been abbreviated to only those sections that directly relate.

Cayce's Most Specific Statements About Ancient America

1. Parts of Utah, New Mexico, and Arizona were occupied 10 million years ago.

2. Cave drawings in northwestern New Mexico remain from these very early people.

3. People were present in the Americas prior to 50,000 B.C. in the southwest and California.

4. Large, dangerous animals freely roamed the Americas prior to 50,000 B.C.

5. A temple dedicated to the sun and moon was established near present-day Santa Barbara, California prior to 50,700 B.C.

6. People from Mu (and Atlantis) migrated to America at the time of the first disturbances in Mu and Atlantis (50,000 B.C.).

7. These people migrated to areas of Pennsylvania around 50,000 B.C.

8. They also migrated to areas of Ohio around 50,000 B.C.

9. People from Mu established the custom of totem, or family trees, in Oregon prior to 50,000 B.C.

10. Women ruled during the time of the great Mu migration (50,000 B.C.).

11. People from the South Seas came to the four corners area and began the "cliff dweller," or pueblo culture, about 50,000 B.C.

12. In 28,000 B.C. some people from Atlantis migrated to Nevada and Colorado.

13. People coming "across the Pacific" entered ancient America in 28,000 B.C.

14. People coming from China entered ancient America in 28,000 B.C.

15. The Iroquois, especially those of noble blood, were pure Atlantean.

16. Pure Atlanteans also migrated to Iberia, especially to the Pyrenees Mountains.

17. An Atlantean priestess who had moved to Egypt visited southwestern America sometime around 10,000 B.C.

18. A group of 2nd generation Atlanteans and others who moved to the Yucatan about 10,000 B.C. migrated north to begin the Mound Builder culture. This occurred sometime after 3,000 B.C.

19. The mounds were replicas of the Yucatan, Atlantis, and Gobi experiences.

20. Remnants of the "Lost Tribes" of Israel came to ancient America in 3000 B.C. in boats. They went first to the southernmost US.

21. After staying for a brief time in the southern part of America, the Lost Tribes moved to the area around Mexico City where they impacted the pyramid-building culture already present.

22. Portions of the Lost Tribes then migrated north merging with other groups to become the Mound Builders in Ohio.

23. Some Israelites escaped the captivity by fleeing to southwestern America from the West across the Pacific. They crossed through areas (perhaps utilizing islands) that were once a part of Mu. They established temples in the southwest. They are referred to as a "lost" or "strayed" tribe."

24. The mound builders were a mixture of influences from Atlantis, Mu, Lost Tribes, and others.

25. The Norse made many trips to ancient America and actually settled here.

26. Some of the Norse merged with the mound builders.

27. The location of the Norse settlement in America, Vinland, was placed in Rhode Island, Massachusetts, and Connecticut by Cayce.

28. Providence, Salem, and Newport are specifically named as modern cities where Vinland was located.

29. The Norse reached Montana in the 1500s via the Great Lakes. An artifact, a knife supposedly belonging to Eric the Red, was recovered in Wisconsin around 1940 that would prove this excursion. In addition, a Norse excursion reached Minnesota.

30. Cayce mentions the Five Great Nations, Chief Powhatan, and a meeting in the "Octagon" by the Ohio River.

Chapter 3

The Genesis of Mysterious America —
A Suppressed History Emerges

Every school boy knows that at the time of its discovery North America was the Red Man's continent. ... We are confident in our knowledge of where man came from to the New World and how he was able to make this trip. ... American Indians... are most closely related to the present inhabitants of eastern Asia... They came to this country as its first inhabitants some 12,000 to 15,000 years ago...
Pope (1956) *Ocmulgee*

The traditional theory held that the first Americans crossed the land bridge from Siberia to Alaska around 11,500 years ago and followed an "ice-free corridor" between two large Canadian ice sheets (the Laurentide and Cordilleran) to reach unglaciated lands to the south.
Encyclopedia Smithsonian (1999)

When, exactly, does history begin? It's a simple question, but it has several answers. History is the story of the past, but it requires that someone knows that story and can tell it. At least, that's always been the idea behind history books. But history is sometimes reshaped and changed for political purposes. It can be slanted to fit agendas or simply fictionalized. It also depends on who is writing that history and what events they wish to choose as the "beginning." And sometimes, we just don't know what happened.

In history books the beginning of ancient America used to be the "discovery" of the New World by Columbus. But for many of the Native American tribes, that was the beginning of the end of their history. In truth, Native Americans have had a rich tradition of history passed on from generation to generation in oral stories and mythology. Many tribes had a written record of their past, but few of these records have survived.

As archaeology began as a true science in the 1900's, it gradually began piecing together the story of ancient America from evidence recovered from excavations. Archaeologists listened to the oral stories from Native American tribes, but discounted the tales when they contradicted the evidence. With the advent of better and better dating techniques, a chronology of events emerged in the Americas. This chronology became the accepted "history" of the Americas in the 1930s and remained the story told in academic history textbooks until the late 1990s. And then, like a house of cards, it all collapsed. Nearly everyone is now realizing that the events that occurred in the Americas in the remote past were far more complex than had ever been imagined. And the emerging chronology of events is becoming more and more similar to the fantastic picture painted by Edgar Cayce's readings.

Archaeology's Traditional Story of Ancient America's History — Prior to 1997

For the past seventy years, academic archaeologists have told us with authority and absolute certainty their chronology of the events that shaped ancient America. It has become a fairly simple proposition that has been rigidly and steadfastly defended. An outline of this story follows but it should be kept in mind that the essential foundation upon which it has been based is now disproven. The emerging theories and the evidence upon which they are based will be presented later in this chapter and in those that follow, but a familiarity with the long-term beliefs of archaeology is important.[1, 2, 3]

During the last ice age, the Bering Straits, a shallow, 55-mile wide divide separating Alaska from Siberia, was dry land. With so much water held in ice, the ocean levels were then 300 feet lower creating a huge, 1500-mile wide corridor (called Beringia) connecting the two continents. But mile-high glaciers blocked the passage. Then, in about 9500 B.C., an "ice-free corridor" opened as the glaciers began to melt. (See figures 7 & 8.) Hordes of Siberian nomads stampeded into the Americas hunting the mammoths and other big game that had no experience with man as a predator. By 8500 B.C., these nomads had reached the southern tip of South

Figure 7
During the last ice age, the Bering Straits, a shallow, 55-mile wide divide separating Alaska from Siberia, was dry land. With so much water held in ice, the ocean levels were then 300 feet lower creating a huge, 1500-mile wide corridor (called Beringia) connecting the two continents. But mile-high glaciers blocked the passage. The seaboard extended further into the ocean. In some places, like Florida, this greatly increased the land mass.

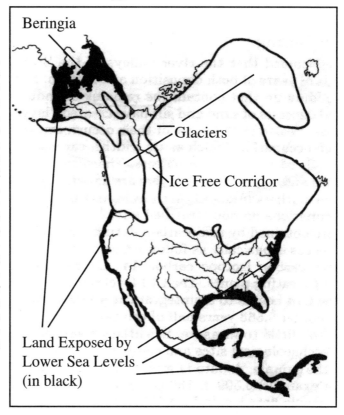

Beringia

Glaciers

Ice Free Corridor

Land Exposed by Lower Sea Levels (in black)

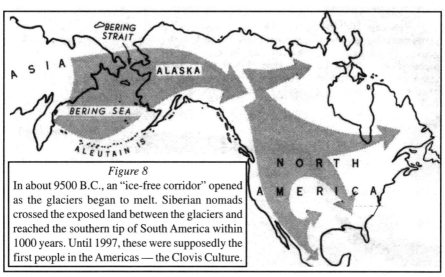

BERING STRAIT

ASIA

ALASKA

BERING SEA

ALEUTAIN IS

NORTH AMERICA

Figure 8
In about 9500 B.C., an "ice-free corridor" opened as the glaciers began to melt. Siberian nomads crossed the exposed land between the glaciers and reached the southern tip of South America within 1000 years. Until 1997, these were supposedly the first people in the Americas — the Clovis Culture.

America at Tierra del Fuego leaving behind distinctive implements archaeologists refer to as the "Clovis Culture." Within a thousand years, the Clovis people — assumed to be nomadic hunters from Siberia — had spread throughout all the Americas. Over time, these ancient people gradually developed their own distinctive regional language derivations and cultures.

According to earlier archaeological beliefs, the first vestiges of mound building in America occurred about 3000 B.C. in New England and the coastal regions of Canada. There, the "Red Paint" people performed burials in small mounds. Large amounts of red hematite (ochre) were spread over the dead before dirt was piled over them to form small mounds.

Mound building next took an unusual and strange turn in 2000 B.C. in Poverty Point, Louisiana. An enormous complex, consisting of over 11 miles of a series of semi-octagonal earthen embankments, was erected there. The embankments focused on a huge bird effigy mound. The bird mound remains 70 feet tall today and measures 710 feet from head to tail and 640 feet from wing tip to wing tip. Poverty Point was believed to be the capital of an early culture that flourished along tributaries of the Mississippi River

Figure 9
U.S. Geological Survey aerial infrared photo of Poverty Point.

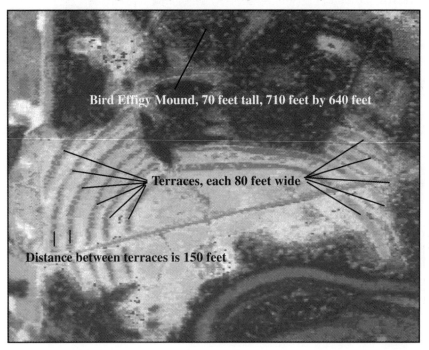

Bird Effigy Mound, 70 feet tall, 710 feet by 640 feet

Terraces, each 80 feet wide

Distance between terraces is 150 feet

from about 2,000 B.C. to about 700 B.C. It is believed that up to 10,000 people lived at this incredible site. Huts were built atop the multiple 6-10 foot high, semi-octagonal embankments. The terraces formed by the embankments were 80 feet wide and spaced 150 feet apart. (See figure 9.) The terraces, most of which are still visible today, were built in a short time frame and once contained enough earth to fill the Great Pyramid at Giza 35 times. The Poverty Point mound complex — its origin as well as the motives of its builders — remains one of the most enigmatic events in ancient North American history.

Five hundred years later, mound building became a way of life in the Eastern half of the United States with the emergence of the Glacial Kame and Adena cultures centering in Ohio. Mound building became more complex with the emergence of the Hopewell culture not long after the Adena tradition began. By A.D. 500, the dominant mound building was termed Mississippian and mound sites were located throughout the entire Eastern half of the United States. Collectively, some archaeologists prefer to term these as "Middle Woodlands" cultures. (See figure 10.)

Figure 10

The traditional timeline of ancient America asserts that the first people entering the Americas came across Beringia from Siberia starting in around 9500 B.C. The first vestiges of mound building occurred with the Red Paint people and the Old Copper Culture around 3000 B.C. Poverty Point began around 2000 B.C. followed by Adena in 1500 B.C. and Hopewell in 500 B.C. Mound building ended just before A.D. 1500 as the Mississippian Culture collapsed.

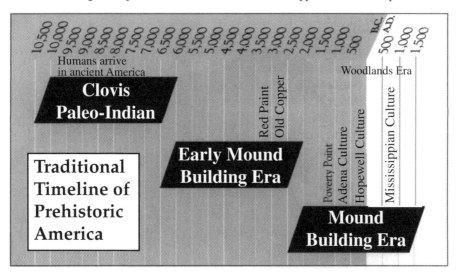

How Archaeology
Has Explained the Mounds

According to conventional wisdom, the mounds were built by the descendants of the Clovis people. The purpose of mounds has always been explained by archaeologists as threefold. First, some mounds, especially the smaller conical mounds, served as burial graves. In general, the larger the burial mound, the more important the burials it contained. Secondly, archaeologists have always argued that mounds, especially the flattop, or truncated pyramid shaped ones, were utilized for religious rituals and often served as the residence for priests. Other than describing a few rituals that were still being practiced by Native Americans when the first European settlers arrived, archaeologists have provided little insight into any ritualistic ceremonies practiced by mound builders. Finally, the mounds served political purposes and were used as place of residence for chiefs. As such, they were a center for political events. (See figure 11.)

Figure 11
Typical Mississippian site. Note the temples atop the flat-topped mounds. The tribal chiefs and priests lived in these temples. The flat plaza in the center of the mounds served as a gathering place and game area. The area surrounding the mounds would have smaller houses built for the populace. *From the Southeast Archaeological Center — National Park Service.*

For many years, archaeologists believed that the placement of mounds was random or designed to allow for defense or easy access to water. Gradually, it was conceded that some mound sites were designed to allow for observation of the movements of the sun. The purpose of the solar alignments was to maintain a planting calendar and mark the time for celebrations — especially around the days of the solstices.

Archaeologists have found that the area immediately around the mounds served two purposes. First, a large plaza was usually present where games and other large events could be held. Secondly, the mound complexes were often the focal point of daily life for the villages and towns that formed around them. Many of these complexes were palisaded for safety. That is, a tall wooden stockade was often built around them essentially making them a fortress. (See figure 12.)

A number of mound complexes and earthwork "anomalies" have remained somewhat of an enigma. Some of these are gigantic. For example, in Chapter 1, the Hopewell site of Portsmouth, Ohio was briefly described. At Portsmouth, the Scioto River joins with the Ohio. (See figure 13.) Sets of parallel walls forming 160-foot wide walkways ran for 20 miles connecting a circular mound complex in Kentucky to an amazing complex of earthen structures high above the Ohio River on the Ohio side of the river. The walkways then continued back across the Ohio River into Kentucky to a massive strange, square enclosure. This site will be extensively detailed in a later chapter, however, mainstream archaeology has tended to

---

Figure 12

The Town Creek, North Carolina site has a partially reconstructed wooden stockade erected around portions of it to show how the complex was a fortress. The original wall was probably much higher than the 10 feet shown in this photo. *Photo — Greg Little.*

shy away from such mysterious locations. They are "explained" away as "Hopewell earthworks and enclosures" used for rituals. Many other anomalous structures, just as enigmatic as Portsmouth, remain in existence.

There are probably hundreds of variations on terms that archaeologists use to describe cultural groups and their traditions. Most of these terms are derived from local names or towns and are used to classify styles of pottery, weapons and points, and symbolic designs frequently found. In the interest of clarity and simplicity, only a few of these terms will be utilized.

It should be noted that the actual names of the mounds, their eras, their cultures, and even all of the artifacts associated with each are unknown. Archaeologists have usually applied the name of the nearest town or settlement to whatever specific artifact or mound complex they uncover. For example, Poverty Point in Louisiana describes a truly unique, highly advanced culture that constructed anomalous earthworks, large mounds, and made unusual cooking implements. The "Poverty Point" people are named for the Civil War-era plantation on which the complex was discovered. No one knows what these ancient people actually called themselves

---

Figure 13
The Portsmouth Earthworks was an incredible collection of embankments and walkways extending for miles between Ohio and Kentucky. Note the circular earthworks in Kentucky (lower right side) and the square (lower left side). The purpose of such earthworks is simply described by archaeology as "ritualistic" — that is, almost completely unknown. *From Squier & Davis (1848) Ancient Monuments of the Mississippi Valley.*

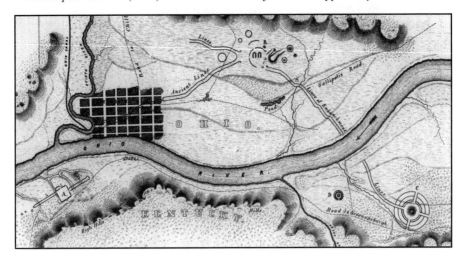

or where they came from. The term "Poverty Point" is no more or less accurate than the term Mu would be if it had been applied to the site. The famous Hopewell and Adena mound building cultures are both named after the large estates on which the first excavations were made of each distinct culture. These could have just as easily been named Og or Zu cultures without being any less accurate. The point is that the authoritative terms used to describe and explain past cultures are not in and of themselves accurate. They are terms simply used to describe and categorize. But they do not truly explain.

Exceptions To The Rules

According to academic archaeology, from the time the first nomadic hunters entered America in about 9500 B.C. until the first European explorers came in the early 1500s, no one else ever entered or visited the Americas. All of America was a vast, uninhabited land before 9500 B.C. One grudging exception has usually been made. At the southern tip of Newfoundland, at a barren coastal location called L'Anse aux Meadows, the Norse made a brief encampment in 1001 A.D. According to archaeological belief, this is the site of Leif Ericson's Vinland. (See figure 14.)

Figure 14
A reconstructed L'Anse aux Meadows in Newfoundland where it is believed that Leif Ericson made a brief encampment starting in 1001 A.D. *Photo — Canadian National Park Service.*

A few archaeologists have argued that it is possible that some Siberian nomads could have entered the Americas around 26,000 B.C. and perhaps a bit earlier. They believe that Beringia had already formed before the glaciers completely blocked the passage, but the time frame then was narrow — perhaps less than 1,000 years. However, the vast majority of archaeologists have accepted the 9500 B.C. date as the earliest entry date and academic textbooks have invariably presented this idea. The 9500 B.C. date has been termed the "Clovis Barrier" and shall be discussed in more detail shortly.

A few archaeologists have argued for an Olmec presence at the Poverty Point mound site in Louisiana. However, this remains controversial. In addition, some massive mound complexes in America are known to be completely ceremonial in that no one actually lived there. These sites were periodically used for "rituals," but that statement is typically the full extent of the usual explanation. Until fairly recent years, archaeologists have not proposed that mounds were arranged according to star patterns or star risings and strongly attacked such claims.

Ancient America Was A Closed Continent

After the last Ice Age ended, ocean levels rose and again covered "Beringia," permanently sealing off any entry into the Americas. According to academic archaeology, all of the unique and distinctive cultures in all of the Americas developed on their own — without any outside influence or intrusion. The Incas, with their unique building style, pyramids, dress, and physical appearance were from the exact same racial group as all other ancient Americans. The Maya, Aztec, Pueblos, Navaho, Hopi, Eskimos, Plains tribes, Cheyenne, Seminoles, Cherokee, Iroquois, Algonquin, and all other tribes — both known and long-forgotten — all came from the same racial background. All developed their individualized styles of dress, pottery, language, customs, building, and pyramid or mound building on their own. Even their distinctively different facial and physical appearances simply evolved because of physical separation from the other groups and the passage of time.

Mainstream archaeology has utilized a very effective technique for disposing of all arguments that contradict its primary doctrine. Artifacts and finds presented as evidence questioning archaeology's major beliefs are simply denied as fakes or misinterpretations. Carbon dates that go against preconceived beliefs are labeled as "questionable" and contaminated. Theories proposing any cultural diffusion into the New World are branded as "racist." George Carter, an archaeologist and geologist who has long asserted that humans were in America long before the Clovis people, has sarcastically written that, "the ocean suddenly becomes an impervious barrier" when American archaeologists consider the possibility of transoceanic contacts. Carter asserts that the early ideas that were proposed about the mounds being built by a vanished race led to the frequent allegations of racism since the idea of outside cultural influence was a racial slur against the indigenous peoples. But Carter also points out that no civilization has risen in isolation and that the charges of racism stop sincere efforts to uncover truth.[4]

The Clovis Barrier

Until the mid-1920s, archaeologists believed that the Native American Indians had only been in the Americas for a few thousand years. This suddenly changed in 1927 with a significant discovery near Folsom, New Mexico. During an excavation, a large spear point was found between the bones of a long-extinct bison. Similar points are now known as Folsom points. Further investigation at the site convinced archaeologists that humans had, indeed, been in the Americas at the same time as the huge animals and had hunted them. The bison was known to have become extinct in about 8000 B.C.[5]

For a brief time, the term "Folsom" seemed to describe the first Americans who entered sometime just prior to 8000 B.C. But only a few years later archaeologists found a different spear point style that would redefine their ideas about when the first Siberian nomads entered America. This point, called Clovis, pushed the date of man's entry into America to about 9500 B.C.

In the early 1930s, two amateur archaeologists, C. W. Anderson and George Roberts, were searching and collecting artifacts from the surface of sand dunes at Blackwater Draw located about halfway between Clovis and Portales, New Mexico. The two men found a number of unusual, large projectile points lying among mammoth bones. In 1932, Anderson got archaeologist Edgar Howard to visit the site. Anderson was so impressed and struck by the importance of the site that he immediately organized excavations and subsequently uncovered more of the unusual points. These bifaced points were termed "Clovis" for their proximity to the town of

Clovis. The mammoths, enormous elephants with long body hair, had been killed in about 9200 B.C.[5] (See figure 15.)

Clovis artifacts have been found in virtually all states, usually at or near the surface level, and have always been dated at no earlier than 9500 B.C. Since this date coincided with the opening of the "ice free corridor" through Beringia as the last Ice Age waned, archaeology suddenly had a neatly formed theory. The Clovis people were first in the Americas and they went virtually everywhere. They crossed from Siberia in 9500 B.C. No evidence of pre-9500 B.C. habitation in the Americas could possibly be found then, since the Clovis Culture was a barrier. Archaeology refers to these ideas as the "Clovis Barrier" or as "Clovis first, Clovis everywhere." This idea has held a stranglehold on archaeology for 70 years.

Figure 15
The hunting and killing of mammoths or mastodons is now known to be far more difficult than originally believed. These large, dangerous animals had free reign over the Americas until they were essentially wiped out by Clovis-era hunters after 9000 B.C. *Illustration — Louisiana Prehistory.*

The Clovis Barrier Crumbles In 1997

Despite widespread academic acceptance of the Clovis barrier, there have always been those who disputed it. Geologist George Carter, mentioned previously, suggested that man was in California as long ago as 100,000 years ago in his 1957 book, *Pleistocene Man at San Diego*. In his 1980 book, *Earlier Than You Think*, Carter reported that he essentially "withdrew" from the professional scene for 15 years after *Pleistocene Man* came out. The flak he received from other archaeologists was the reason. Louis S. B. Leakey, the famous British paleontologist who died in 1972, became the scorn of archaeologists when he reported that the area around Calico Hills, California showed definitive evidence that it had been occupied at least 200,000 years ago. Many, many others who dared to take on the Clovis barrier saw their careers ended or stalled by the effort. In a 1999 interview, the Director of the Mercyhurst Archaeological Institute in Erie, archaeologist James Adovasio, termed Clovis-first as the "holy writ" of American archaeology. Adovasio added that even suggesting the Clovis model could be wrong was considered a "heresy" in archaeology.[6] But in 1997, a blue-ribbon panel of 12 archaeologists (including several prominent skeptics) was formed and dispatched to a site in South America where an academic archaeologist had found definite pre-Clovis evidence.

Starting in the 1980s, University of Kentucky archaeologist Tom Dillehay has routinely led a team of excavators digging at the Monte Verde site in southern Chile. Over the years, Dillehay and his team had uncovered evidence of a pre-Clovis habitation there. Finds at Monte Verde included many stone, wood, and bone artifacts as well as the remains of hide-covered huts. A child's footprint and several collections of both medicinal and edible plants were also uncovered. Radiocarbon dates consistently put the find at 10,500 B.C. — a full 1,000 years before Clovis. The full panel of archaeologists was impressed and completely won over by their visit. Incredibly, as the panel held their press conference in February 1997 announcing that the Clovis barrier had officially been broken, Dillehay uncovered a deeper layer of artifacts at the site showing that it may have been occupied as early as 35,000 B.C.

The effects of the Monte Verde site on American archaeology were profound and instantaneous. In the press release on the panel's findings from the Dallas Museum of Natural History, Alex Barker of the Museum stated, "It's hard to overstate the importance of the team's consensus. For 60 years, the Clovis-period entry of humans into the New World has withstood all challenges. Now the Monte Verde site establishes that humans arrived earlier." George Stuart, the National Geographic's chief archaeologist and chairman of the Society's Committee for Research and Exploration, said, "The Monte Verde conclusion is as definitive as archaeology gets." David Meltzer, professor of anthropology at Southern Methodist University, added, "While it's only a thousand years older than the previously accepted dates, its location 10,000 miles south of the Bering land bridge route that the first Americans took into the New World implies a fundamentally different history of human colonization of the Americas." (Note: Appendix B contains the full text of the important Monte Verde Press Release.)

Foreshadowing the flood of new information that was to follow the acceptance of Monte Verde's pre-Clovis dates, Dennis Stanford, curator of North American Archaeology of Smithsonian Institution stated, "I suspect we'll start finding earlier sites coming out of the woodwork." And this is precisely what occurred. With the sudden crumbling of the Clovis barrier, a flood of new dating information appeared on the archaeological scene. One factor that helped to maintain the Clovis-first idea was expressed by a University of South Carolina archaeologist at an October 1999 conference in Santa Fe on the new pre-Clovis evidence. Albert Goodyear had earlier excavated a Clovis settlement at a location called Topper near the Savannah River. Goodyear went back to the site after the Monte Verde information emerged. Goodyear explained that after he initially found the Clovis level, he just stopped digging: "You don't look for what you don't believe in." But when they looked, Goodyear and his team found settlement levels below Clovis. Another archaeologist, Michael Johnson, did the exact same thing. At Cactus Hill, a ridge 50 miles south of Richmond, Virginia, Johnson and his team had earlier excavated a Clovis site. But they stopped at the Clovis level because nothing else could be below it. After the Monte Verde findings were issued, Johnson immediately returned to Cactus Hill and dug deeper. He found stone points at a level 5,000 years older than Clovis.

Current Radiocarbon Dating Evidence in Ancient America

Although Monte Verde convinced the vast majority of archaeologists that America was inhabited before 9500 B.C., a few hardened skeptics have remained. One of the most strident is Stuart Fiedel, a private sector archaeologist. In early 2000, Fiedel published a review of the sites he believes that show the best evidence of being pre-Clovis.[7] The dates that follow represent the approximate range of corrected radiocarbon test results from these sites in order from the oldest to the most recent as reported by Fiedel. We have utilized the dating label of B.C. because Cayce's readings used it and listed the mid-point of carbon dates. It is important to keep in mind that Fiedel is a skeptic of pre-Clovis sites. In addition, some of the most interesting sites were ignored by his article. These other sites are discussed in the following section.

38,000 B.C. — 15,000 B.C.
Brazil: Pedra Furada

Hearths, charcoal, tools, and numerous quartz artifacts were recovered at this rock shelter where numerous cave paintings are found.

35,000 B.C. — 10,500 B.C.
Chile: Monte Verde

Numerous habitation artifacts were found as discussed in prior sections. The 35,000 B.C. date came from carbon samples recovered from fire hearths found below the earlier reported level.

26,000 B.C. —13,000 B.C.
Yukon — Bluefish Caves

A variety of stone artifacts were found with bones from mammoth, horse, bison, and other extinct animals.

22,000 B.C.
Mexico: Valsequillo

Five separate sites exist at this location. Stone artifacts, freshwater shells, points, knives, scrapers, blades and many other artifacts have been recovered.

20,000 B.C. — 14,000 B.C.
Pennsylvania: Meadowcroft Rockshelter

In a deep strata of this long-used rock overhang, blades, reworked points, and other items were found. Radiocarbon dating was done on material found adjacent to the artifacts.

17,000 B.C. – 16,000 B.C.
Virginia: Cactus Hill
This ridge shows long-term habitation evidence with multiple layers of artifacts. Several inches below the Clovis layer quartz blades, pentagonal points, and charcoal have been found.

16,700 B.C. — 12,500 B.C.
Venezuela: Taima-Taima
A point in mastadon bone was found with other mastadon bones, points, scrapers, and even the contents of a mastadon stomach.

16,000 B.C.
Idaho: Wilson Butte Cave
A knife, blade, flake, and bones were found.

14,000 B.C. — 13,000 B.C.
Wisconsin: Chesrow Complex
Mammoth bones, blades, flakes, and wood artifacts have been recovered near this site.

Other Archaeological Evidence Of People in Ancient America

During the past few years, additional evidence has emerged indicating that America was settled in pre-Clovis times. All of these sites contain strong evidence and have been fully investigated by archaeologists as well as geologists and forensics experts. In addition, all have been reported in the professional archaeological literature.

50,000 B.C.
New Mexico: Pendejo Cave
Archaeologist Richard S. MacNeish has been one of the most persistent detractors of the Clovis-first model. Beginning in 1992 he began excavations in a desert area of New Mexico utilizing a team of other archaeologists and forensic scientists. Human hair, 14 hardened clay molds of human fingers and palm prints, a clay effigy, bison and horse bones, and various points and stone artifacts have been recovered at the site. The cave shows evidence of continuous occupation. The levels of occupation, stratig-

raphy layers, were well preserved and well defined. Radiocarbon dating was done on 45 different material samples. The results showed that the cave was in use as early as 50,000 B.C. and was continuously used until about 500 years ago.[8]

18,000 B.C — 16,000 B.C.
California: Manix Basin, Mojave Desert

Numerous points, flakes, cores, anvils, picks, hammmerstones, and other artifacts have been found at this location. They are at least 18,000 years old. [9]

200,000 B.C. — 150,000 B.C.
California: Calico

Nearly 900 stone tools and other artifacts have been recovered from what archaeologists believe was a quarry from which rock was used to form various tools. Dating of the levels has been accomplished by soil-geomorphology and uranium-thorium dating technology. Nearby sites have been dated to 185,000 B.C. [9]

100,000+ B.C.
California: San Diego

Metates, ancient stone grinding blocks, have been found in underwater alluvial layers of the continental shelf. During the Ice Ages these locations were dry land as the ocean level was at least 300 feet lower than today. Geomorphology dating has shown that these embedded grinding stones are older than 100,000 years. Other locations in San Diego, including areas virtually in the downtown area, have yielded similar finds.[10]

100,000 B.C. — 25,000 B.C.
California: Santa Barbara

Evidence recovered from a host of sites indicates that the continental shelf area was densely occupied during periods of lower ocean levels. Santa Rosa Island, San Nicolas Island, and Tecolote Canyon have turned up hearths, mastadon bones, metates, other grinding stones, and stone bowls. Geomorphology and other dating techniques place the finds at 27,000 to 100,000 years old. [10]

293,000 B.C.
Brazil: Esperanca Cave
Pebble tools were found with fossil bones in this cave showing long-term habitation. Uranium-thorium dating was performed on the bones. [7]

America BC: 200,000 Years of Occupation?

With the fall of the Clovis barrier, it is now apparent that America was occupied far earlier than 9500 B.C. The evidence shows that both North and South America were extensively inhabited by 25,000 B.C. The West Coast areas and the southwestern United States were inhabited far earlier than that, however. Several locations date to 50,000 B.C. and the coastal areas of California date far earlier — extending back to as early as an astonishing 200,000 years ago.

Carbon dating is far from exact. One problem with carbon dating is that it loses accuracy as the material that is tested approaches 50,000 years of age. Carbon dating of material that is suspected to be older than 50,000 years is problematical. In addition, evidence uncovered in 2001 has brought the accuracy of all radiocarbon dating into question. It appears that all dates over 3000 years old may be much older. This finding awaits further clarification. However, newer technologies such as geomorphology and uranium-thorium dating have proven valuable tools. In addition, there are even more advanced dating methods under investigation.

In the coming years it is likely that many known Clovis sites will be re-excavated to levels below the Clovis layer. It is a near certainty that many of these, if not the vast majority, will reveal earlier habitation.

Revisiting Cayce

Of the 30 specific statements Cayce made about ancient America, 18 of them took place prior to 9500 B.C. Thus, as long as mainstream archaeology continued to accept the "Clovis-first" date of 9500 B.C. as the beginning of human history in America, it would be absurd to expect any archaeologists to take any of his statements seriously. And since the majority of people believe in the veracity of the history presented in our textbooks, it should be expected that relatively few people outside the Cayce community would give much credibility to Cayce's history. However, with the post-1997 evidence, Cayce's statements take on a different perspective.

While Cayce asserted that humans were present in the southwest 10 million years ago, there is no current evidence supporting this contention. But the age of humanity is progressively being pushed further and further back in time. As stated in Chapter 1, the most recent evidence supports a 6 million year history for human-like ancestors. However, this area of paleontology remains unsettled. The truth is that science simply doesn't know the age of humans. Evidence shows that hominids were in Eastern Asia nearly 2 million years ago, but very few remains of man have been found extending back a million years. As to Cayce's assertion that these very remote people made cave drawings, it could be unreasonable to expect those caves to remain in existence for so long. Cave drawings have been found in New Mexico, but none of these are 10 million years of age. In

Figures 16-19
Examples of ancient cave drawings from Utah, Arizona, and New Mexico. Few of these are dated prior to 1000 B.C. *From — Art Today.*

short, these two contentions about ancient America are currently not verifiable nor are they disproven. Time will tell.

Cayce mentioned 9 events in America occurring around 50,000 B.C. He specifically named California, Santa Barbara, Oregon, Pennsylvania, Ohio, and the Four Corners area. In addition, he mentioned the large animals freely roaming the world and efforts to exterminate them.

Ancient America certainly had very large, very dangerous animals at that time. In fact, the rapid extermination of the megafauna played a role in the development of agriculture in the Americas. The hunting of these enormous animals was efficient and done on a mass scale. Almost all of them were extinct by 8000 B.C. with man the cause of their demise. (See figure 20.)

Three (California, Santa Barbara, and the four corners area) of the six locations Cayce stated were inhabited by 50,000 B.C. have had excavations verify this claim. In addition, one other location (Pennsylvania) has yielded a site only recently redated to 20,000 B.C. The real problem is that archaeologists have not yet had sufficient time to go back to the known Clovis sites and dig deeper.

While Cayce's early dates for humans in America appear valid, that does little in assessing his claims about the origins of these migrants. Despite the demise of the Clovis barrier, many archaeologists continue to assert that, despite the early dates of habitation in America, all of these ancient people came from Siberia. However, a completely unexpected technology appeared in archaeology in the late 1980s — genetic testing. At that time, genetics was still a developing field, but with the swift improvements in genetic technology, startling findings about the people of ancient America emerged. It is to this remarkable evidence we now turn.

Chapter 4

Who Settled America? When Did They Do It?

The first Americans must have entered the North American continent by way of a land bridge across the Bering Strait. … There was, and is still, no reason to doubt the Asian origins of the American Indians.

Dean Snow (1976) *The Archaeology of North America*

For at least 100 years, archaeologists have been certain that Native American Indians originated from Siberian Asia. In fact, the idea was proposed over 400 years ago. In 1590 Friar Joseph de Acosta deduced that the continents of Asia and North America were somehow connected because certain animals had apparently migrated from Asia to the New World. Acosta reasoned that nomadic Asians must have also walked across this connector and published his theory in his book on the Americas, *The Natural and Moral History of the Indies*. But it wasn't until the late 1720s that the Russian explorer Bering discovered the narrows of water separating Asia from North America. With that discovery, it became accepted that the Bering Straits had been the ancient gateway to the New World. In 1794, Ignaz Pfefferkorn wrote, "It is almost certain that the first inhabitants of America really came by way of the strait."

Although the Clovis barrier has now fallen, many have continued to argue that all Native Americans are of Asian origin. But a problem with their theory is that glaciers prevented the nomads from migrating across Beringia (first discussed in Chapter 1) between 28,000 B.C. and 10,000 B.C. To accommodate their beliefs, many Clovis supporters now embrace a water crossing theory despite arguing for the last 50 years that it was impossible for ancient man to cross an ocean. They now assert that Siberian nomads used small hide-covered boats and gradually worked their way down the Pacific coast around 20,000 B.C. Evidence of those voyages may be underwater because the continental shelf would have been the coastline during the ice age. There is no doubt that the majority of ancient American inhabitants came from Siberia and early coastal migrations certainly could have occurred. But this cannot be the only explanation for the many early habitation sites in America and it ignores an astonishingly large and wide-ranging accumulation of contradictory evidence. This evidence includes ancient human skeletal remains that are not Siberian in origin, viral evidence matching ancient Americans to other populations, proof of an active trading network between ancient America and India, Africa, and Europe, and complex genetic matching. Ancient America was a melting pot of people — just as Edgar Cayce stated back in the 1920s. Let's explore the scientific evidence.

Skeletal Evidence — "Skull Wars"

For over 200 years, human skulls and skeletal remains have been recovered in the Americas by amateurs and archaeologists alike. In 1990 a new federal law required museums to return the remains of the ancient Native Americans to tribes that claimed ancestory. (The law is called NAGPRA, short for Native American Graves Protection and Repatriation Act.) As a result, archaeologists quickly intensified ongoing efforts to produce a statistical profile of skulls before they lost them to reburial under the law's provision. Over 90 different measures have been taken on several thousand skulls producing a "craniometric profile" of early Americans. The results have created a controversy in archaeology that many refer to as "Skull Wars."

While most ancient skulls fit the East Asian profile, a disturbingly large number have been found that are clearly different. They do not fit the expected East Asian profile, but rather fit the known profiles from other racial groups. Archaeologists on one side of the issue have argued that some extreme deviations should naturally be expected from the standard "skull" profile.

In truth, the oldest skulls found in America do not show the expected "Mongoloid" (east Asian) appearance. In fact, the profile that has emerged from these old skulls does not match any modern Native American Indian tribe. Two anthropologists, the University of Tennessee's Richard Jantz and Doug Owsley of the Smithsonian, recently completed an evaluation of 11 ancient skulls from America. They concluded that at least three distinct racial groups were present in America 10,000-12,000 years ago including groups related to the aboriginal Anui of Japan, Polynesians, Europeans, and perhaps even Africans.[1]

In Brazil, archaeologist Walter Neves has long studied skulls found in South America. In the late 1999 BBC documentary, *Ancient Voices*, Neves discussed a skull from a female found at the 50,000 year-old habitation site at Serra Da Capivara. Cave drawings at the site depicted giant armadillos which became extinct prior to the last Ice Age. The skull of the female recovered at the site was that of a Melanesian or Australian aborigine. Meanwhile, in Australia, rock art at least 17,000 years of age, but possibly as old as 50,000 years, depicts a high prow ocean-going ship. The prow is the front end of a boat and a high prow is an upward projection that can push waves to the sides allowing movement through rough water. Some archaeologists now speculate that Melanesians may have sailed to South America tens of thousands of years ago. Amazingly, today on the islands of Tierra del Fuego, it is now known that Melanesian descendants, called the Fuegans, still survive. (See figure 20.)

Figure 20
Rare photo taken circa 1900 of the Fuegans at Tierra del Fuego. *From — The Stream of History (1928).*

In the United States, archaeologists have investigated several skulls that have deeply divided factions within the field as well as pitted them against Native American tribes. The famous Kennewick Man, discovered in Washington State in 1996, provided a major tug of war between scientists and Native American groups in a test of the 1990 (NAGPRA reburial) law. Before a federal court order sequestered the remains in Seattle's Burke Museum, scientists investigating Kennewick Man determined he was probably a Polynesian or Japanese Ainu. Other skulls have deepened the mystery. In Nebraska and Minnesota 8,000-9,000 year-old skulls appear to be European or southern Asian. "Burl Woman," an 11,000 year-old female skull found in Idaho is apparently Polynesian. "Spirit Caveman," a 9,400 year-old skull found in Nevada is probably an African bushman!

Viral Evidence

For nearly 10 years, Japanese cancer researcher Kazuo Tajimi has been attempting to unravel the mystery of why a particular type of leukemia virus is not evenly distributed within different populations. A subtype of the HTLV-1 virus, termed "Cosmopolitan A," has been found in the Chilean Andes and with the Atacamanian people, a small subpopulation of Japan. The disease spreads by direct human contact and causes infection in about three percent of those who carry the virus.

Seeking clues, Tajimi and her group from the Aichi Cancer Center Research Institute in Nagoya, Japan, scanned 104 mummies found intact in the Andes. After removing DNA from a 1,500 year-old mummy's bone marrow, they were able to identify viral DNA strands. Several comparisons between the Japanese and Chilean version of the virus showed they were identical. Yet, this specific virus is found in no other areas of the world. Aside from the implications for cancer research, scientists concluded that perhaps 25,000 years ago the racial group from which both the Chilean and Japanese populations had derived split into two. One group went to Japan while the other went to South America.[2]

In another study, in 1997 researchers from the National Institutes of Health decided to trace the genetic lineage of the human polyomavirus JC (JCV). This virus causes a progressive central nervous system disease. The researchers recruited 68 Navaho Indians from New Mexico, 25 Flathead Indians from Montana, and 29 Chamorro Tribe members from Guam. Strains of viral DNA were collected from urine samples and subsequently isolated and matched. All three groups were discovered to carry a unique subtype of the virus found only in China and Japan. As a result, it was concluded that these groups had a racial linkage that could have separated as long ago as 50,000 years to more than 100,000 years.[3]

The implications of this research could be profound. Most archaeologists prefer to explain the findings by their standard belief. That is, all of these groups started out in Asia; from there, some migrated to Japan or China. Others crossed Beringia into America while a few migrated to Guam and nearby islands. However, it may be more likely that the groups identified by this research entered America directly from Japan, China, and Guam. An even more interesting possibility is that a simultaneous migration occurred to ancient America, Japan, China, and Guam from an unknown location somewhere among these vastly-separated areas.

Cocaine and Nicotine Mummies From Ancient Egypt & Europe

Some of the most provocative evidence all but "proving" contact occurred between ancient America and the Old World was first published in the respected medical journal *Lancet* in 1993.[4] It all began when three researchers at the Institute for Anthropology and Human Genetics in Munich, Germany began studying mummies excavated from several widely different areas. The research was conducted to identify the extent of drug usage in ancient times. Toxicologist Svelta Balabanova was employed to conduct unusual drug usage testing on the remains. Balabanova had pioneered testing methods to detect the presence of drugs in hair and sweat, which are in widespread use today. The mummies examined included 72 from Peru (dated at 200-1500 A.D.) and 11 from Egypt (dated at 1070 B.C.-395 A.D.). In addition, skeletal tissue from 10 German remains (dated at 2500 B.C.) and two remains of Sudanese (dated at 5000 B.C. and 1400 A.D.) were examined. Tests designed to pick-up traces of cocaine, hashish (marihuana), and nicotine were performed on all of the remains.

The results were startling. German and Sudanese remains contained nicotine. Both cocaine and nicotine were found in the Peruvian and Egyptian mummies. Since cocaine and nicotine are from plants native only to the Americas and have not been found to ever have grown anywhere else, Balabanova first believed she had somehow contaminated the samples. So she had all of her equipment cleaned and recalibrated. But the new tests came back with the same results. She repeated the tests again with the same results. She then sent the samples to several other labs for testing. All of their test outcomes verified earlier results. When Balabanova published a paper on her findings, she suddenly found herself at the center of a storm of controversy. She received open threats, insults, and accusations of fraud from other scientists and archaeologists. The subject was so intriguing that a television documentary was made from the research and subsequent events.

What makes this research so significant is that Balabanova's credentials and techniques are so scientifically impeccable. Balabanova is an experienced forensic toxicologist who works with police, criminal investigations, and as a researcher. The method she developed for extracting drug metabolites from the protein in hair shafts is considered infallible. Drug metabolites can only become incorporated into the protein structure of hair by being consumed by a living person where it eventually grows into the hair shaft. It is impossible for any drugs to be absorbed into the hair shaft structure after the death of the individual. Thus, Balabanova then suspected that the mummies and remains she had been given to test had somehow been misidentified or were fakes. However, the museum responsible for the remains verified that all of them were genuine and uncontaminated.

One skeptic was Rosalie David, Keeper of Egyptology at the Manchester Museum in England. She had hair samples and tissue from several of the Egyptian mummies housed in her museum collection sent out for testing. Three came back positive for nicotine — a result which stunned her. At the same time Balabanova decided to have the remains from 134 naturally preserved bodies in Sudan's desert sent to her for analysis. These remains dated to about 1100 A.D. One-third of them tested positive for nicotine and cocaine. These results confirmed what was once unthinkable. People were traveling between America and other areas in the world in ancient times.

Several international archaeologists have long believed that a vast ancient trading network occurred between the Americas and the rest of the world. They have long asserted that North American archaeologists discount such evidence because it refutes their "Clovis-first" theory. With this evidence, many American archaeologists have conceded that ancient trading did occur. However, many others remained not just skeptical, but openly hostile. But Balabanova discovered an additional curious fact that had been suppressed in 1976. On September 26, 1976, the mummy of Ramses II arrived in Paris for an exhibition. Ramses II had died in 1213 B.C. and the mummy had been carefully preserved. However, when it was examined in Paris, several experts had to be called in to repair damage to the wrappings. Pieces of the deteriorated wrapping were removed and sent out for analysis. Filaments of tobacco and nicotine crystals were found embedded in the wrappings. Michelle Lescot, an analyst and anthropologist at the Natural History Museum of Paris, investigated the wrapping pieces and the tobacco found in them. She stated that she couldn't believe the results and ran the tests again and again. It is now believed that part of the mummification process utilized tobacco because nicotine is an antibacterial agent as well as insecticide. In addition, this research shows that there is no doubt that people throughout the ancient Old World had access to tobacco and smoked it.

That both tobacco and cocaine were used by some ancient Egyptians as well as other ancient people in Europe and Asia is an incredibly important finding for New World archaeology. Botanists are certain that there were no variations of the Coca plant anywhere else in the world. The only possible source for Coca (cocaine) was South America. And tobacco was only grown in the New World. This means that ancient contact between America and Egypt had to occur. The oldest mummies and remains tested in these studies were about 5,000 years old. Some researchers believe that it is highly likely that trading networks between the Old and New worlds existed far earlier than that date, but testing of older remains has not yet been done.

Corn in India

Carl L. Johannessen is a retired professor from the University of Oregon who served as chairman of the Geography department there in the late 1970s and early 1980s. During the 1990s, Johannessen devoted his attention to investigating the reason maize (ancient forms of corn) is depicted on temple sculptures in India. It is well known that maize was indigenous only to the Americas and was supposedly carried to the Old World only after Columbus' voyages.

Johannessen found that virtually all of the 35 temples he visited from the Hoysala Dynasty in Karnataka State of India had statues with maize depicted. Most temples had dozens of these statues. For example, the temple at Somnathpur has 82 figures holding maize. In addition, each statue is unique and each depiction of maize is unique. (See figure 21.) Some statues depicting the entire corn plant were also found. Although these temples date to about 1200 A.D., the maize depicted was of an ancient variety believed to have existed only in America as long as 7,000 years ago. Johannessen also found statues of Hindu gods in west central India holding maize in their hands. The temples with these figures are known to have been built in about 600 A.D.

Figure 21
Close-up view of an ear of corn held by 3-foot tall figure at Somnathpur, India. This is only one of over 100 such statues. *After Johannessen.*

Johannessen is convinced that an active trading network between ancient America and India had to have existed. The earliest date this trading network existed is unknown, but it could be as long ago as 5,000-7,000 years.[5]

Native American DNA — Modern & Ancient

DNA analysis on Native Americans began in the 1980s, but with rapid technological improvements, research intensified in the early 1990s. Several teams of genetics researchers at prominent American universities have been conducting numerous studies. Although results from early studies showed the expected Siberian-Asia ancestry of the majority of modern Native American tribes, things took an unexpected turn in 1997. At that point it was found that a small percentage of modern Native Americans have an unusual type of DNA then known to exist only in a few locations in Europe and the Middle East. Subsequent research indicated that the European DNA was not the result of genetic mixing after Columbus. In addition, the same DNA was later found in the bone of an ancient American burial confirming that people carrying this unique DNA had entered America in ancient times. However, in July 2001, this unique gene was also found in a small tribe living in the northern Gobi Desert area. The DNA research initially seemed to promise solid proof of not only *where* the ancient Americans came from, but also *when* they came. However, as might be expected, ancient DNA research has become a highly contentious issue with several competing sides.

Most of the DNA research on Native American Indians has been done utilizing mitochondria. Every cell in our body contains hundreds to thousands of these tiny, football-shaped organelles. The mitochondria process glucose (sugar) into a usable form of energy for all of our body's functions. The mitochondria are believed to be an evolutional form of bacteria that adapted into a symbiotic relationship with multi-celled life forms. Thus, the mitochondria have their own unique DNA, which is simpler and easier to analyze than the human DNA found in the nucleus.

Mitochondrial DNA (usually abbreviated as mtDNA) is passed to offspring only through the egg. Thus, it is not a combination of male and female genes. It is a haploid gene — meaning that it has only one dose of chromosomes. The haploid mitochondrial DNA shows only the female lineage of a person. Diploid genes are two sets of combined chromosomes, the female set coming from the egg, the male chromosomes from the sperm.

Mitochondrial DNA (mtDNA) is categorized into several types and groups termed haplotypes and haplogroups. That is, there are variations in the genetic code of mitochondria that fit into clusters. These clusters can trace lineage far back into time. There are 39 different, distinct mtDNA groups into which all humans fit.

While mtDNA analysis is not only easier than other forms of genetic testing, it has a further advantage. All DNA mutates over time. But mtDNA has a fairly steady rate of mutation that permits a reasonably accurate estimate of exactly when a particular group of people migrated from their primary group. Thus, two important factors can be determined through analysis of mtDNA. First, a living person (or the mtDNA from the remains of a deceased person) can be tested to determine the specific racial group from which the individual came. Secondly, the approximate time when that individual's ancestors migrated from their primary racial group can be determined.

One way to view mtDNA testing is that it may be able to provide a racial family tree extending back to the beginning of humanity. The current idea in mtDNA analysis is that ancestory on the female side can eventually be traced back to a genetic "Eve." The 39 types of mtDNA were presumably derived from this Eve. Whether this idea will be completely confirmed by research remains to be seen. However, mtDNA testing has confirmed several oral traditions passed down through many generations in several tribes. For example, the indigenous people of Hawaii and Polynesia have long asserted that their ancestors frequently traveled back and forth and that they shared ancestry. Genetic testing showed that these two groups were related and confirmed the migratory legends of these peoples.[6]

Confirming the Siberian Migration

The first research on living Native American tribes showed they were comprised of four distinct mtDNA haplogroups called A, B, C, and D. This means that the Native Americans are derived from four different lineages. These haplogroups were also found in native populations in Central and South America. Later mtDNA research utilizing ancient remains recovered in the Americas validated these four haplogroups. Three of these haplogroups, A, C, and D are found primarily in Siberian Asia. The B haplogroup, however, is found only in aboriginal groups in Southeast Asia, China, Japan, Melanesia, and Polynesia.

Confirming a South Pacific and Japanese Migration

Based on the mutations found in the mtDNA, most researchers think that groups A, C, and D entered America from Siberia across Beringia some time around 35,000 B.C. Group B, they assert, probably came to America from the South Pacific or Japan via boats. It is believed the B groups began this migration not long after the A, C, and D groups arrived. However, the majority of the B group arrived about 11,000 B.C. This leaves open the possibility of several migrations by the B group from different locations.

It should be noted that a few geneticists have proposed that each of these four haplogroups came in four separate migrations. And many Clovis supporters argue that all the groups migrated together. However, the most popular theory is that there were three distinct waves of migration. This idea is referred to as the "Greenberg Hypothesis."

Joseph Greenberg, a retired professor of linguistics and anthropology from Stanford University, found that the primary mtDNA types matched the types of tooth structure and primary language spoken in different Native American tribes. Greenberg showed long ago that the 500 different languages spoken by indigenous American tribes essentially fell into three major linguistic groups. Amerind was spoken by most American Indians, Eskimo-Aleut was found in Aleutian Islanders and Eskimo tribes, and Na-Dene was spoken on the Northwest coast of Canada and the United States. In addition, there was a different primary type of tooth structure found among these three groups. As a result, Greenberg believes that there were three different waves of migration into the Americas.

An Unknown and Unexpected Migration Group Confirmed

In 1997, a fifth mtDNA haplogroup was identified in Native Americans. This group, called "X," is present in three percent of living Native Americans. Haplogroup X was not then found in Asia, but was found only in Europe and the Middle East where two to four percent of the population carry it. In those areas, the X haplogroup has primarily been found in parts of Spain, Bulgaria, Finland, Italy, and Israel. In July 2001, a research letter was published in the *American Journal of Human Genetics*, relating that a few people with the "X" type had been identified in a tribe located in extreme southern Siberia. These people, called the *Altasians*, or Altaics as Russian geneticists refer to them, have always lived in the Gobi Desert area. Archaeologists and geneticists are certain that the presence of "X" in America is not the result of historic intermarriages. It is of ancient origin.

Among Native American tribes, the X haplogroup has been found in small numbers in the Yakima, Sioux, and Navaho tribes. It has been found to a larger degree in the Ojibway, Oneota, and Nuu-Chah-Nulth tribes. The X haplogroup has also been discovered in ancient remains in Illinois near Ohio and a few other areas near the Great Lakes. It has not (so far) been found in South or Central American tribes including the Maya.

The X haplogroup appears to have entered America in limited numbers perhaps as long ago as 34,000 B.C. Around 12,000 B.C. to 10,000 B.C. it appeared in much greater numbers. It is important to note that not all Native American tribes have been categorized by mtDNA analysis and that relatively few ancient remains have been tested.[7-14]

The Significance of mtDNA Research

The mtDNA research confirms most of the other new findings in archaeology. The Americas were settled early and many different racial groups came. Several different waves of migration probably occurred. The initial wave seems to have occurred around 35,000 B.C. However, it may have been far earlier since some of the recent radiocarbon dates that have emerged from areas like California and the southwest point to 50,000 B.C. But it must be kept in mind that mtDNA analysis is still in its infancy. Not all current Native American tribes and very few remains have been tested. But the picture the mtDNA research findings paint of ancient America is astonishing.

It may seem that the apparent widespread presence of the X type (from Canada and Washington State, to Arizona, to the Plains, to the Great Lakes area) could indicate a wide initial dispersal. However, the history of several of these tribes tells a different story.

The Sioux, who show the X type, were the ancient enemy of the Chippewa. They were driven to the Western Plains from the Great Lakes area not long after the first European explorers entered America. Prior to living in the Great Lakes area, the Sioux resided in the southern Ohio area and neighboring parts of Kentucky and Indiana. It is strongly believed that the Sioux have Iroquois' origins.[15] The Chippewa, the mortal enemies of the Sioux, are also known as the Ojibway — another tribe with the X type. The place of origin of the Ojibway is not known, but it is known that they routinely battled with the Iroquois before they moved to the Great Lakes area. [15]

The Oneotas, also an X type, are actually a cultural blend of ancient tribes originating in Ohio as well as near the beginning of the Mississippi River and in Iowa and Wisconsin. They are part Sioux and are known to have been involved in the Hopewell and Adena moundbuilding eras. The Oneotas also are believed to be Iroquois in origin. [16]

The Yakima and Nuu-Chah-Nulth tribes reside in the far Northwest corner of America and in Northwest Canada. Their origins are almost completely unknown except it is assumed they must have crossed into America from Siberia. The presence of the X type within their tribes deepens the mystery. The finding of the X group in the north Gobi-dwelling Altasians is hailed as proof that all American migrations came from Siberia via the Bering Straits, yet it seems unlikely. With the X type being present in the Middle East, Europe, and America, a migration from the Gobi to all of these areas is doubtful.

The Cayce readings cite a series of large and small migrations of Atlanteans to very specific parts of the world. These migrations occurred at several times, but especially during the years approaching 10,000 B.C. One of these places was to the Gobi in extreme southern Siberian Asia. If we assume that haplotype X originated from Cayce's Atlantis, some of the X haplotype should be found in the Gobi region — but very little of this group should be found elsewhere in Siberia. This is what has been found.

The presence of the X type in ancient remains from the Great Lakes area as well as in modern Great Lakes tribes indicates that the X in America may well be Iroquois in origin. The Iroquois were initially a vast collection of tribes originating in the regions around the St. Lawrence region. These 15 to 20 tribes occupied most of the Eastern seaboard of Canada as well as Eastern America all the way to the Great Lakes.[17] They were the early "Red Paint" people (circa 3,000 B.C.) who made small burial mounds and spread large amounts of red ochre (hematite) on the remains. The ancient Iroquois experienced constant violent conflict within and between their tribes. The result was that the tribes eventually migrated far away from their enemies gradually moving everywhere in America and Canada. The Cherokee are Iroquois in origin as are many of the remaining tribes in the Great Lakes region as well the Northeastern United States.

Reflections on Cayce's Statements

Cayce stated that people entered the Americas in three distinct waves tied to cataclysmic events. The first wave took place in about 50,000 B.C. The vast majority of these people came into the Americas from the west from Mu. According to Cayce, many of the people of Mu also went to China, Japan, and South America. About the same time, Cayce stated that some people entered the Americas from the east from Atlantis. In addition, a small group from the South Pacific entered the southwest of America and established the cliff-dweller culture.

The second wave of migration took place in 28,000 B.C. These he describedas people who "crossed the Pacific" as well as people from China and Atlantis. The Atlanteans who entered America eventually congregated in the Ohio area and also became the ancient Iroquois. Later they became the mound builders. Another group of these Atlanteans went to Iberia with the majority of them moving into the Pyrenees Mountains, and a few went to the Gobi. The third wave of migration occurred in about 10,000 B.C. from Atlantis. These Atlanteans migrated to the American northeast and southwest with a very small group going to the Yucatan. Large groups of Atlanteans also went to Egypt, Iberia, and the Gobi. Civilizations pre-existed in both Egypt and the Gobi at that time.

Evidence from skulls, viral research, and mtDNA analyses essentially support all of Cayce's contentions regarding the timing and direction of migrations into America. Migrations into America did occur from China, from across the Pacific (Japan), and from South Pacific Islands (Polynesia and Melanesia). In addition, the largest migration into the Americas occurred from the west as Cayce stated.

B Haplogroup may Originate from Mu

The B haplogroup, found only in aboriginal groups in Southeast Asia, China, Japan, Melanesia, and Polynesia, may represent Cayce's people of Mu. Both Chinese and Japanese archaeologists take the idea of Mu seriously, and the B haplogroup findings closely match the story Cayce told about the continent. Most of the people of Mu who escaped the destruction in 50,000 B.C. escaped to China, India, and Japan. Some time later, descendants of these peoples could have traveled to America. While Cayce said that some people from Mu entered the Americas about 50,000 B.C., he did not indicate that date as the time period when the majority of them came. We only know that it was after 50,000 B.C. and prior to 28,000 B.C.

A, C, & D Haplogroups —From Siberia?

The Cayce readings do indicate that people entered the Americas from both the east and west in 28,000 B.C. These migrants came from Atlantis, China, and from "across the Pacific." The 28,000 B.C. date matches well with the haplogroups A, B, C, and D proposed dates of entry into America. The Cayce readings do have references to the Bering Straits, but Cayce did not relate that there were migrations across it. In fact, no one ever thought to ask him about this, so it remains an open question in the Cayce story. But the A, C, and D haplogroups clearly originated in Siberia just as the archaeologists have speculated. Cayce stated that the "yellow" or Mongol race of humanity originated in the Gobi and gradually spread throughout Asia. Thus, according to Cayce, haplogroups A, C, and D probably originated in the Gobi and would be the migrations Cayce cited as coming from "across the Pacific."

The Atlantean Haplogroup may be X

Cayce indicated that the largest migration from Atlantis occurred just before 10,000 B.C. The majority of these Atlantean survivors went to the Northeastern coastal areas of America and Canada becoming the Iroquois. It should be recalled that Cayce also stated that not *all* of the Iroquois were Atlantean. The Atlanteans migrating to the Americas merged with the people already present in America by that time. The Atlanteans became leaders of the tribes. Cayce's story makes it clear that the the Atlanteans had serious disputes among themselves that were reflected in ongoing violent conflict. (This was the struggle between the Belial and Law of One groups.) This is confirmed by the Iroquois' ancient history that tells of constant battles resulting in distant displacements of entire tribes to ensure their survival.

Perhaps the most astonishing confirmation of Cayce's story of ancient America is the presence of haplogroup X. Geneticists at first assumed that the source of X was in the Caucasus Mountains. Why? Because a few people with the X haplotype are there and the standard story is that *all* people came out of Africa into Asia — and all of the Native Americans came from Asia. But in truth, the actual source of the X haplogroup is completely unknown. What is known is that the X haplogroup first showed up in America perhaps 34,000 years ago, but its main entry occurred in 10,000 B.C. These dates match Cayce's timeframe for Atlantean migrations as well as the occurrence of X in the specific tribes predicted by his statements. The X group also appears to have shown up in ancient Iberia about the same time as well as in the Gobi. These dates match Cayce's story of the final two destructions of Atlantis and the resulting migrations to these areas. In fact, the existence of the X group in tribes that were located in Ohio, the heart of the mound builder culture, perfectly matches Cayce's story. In addition, Cayce was careful to state that the Atlanteans merged with the indigenous peoples already present in the area. Thus, the primary DNA in these tribes would not be Atlantean. And that is exactly what has been found.

Another interesting statement by Cayce was that the Iroquois of noble blood were pure Atlantean. To our knowledge, no mtDNA testing has occurred yet with the modern Iroquois remaining in Northeastern areas. However, tribes that were in the exact same geographical area as the Iroquois do show the X type as well as tribes that were once Iroquois.

One more interesting issue merits mention in regard to the X haplogroup in modern Native Americans. The X type has not yet been found in any Central or South American natives. While Cayce stated that Atlanteans went to the Yucatan in about 10,000 B.C., this group consisted of an individual named Iltar and only 10 other people.[18] Their purpose was to build a "Hall of Records" that would contain a history of humanity. The location of this site is strongly believed to be at Piedras Negras in Guatemala. Because of conflicts with the groups already present in the area, the Atlantean descendants of Iltar's group eventually left the Yucatan and moved to the Ohio area.[18] Thus, the X type may not be present in modern Mayan people. However, it may well be that mtDNA analysis of ancient human remains excavated from Piedras Negras or nearby sites associated with it would show the X type. Such research has not yet been conducted but would obviously present intriguing — if not incredible — possibilities.

Evidence of Atlantean Migration to America and Europe

It is logical to theorize that the X haplogroup entered the Americas as well as Europe at roughly the same time. A central location between these two continents would be the logical place from which such a migration would occur. Another finding also supports this idea. One of the most compelling facts that has been ignored by American archaeologists — until recent times — is that a culture in France and Spain, called the Solutrean, was virtually *identical* to the American Clovis Culture. The Solutrean Culture began in about 15,000 B.C. in the areas of Europe where Cayce said many Atlanteans fled. These areas centered on the Pyrenees Mountains between Spain and France. Clovis, considered to be the most advanced of the ancient American cultures, emerged suddenly in the Americas in 11,000 B.C. Both of these identical cultures may have originated from the same source. Once again, it is logical to theorize that a central location between America and Europe existed and that migrations from it led to the development of identical cultures on the two continents.

The evidence emerging from a host of new research areas is showing how true Cayce's "impossible" assertions about America may well be. Numerous findings have now verified the timeframe and background Cayce gave for ancient American migrations. When Cayce gave his readings on ancient America (1924-1945), no one seriously considered that people entered the Americas prior to 11,000 B.C. And multiple migrations into America from different locations were considered impossible. The idea of ancient contact between America with China, Polynesia, Japan, and other areas in the South Pacific was ludicrous. The idea that a tribe such as the Iroquois could show an ancient racial heritage linking them to people in Europe and the MiddleEast was preposterous. Yet Cayce calmly told these stories and gently endured ridicule. In later chapters, we will revisit much of this research. However, some of Cayce's most impossible statements referred to the mound builders, and that is where we will go next.

Chapter 5

Builders of High Places

It is difficult now to understand how intensely interested people were in the mounds and their builders a century and more ago, and we have trouble realizing why people were so eager to believe that the mounds were the creations of superior beings hidden in the mists of time. The old myths are dead, and archaeologists smile at the fancies of yesteryear.

Robert Silverberg (1968) *The Mound Builders*

M odern archaeology has never recognized the term "mound build- ers" as meaning anything more than *people who built mounds.* But when the American mounds first came to the attention of the early Euro- pean settlers, everyone was so impressed with the size and complexity of them that a myth of a lost race of advanced mound builders arose. Euro- peans entering the New World could not believe that the "savage Indians" who were being driven further and further West were related to the mounds. Gradually, the idea of a lost race of mound builders came to be viewed as a slur on the Native Americans and has been cast as racism. We do not wish to enter such arguments, but simply seek to examine the cur- rent scientific evidence regarding ancient America.

It can be said with some confidence that the mounds were built by the ancestors of modern Native Americans. But, as the prior chapters have shown, ancient Americans came from many places and arrived at many different times. America, it seems, has always been a melting pot.

The Genesis of
American Mound Building
The Red Paint People

Mounds for the dead were constructed everywhere in the ancient world. Mounds and similar structures are found in Siberia, China, Korea, Japan, Africa, and all of Europe. Archaeologists are uncertain of exactly where the idea of mounds originated, but it is generally thought that various cultures began constructing mounds at the same time.

In the *Iliad*, Homer wrote how burial mounds were constructed for Achilles' friend Patroclus and Hector. In 450 B.C., Herodotus wrote how a huge mound was erected for a Scythian king in Russia. Alexander the Great had a gigantic mound built over the remains of Hephaestion. In 362 A.D. Emperor Julian was buried under a huge mound after dying in a war against the Persians. In both Scandinavia and the British Isles mounds nearly identical to those in North America have been fascinating curiosities for thousands of years.

The erection of mounds for ritualistic and ongoing ceremonial purposes seems related to burial mound practices — but at the same time "different." In the Bible, the Canaanites worshiped God in "high places" and scattered references to ceremonies and altar use at these "high places" are also found. In America some mounds represented artificial "high places" and were usually built near conical burial mounds. In a later chapter, we'll go into some depth discussing the significance of these "high places."

The traditional story of American burial mounds has been thought to begin in about 3,000 B.C. in the New England area by the ancestors of the Iroquois. There, an enigmatic group called the "Red Paint People" began burying their dead in small mounds. (Note that the term "Red Paint People" is no longer in favor in archaeology. The term "Moorehead burial tradition" is now used.) A shallow pit was first dug and then lined with red hematite (ochre). The remains of the deceased were then placed in the pit. Next, personal objects were arranged carefully beside the deceased. These artifacts were often elaborate and exquisite. "Most graves contain celts (axes), adzes and gouges, often highly polished and sometimes still sharp enough to inflict a deep cut on a careless archaeologist."[1] Fire-making kits of pyrite and flint, exquisite, long and pointed whetstones, very long, perfectly formed thin slate spear points, and beautiful points made of translucent quartzite are frequently found in these burials. The slate spear points are similar to bayonets and are often covered with exquisite markings. These markings typically form a repeating hexagonal pattern. The burial was completed by spreading large amounts of ground-up hematite on the remains and artifacts after which a small mound of dirt was heaped atop it.

Archaeologists have long believed that the red color of hematite was symbolic of blood. The use of it in burials was, according to this line of reasoning, a means of aiding existence in the afterlife. As with ancient Egyptian practices, an individual was buried with his or her possessions and tools so that they would accompany the person to the afterlife.[1]

The Yucatan & The Red Paint People — A Cayce Connection?

The Cayce readings stated that just prior to 10,000 B.C. a group of 11 Atlanteans went to the Yucatan and established a center to house their ancient records. At the same time, many Atlanteans migrated to the Northeastern coast of America where they eventually became the historical Iroquois. In *The Lost Hall of Records*, the site of Piedras Negras, Guatemala is identified as the location where Iltar and 10 other Atlanteans probably built the Hall of Records. In his many readings on the Yucatan Hall of Records, Cayce stated that a six-sided figure would be found near the temple housing the records. This hexagonal figure, according to Cayce, was an "emblem" representing the Atlantean "firestone." The firestone was a crystal utilized as a power source in Atlantis as well as a means of communication between man and God.

A hexagonal carving does, in fact, appear on a massive stone slab at Piedras Negras in a manner clearly fitting Cayce's description of it. In addition, a number of unusual hematite artifacts were recovered at the site. Hematite (red ochre) is paramagnetic in nature. In his readings, Cayce stated that the Atlanteans brought "stones of the magnetized influence" along with them and that the firestone itself "was a crystal: 'in the form of a six-sided figure.'" Hematite forms 6-sided crystals at its molecular level.

The importance of hematite at both locations where Cayce said the Atlanteans fled in 10,000 B.C. is intriguing. The exquisite hexagonal engravings on the finest artifacts recovered at the 3,000 B.C. Red Paint People burial sites may well be related to the hexagonal carving at Piedras Negras.

Old Copper Culture

About the same time that the Red Paint People were building small burial mounds on the east coast, in the area of the northern Great Lakes another group also constructed small mounds. At Isle Royal and nearby areas on the southern shore of Lake Superior, the remains of the "Old Copper Culture" are found. Burials were similar to those in the Northeast and small naturally-occurring hills, called kames, were also utilized for burials.

Over 100 books have been written on the Old Copper Culture. Many of these have been written by mining engineers as well as archaeologists. However, many other books on this intriguing culture are highly controversial. The reason is that much more copper was mined from this area than can be accounted for by its usage in artifacts in America. Estimates are that, for every amount of copper utilized by Native American Indians, 2000 times as much copper is unaccounted for or went "somewhere else." That "somewhere else" has been theorized to be Europe and Egypt. The

Figure 22
Ancient mining at Lake Superior as depicted by *Schoolcraft (1855)*.

most controversial theorists assert that the Bronze Age in Europe (as well as in ancient Egypt) was fueled by copper mined from Lake Superior. The amounts of copper removed from this area have been estimated by the number of ancient mines found and the amount of material excavated from them. The most conservative estimate is that 100 million pounds was removed while the highest estimate is 1.5 billion pounds.[2]

On Isle Royal alone, over 2000 ancient mining pits can be seen today along with over 200,000 ancient hammer stones that were used to cut raw copper out of huge veins running deep into the earth. (See figure 22.) The world's largest source of almost pure copper is found along a 150-mile long 4-7 mile-wide swath along Lake Superior. The largest copper "nugget" found there in historic times was reportedly 46 tons. It had been dug out of a mine by ancient miners but it was too large and heavy to be moved. Numerous other copper nuggets have been found including one nearly 7 tons in weight. It was found 18 feet down a mineshaft but it had been raised and propped up 5 feet above the mine floor with logs.[2]

Carbon dating of materials associated with the ancient miners has been done many, many times. The vast majority of the dates center around 2500 B.C. with some dates at 3000 B.C.[3] The skill and determination of these people is apparent in their mines. The average mine pit was about 20 feet in diameter and 30 feet deep. However, many mines dated to 2500 B.C. are much larger. For example, huge trenches 100 feet across were sunk up to 60 feet deep into solid rock.[4]

Research has shown that the people of the Old Copper Culture were definitely related to the Red Paint People — both groups were the ancestors of the historic Iroquois.[3]

Cayce & The Old Copper Culture

The word "copper" appears 1205 times on the Cayce Readings CD ROM in 618 different documents. All of these were examined. The vast majority of these occurrences describe the use of copper sulfate and small copper plates in health applications. Many readings detail the significance of copper in electrical and magnetic conduction and in understanding the vibrational qualities of the metal. Two readings (661-4 and 1931-3) mentioned the vast copper deposits near Lake Superior but did not go into any further detail.

While Cayce was silent on details of the Old Copper Culture, the suggestion by modern writers that the Lake Superior copper deposits were taken to ancient Egypt is addressed indirectly in the readings. Two readings (both in the 294-142 to 294-153 series) discussed the use of copper in ancient Egypt. These readings indicated that the copper used in Egypt came from mines in Upper Egypt and stated that the actual ancient mine locations had not yet been discovered in modern times. As to the possibility that copper from Lake Superior helped fuel the Bronze Age in Europe, the Cayce readings are completely silent. Several readings do mention copper mines in Europe, but nothing else of relevance. Large amounts of copper being transported to Europe thousands of years ago would have been rather significant. If this had occurred, it is likely that Cayce would have mentioned it. We can assume with some confidence that the implication from the Cayce readings is that it didn't occur.

According to other Cayce readings, copper was an important metal in Atlantis. The Iroquois, as descendants from Atlantean migrations, would certainly have found and mined metals everywhere they went. Thus, it should not be surprising that ancient Iroquois tribes mined copper. In summary, the presence of the early Iroquois in the Old Copper Culture is consistent with the Cayce readings.

Poverty Point Earthworks & Mounds: 2500 B.C. — 1500 B.C.

While both the Red Paint People and the Old Copper Culture peoples constructed small burial mounds, neither group is considered to be a true "mound building culture" since they didn't construct earthworks, large burial mounds, or ceremonial mounds. The distinction of the first "mound builder culture" has been bestowed upon an amazing site near Epps, Louisiana. Since its discovery on an aerial photograph by James Ford in 1953, the Poverty Point, Louisiana site has been considered to be the first genuine "mound builder" site. (This, however, is no longer true as we shall see in the next section.)

In 1953 Ford was given an aerial Army photograph of the Poverty Point area that was taken in the 1930s. Knowing that many artifacts had been found at this location, Ford carefully examined the photo and spotted several curiosities. He noticed what looked like a mound and a parallel series of ridges forming a semi-octagonal pattern. The ridges were uniform and obviously man-made and ended at a bluff along what was once the Arkansas River. After investigating the site, archaeologists were astonished. They quickly discovered a huge bird effigy mound that was facing a three-quarter-mile wide series of semi-octagonal embankments forming terraces.

The effigy mound is 72 feet tall and, from wing tip to wing tip, measures 640 feet. The mound measures 710 feet from the effigy's head to its tail. Several other smaller mounds still remain at the site.[5] (See figure 23.)

Carbon dating revealed that the people who developed what has become known as the Poverty Point Culture lived there by 2500 B.C. They constructed the mound effigy and embankments sometime around 1800 B.C. Up to 10,000 people lived at this complex site until around 600 B.C. Huts were built atop the multiple 6-10 foot high, semi-octagonal embankments. The terraces formed by the embankments were 80 feet wide and spaced about 150 feet apart. The terraces, most of which are still visible today, were built in a short time frame and have a total linear length of over 7 miles.[3]

As can be seen in figure 23, the mounds and the inhabited terraces had several straight aisles formed through them. These aisles allowed observations of the rising and setting sun on the equinoxes.[3] Other alignments to solar, lunar, or stellar observations are suspected at the site.

Figure 23
A fascinating reconstructive drawing of what Poverty Point probably looked like circa 1000 B.C. Note the many walkways and the wooden posts used for alignments. Circular houses can be seen on the embanked terraces. The giant bird effigy mound is in the upper right center side. *From — Poverty Point by Jon L. Gibson (1983).*

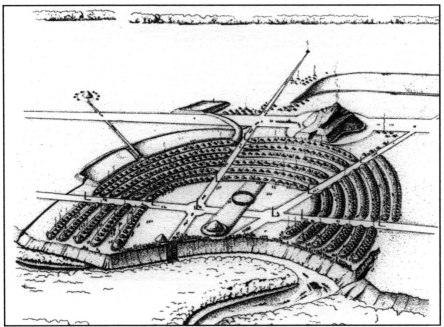

Artifacts recovered at Poverty Point have shown that the Poverty Point people traveled and traded widely. Hunters at ancient Poverty Point used a special device called a bola to catch birds and small game. The bolas consisted of three or more weights polished into a teardrop shape attached to each other by leather or rope. The weights were made of a special hematite found only in Missouri or Southwestern Arkansas. From North Carolina unique soapstone was brought in to be used for pots. Lake Superior copper, Lake Michigan slate, Ohio flint, and tons of steatite from Georgia and Alabama have been found at Poverty Point.[3, 5]

Archaeology has long accepted a possible Olmec influence at Poverty Point.[1] (It is the only ancient American site to have this distinction.) Some of the artifacts found at Poverty Point closely resemble artifacts found at early Olmec sites along the Gulf Coast of Mexico. Poverty Point's layout has some resemblance to the Olmec sites of La Venta and Corral both of which were occupied by this time. "It is difficult to avoid concluding that Poverty Point was a product of Olmec influence, and the gateway through which the idea of monumental architecture passed into the Eastern Woodlands."[1]

The 1997 Watson Brake Mound Announcement — The New Beginning of American Mound Building

In the 1970s, logging operations began to clear-cut an area about 20 miles southwest of Monroe, Louisiana. This location, known as Watson Brake, lies about 60 miles from Poverty Point. Only three or four mounds were discovered at that time and since Louisiana is literally dotted with mound sites, no one was surprised or took particular notice. In 1981, more logging operations at the site revealed a fairly large number of mounds and a strange circular embankment. An amateur archaeologist and an interested citizen (Reca Bamburg Jones and John Belmont) became convinced that the site was important. Jones met with the logging company and urged them to leave the mounds and earthworks intact. After the logging company agreed to bypass Watson Brake, Jones and Belmont tried to convince academic archaeologists to examine the site. Archaeologists visited the site, but left unimpressed. Undaunted, the two continued to urge formal archaeological investigation of the site as Jones gradually discovered a circular embankment that supported many mounds.

In July 1993, Joe W. Saunders, the state's archaeologist for that region, cored the first sample from the tallest mound at the site (26 feet). Saunders was astonished to find that the core indicated that the site was much older than he expected. He subsequently spent several years studying the site taking more samples for carbon dating and geological analysis. In 1997, Saunders reported in the journal *Science* that Watson Brake was now the oldest known mound site in America. He dated it to about 3400 B.C.[6] The announcement took archaeology completely by surprise and required a substantial revision in how scientific, mainstream archaeology viewed the "hunter-gatherer" culture supposedly dominant at the time.

Watson Brake is constructed as a gigantic, egg-shaped oval embankment enclosing 22 acres. The embankment is several feet high and extends 300 yards from end to end and 200 yards across. Just over half of the oval embankment was formed by a natural ridge that stood on the edge of a tributary of the Arkansas River. Constructed on the oval embankment are 11 mounds up to 26 feet high. (See figure 24.)

In 1999 Douglas S. Frink of the Archaeology Consulting Team, Inc. in Essex Junction, Vermont presented a paper on Watson Brake at the 53rd

Figure 24
Reconstruction of the Watson Brake Mounds. The oval encloses 22 acres and has 11 mounds constructed on it. The dating of the site between 3000 B.C. - 3400 B.C. was completely unexpected. *From the Southeast Archaeological Center — National Park Service.*

Annual Meeting of the Southeastern Archaeological Conference in Birmingham, Alabama.[7] Frink's group collected 200 soil samples from the mounds and the embankment in 1995. The samples were taken to Vermont and subjected to a newer, highly accurate form of carbon dating. The results confirmed that Watson Brake was constructed between 3000 B.C. and 3400 B.C. Carbon dating also indicated that it was abandoned sometime between 2810 B.C. and 3210 B.C. The mid-point dates of the building and abandonment of the site were 3200 B.C. and 3010 B.C., respectively. Thus, it seems that the people of Watson Brake probably utilized the site for under 200 years before moving on to parts unknown.

Artifacts found at Watson Brake include points (spear points and arrowheads made from local materials), gravel used as cooking stones, seeds from local weed species, small beads, and over 175,000 bone pieces. The bones were mainly from fish, but bones from deer, turkey, and other small game were found. One other curious type of artifact was found there in large quantity. These are small, "fired earthen objects" in a variety of undecorated shapes.

In 1998, Saunders and his team reported that 427 of these had been recovered at Watson Brake and an additional 448 were found at two related mound sites near there. The shapes of these objects are primarily block-like — cubes or rectangular blocks. Some are shaped into cylinders or spheres. The average dimensions of these curious blocks are 1.7 inches, by 1.6 inches, by 1.4 inches. The largest are 2.3 inches, by 2.3 inches, by 2.1 inches. They have been found stacked or arranged in fire pits. (For example, 16 of them were discovered in a fire pit. They were carefully placed together forming a cube of 4 x 4 x 4). Charcoal found with the blocks has been carbon dated to the period of Watson Brake's construction. Thus, the blocks were used by the people of the Watson Brake mounds at the same time the mounds were being constructed. Testing showed that the blocks were definitely not used in food preparation and were unrelated to Poverty Point artifacts. The purpose of these objects is completely unknown, but a "guess" by archaeologists is that they might somehow have been employed in the making of beads.[8]

It is speculateed that Watson Brake was used seasonally before it was abandoned sometime between 3210-2810 B.C. Since the 1997 announcement about the site, several other smaller mound locations have been linked to Watson Brake. These are about 20 miles away and all show similar carbon dates. The oval mound arrangement at Watson Brake is now used to exemplify a "circular shell-mound culture" that is also believed to have been in Florida somewhat later.

The significance of the Watson Brake site is far greater than might be realized at first glance. Poverty Point's date of establishment (circa 2000 B.C.) has long been accepted as the arrival of a sophisticated and organized society capable of making the kind of group effort required to construct such a monumental site. But Watson Brake predates Poverty Point by well over 1000 years — during a time period called the hunter-gatherer era. The site even predates the Olmec culture which is believed to have emerged (seemingly from nowhere) just before 2000 B.C. Watson Brake and a few additional sites have shown that people in the "hunter-gatherer" era were much more socially complex and organized than anyone had ever suspected.

One more significant find at the site is more appropriately termed a non-find. That is, the Watson Brake mounds were not used for burials. No burials have been found at the site. Thus, these ancient people appear to have been very different from the Red Paint People and the Old Copper Culture who made small burial mounds. An unrecognized genesis of America's mound building culture is now emerging.

Cayce's Chronology of Mound Builders & The Archaeological Record

The Cayce readings provide a fairly specific chronology of events in the emergence of the mound builders in America. Prior to the final destruction of Atlantis in 10,014 B.C., a group of 11 Atlanteans went to the Yucatan area to establish a temple for the safekeeping of the Atlantean records. At the same time larger groups of Atlanteans fled the remaining islands and went to the northeastern coast of America where they eventually became the Iroquois.

According to Cayce, in about 3000 B.C. a portion of the "Lost Tribes" came to the southernmost portion of America by boats. It is assumed that these "Lost Tribes" are from the ancient Semitic and Hebrew lands. Cayce stated that they remained in America for a relatively short time. These people then moved to the areas around Mexico City where they imposed a new form of ritual on the pyramid builders already present. This ritual was the utilization of sacrificial altars.

Over time, the use of altars for sacrifices degraded into human sacrifice. Facing increased violence and danger from the "Belial" ruling groups who had imposed harsh rule and demanded human sacrifice, a migration northward occurred. A "portion" of the Lost Tribes joined with the descendants of the Atlanteans who had been in the Yucatan since 10,000 B.C. This group went north and became the mound builders. According to Cayce, the center of their mound culture became Ohio.

It should be pointed out that the 3000 B.C. date Cayce gave for the Lost Tribes does not fit the traditional dating of that event. Chapter 12 extensively explores that discrepancy as well as reviewing Mormon beliefs about the Lost Tribes in America. In addition, we can neither prove nor disprove that people from Atlantis came to America (but this issue shall also be addressed later). Archaeologists are loathe to even entertain the idea of ancient Israelites in America. Thus, for the moment, we'll ignore the implications of the terms "Lost Tribes" and "Atlantis" and compare Cayce's chronology to the currently known archaeological record.

Watson Brake is a mere 160 miles from the Gulf of Mexico. It could have been easily reached via the Mississippi River and its tributaries or from the Black River via the Atchafalaya River from the Gulf. The Gulf area itself fits Cayce's statement of the Lost Tribes arriving at "the southernmost portion of America." The carbon dates of Watson Brake's establishment (3000 B.C. – 3400 B.C.) fit Cayce's date of the Lost Tribes arrival (3000 B.C). In addition, the abandonment of the site (sometime between 2810 B.C. and 3210 B.C.) appears to indicate that the site was used less than 200 years. This finding is in line with Cayce's statement that the Lost Tribes only stayed in North America for a short time.

One tantalizing clue possibly pegging Watson Brake as a proto-Hebrew or Semitic settlement lies in its shape. According to *The Jewish Encyclopedia* (1902) the ancient Hebrews formed circular camps and temporary settlements where "safety and a sufficient supply of water were the primary considerations determining the choice of locations." The entry continues, "The camp was usually laid out in a circle." In an effort at protection, they gradually made a permanent enclosure in the center and erected "a massive platform of stones" upon which huts were built for lookouts. The entry concludes by stating that the erection of these camps "must be considered as the first step toward the abandonment by the Hebrews of the migratory life with its moveable camps."[9] The Watson Brake location and its shape seem to be, at a cursory level, erected as a circular camp that was initially intended to be a more permanent settlement. Since the site has no stone with which to build a lookout platform, the erection of earthen mounds would certainly be a logical alternative. Another clue possibly linking Watson Brake to ancient Israelites is the lack of burials at the site or in the mounds. The Hebrews and their Semitic ancestors did not perform burials in mounds. Instead, they used stone-lined graves or caves. The use of burial mounds in the both the Red Paint People and the Old Copper

Cultures show that those cultures were not likely influenced by ancient Israelites. However, the lack of burials in the Watson Brake mounds is consistent with the Lost Tribes practices.[9]

In Mexico and the Yucatan, the genesis of human sacrifice on altars atop "high places" (pyramids) has always been a mystery. According to Cayce, the migration of the Lost Tribes from America to the Mexico City area infused the idea of using sacrificial altars upon the people already located there. Initially the altars were used for various nonhuman sacrifices. However, as the Belial influence gained power and control over the culture, the altars were eventually turned to human sacrifice. It was in response to these events that the remaining descendants of the Atlanteans joined with some of the remnants of the Lost Tribes and moved north into America. At that time they established the mound builder culture. Cayce did not provide a date for this event for a simple reason — no one asked him. During his many readings, those supplying questions were often completely unprepared for the astonishing information he gave. The vast majority of people seeking readings were interested in personal information (e.g., who to marry, where to move, what career to pursue). Thus, all we know about the chronology is that the Atlantean descendants from the Yucatan who joined with some of the Lost Tribes migrated sometime after the Lost Tribes came to the Mexico City area. If the Lost Tribes left America (Watson Brake) around 2810 B.C., it means they entered Mexico and remained there for an unknown time period. How long is questionable, but based on what is known about the movements of groups of people in this era, it is reasonable to assume that they did not reenter America for a few hundred years.

The site of Poverty Point appears to fit Cayce's chronology of the return of the Lost Tribes and the Atlanteans accompanying them. The Poverty Point culture seemingly came from nowhere and an Olmec/Yucatan influence seems apparent at the site. It was occupied by 2500 B.C. and completely constructed by 1800 B.C. Poverty Point reached its peak in 1500 B.C. and gradually lost population. By 600 B.C., it was abandoned. During the time Poverty Point lost population and was in "decline," more complex mounds and earthworks were constructed centering in the Ohio region. In fact, Poverty Point has been termed by archaeologists as the "gateway" through which the idea of monumental mound building entered Ohio.[1]

As stated earlier, we cannot yet prove that the people Cayce referred to as Lost Tribes and Atlantean descendants from the Yucatan established the Ohio mound builder culture. However, the fact that the current archaeological record essentially matches Cayce's entire chronology of events leading up to it is mind-boggling. Neither Watson Brake nor Poverty Point were known at the time of Cayce's readings. In fact, researchers were fairly certain at the time of Cayce's readings that mound building began *after* 1000 B.C.

The 1997 collapse of the Clovis Barrier, the 1997 announcement of the discovery of Watson Brake, and the 1997 discovery of the X haplogroup represent a pivotal point in ancient American archaeology. Incredible as this post-1997 turn of events is, the most incredible aspect of Cayce's story is in the purpose of the mounds. Cayce stated that they were representations of the Yucatan, Gobi, and Atlantean experiences. What does this mean? Do the Ohio mounds hold clues to this statement? It is to Ohio and Cayce's most amazing ideas where we now turn our attention.

Chapter 6

The Mound Builder Era Begins in Ohio

Of the early "Mound Builders" the Adena peoples dominated the
Ohio Valley from about 1000 B.C. until their contact and absorption by
Hopewellian peoples in the central Ohio Valley starting about 200 B.C.
Don Dragoo (1963) *Mounds for the Dead*

D irectly across the street from the West Virginia State Penitentiary in
Moundsville, West Virginia stands one of America's most curious
mounds. Named the "Grave Creek Mound" after a nearby stream, it attracted much attention by settlers after its "discovery" in 1770. Originally
encircled by a 40 foot-wide, 5 foot-deep moat, its circumference was 910
feet and it stood 65 feet tall. North of the mound, near the bank of the Ohio
River, a 5-acre earthwork in the shape of octagon was found. Farming rapidly obliterated the octagon and other nearby earthworks. The damage to
these amazing earthworks was nearly complete. Dragoo reported that in
the city limits of Moundsville, 47 mounds had been counted in the late
1700s before almost all were destroyed.[1]

The huge central mound was put to use by the town. It once had a for-
profit museum built *inside* it, a saloon was built on its top, and a racetrack
ran around its base. The state took the site over in 1909 and it is a park
today. (See figures 25 & 26.) Standing on the summit of this massive, sacred mound today can produce contradictory emotions and thoughts. The
penitentiary located less than 100 yards away is an overwhelming, sober-
ing edifice that, in several ways, graphically portrays man's cruelty to man.

Figure 25 (above)
The Grave Creek Mound as depicted by Squier & Davis in 1848.

Figure 26 (below)
The Grave Creek Mound today. *Photo — G. Little.*

In 1838, the Grave Creek site was owned by the Tomlison family. For $2500 the family had a shaft dug straight down from the top eventually digging well below the subsurface level. At the 77-foot level (12 feet below the "bottom" of the mound itself), a log chamber was found covered by stone slabs. A skeleton was retrieved along with mica sheets, copper ornaments, and thousands of shell beads. In addition, a small, engraved tablet was found with the burial. The sandstone tablet was 3/4 of an inch thick and about two inches in diameter. Digging even deeper, at the 111-foot level another log burial chamber was found. It contained two skeletons and nearly 700 shell beads. A rising, horizontal tunnel to the outer base of the mound was then dug. In the process of cutting the tunnel, 10 skeletons and masses of charcoal and cremated bones were found. The interior of the mound was subsequently opened as a museum and tourist attraction. The centerpiece of the attraction was the engraved tablet Abelard Tomlison found during the excavations.[2]

The Grave Creek Tablet caused an enormous stir as soon as its discovery was announced. The 25 characters on it resembled ancient Celtic or Phoenician script. (See figures 27 and 28.) In 1976, Harvard professor and epigrapher Barry Fell professed the tablet to be genuine and translated the Iberian engraving as meaning: "The mound raised-on-high for Tasach; This tile … (His) queen caused-to-be-made."[3] Others continue to assert that the tablet is a fake.

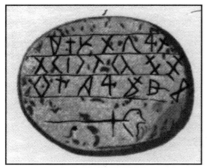

Figure 27
Grave Creek Tablet front side
(actual size). *From
Schoolcraft (1851).*

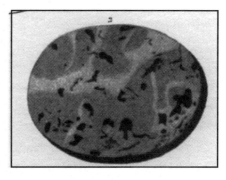

Figure 28
Grave Creek Tablet reverse
side (actual size). *From
Schoolcraft (1851)*

The Adena Culture Is Defined

Excavation of the Grave Creek Mound provided the first look into the construction and usage of the enormous conical burial mounds. It also provided the first opportunity to study the culture that constructed them. Many huge, conical burial mounds had been identified by settlers and early professionals, but classifications of them were unscientific. And, at that time, there was no way that one type of mound could be distinguished from another.

In the late 1800s, Ohio Governor Thomas Worthington allowed an excavation of a huge mound on his Ross County Estate called Adena. (See figure 29.) After excavating the Adena mound, archaeologist W. C. Mills published his results in 1902. Mills applied the term *Adena* to all similar mounds. As a result, the name Adena has since been used to describe mounds of this type. The original Adena mound was completely obliterated by the excavation and its dirt leveled to improve farming. Unfortunately, this has been the fate of the majority of ancient American mounds.

The Adena Era was fully developed by 1000 B.C. and is suspected of being a combination of two cultural influences. First, in the area where the Adena Culture was centered (the Ohio Valley), the Red Paint People and

Figure 29
The original "Adena" mound on Gov. Worthington's estate
prior to its complete obliteration in 1901.

Old Copper Culture extended their use of small burial mounds including the use of red ochre. Secondly, it is believed that people from the Poverty Point culture migrated to the area of the Ohio Valley several times between 1500 B.C. and 600 B.C.

There are over 200 known Adena sites with the majority occurring in Ohio. Most of the other Adena sites are found in West Virginia, Kentucky, Indiana, New York, and Pennsylvania. The majority of carbon dates at Adena sites range from 1300 B.C. to A.D. 900.[2] While the Red Paint People made some crude pottery, the complete debut of pottery in ancient America occurred in Adena times. Archaeologists now refer to this event as the beginning of the Eastern Woodlands Period.

The defining essence of Adena Culture sites is the combination of the huge burial mound and the unique burial traits found in the mounds. Some Adena sites contain circular earthworks and red ochre was used to line the burial pits. Archaeologist William Webb relentlessly excavated Adena mounds in the 1920s and identi-

Figure 30 (right)
Stone pipe recovered from original Adena Mound in 1901 excavation. *Photo — G. Little.*

Figure 31 (below)
Bird effigy pipe from Adena era mound..
From — Dover.

fied 90 "traits" common to the sites. Archaeologists today tend to accept many of Webb's Adena traits, but argue about the significance of some of them.

The Adena dead were usually prepared for burial in a consistent way. The bones were first "cleaned" by exposing the body to carrion-eating birds in trees and on raised platforms. After the bones were clean, they were stored for later burial or buried immediately. Some were cremated, although archaeologists do not know how the decision was made as to the type of burial performed. Tombs were constructed of bark or logs after a small burial pit was dug. Red ochre was often spread into the tomb and the skeleton was placed on its back or sometimes bundled. A variety of artifacts were placed into the tomb. These included tools, weapons, personal adornments, pipes, gorgets (ornaments that hung around the neck), copper artifacts, and distinctive stone tablets. The tomb was then covered with logs or stone and a small mound was erected over it. As the Adena era progressed, the burials became increasingly elaborate. Some of the Adena artifacts placed in graves were spectacular. (See figures 30 & 31.)

Figure 32
The Miamisburg Mound (Ohio) was once the largest Adena mound in Ohio standing 68 feet tall with a diameter of 300 feet.. It contains over 54,000 cubic yards of earth. *Photo — G. Little.*

One of the greatest areas of dispute is the strong possibility that social classes existed during the Adena era. Obviously, a mound containing 3 million basket loads of earth (as the Grave Creek Mound does) requires a great expenditure of effort by many people. It seems logical to conclude that the individuals buried in the log and stone covered tombs under the mound were important. Webb concluded that "special people" were buried in the gigantic mounds and other members of the community were simply cremated after death.[1] Webb also believed that the culture had its beginnings in Mexico. However, the Adena people imported and grew two crops only known in Mexico: gourd and squash. Maize, also imported from Mexico, was grown at Adena-era sites perhaps as early as 500 B.C. Thus, it is obvious that some form of contact, be it a trading network or an actual migration of people, occurred between the Ohio region and Mexico sometime at the beginning of Adena (1300-1000 B.C.) and perhaps again in 500 B.C.[4]

Modern excavations of Adena sites show the mounds were constructed in additive phases. The initial mound was often built over a log-pit burial often covered by stone or logs. Additional burials took place on the mound itself, and, with each burial, the mound increased in size. The Robbins Adena mound, in Kentucky, for example, contained 100 burials — 99 in closed grave pits and only one in a log crypt. The largest Adena mound is the Miamisburg Mound in Ohio. (See figure 32.) In 1869 a shaft was sunk 36 feet down into the 68-foot tall mound. Burials were found at 8 and 36 feet down with layers of ash interspaced between them.

The layers of ash found in the mounds point out another characteristic of the Adena burial mounds. Excavations have shown that the mounds were often constructed over unusual circular homes or a specialized mortuary building. The buildings were burned before the mound was erected above them. Another building could then be erected atop the mound. After a death, the burial was performed in the floor of the house and the building burned. Then the mound was enlarged. This cyclical process was often repeated many times.

The circular earthworks accompanying many Adena mounds are fascinating but enigmatic. They appeared virtually circular and were surrounded by a moat or ditch. Mounds were sometimes located inside the circles. All had an opening aligned to a Cardinal direction. Many sites had clusters of circles in multiples of 2 (2, 4, 6, or 8). A small earthen platform often stood in the center of the circles. The Mt. Horeb mound and earthwork in Kentucky is considered to be a stereotypical example of these. (See figure 33.)

The circular earthworks are generally termed "sacred circles," but the purpose of them is unknown. Some form of ritual appears to have been performed in them.[1, 4]

The Adena Tablets

Over a dozen intact inscribed sandstone tablets have been recovered from excavations into Adena mounds. Another dozen intact tablets (without inscriptions) have been recovered. Almost all of these can be viewed today in the Ohio Historical Society Museum in Columbus. Many other broken tablets and fragments have been found during excavations. For example, when Dragoo excavated the West Virginia Cresap Adena Mound in 1958, 22 tablets were found.

The authenticity of these tablets has been accepted because a few were found during professional excavations. The primary problem with such unusual discoveries is that many artifacts *have* been faked. This has been a recurring problem.

The inscribed Adena tablets are believed to depict zoomorphic images (animals) and geometric patterns. Most of the tablets are rectangular in

Figure 33
The Mt. Horeb mound and earthwork in Kentucky is a stereotypical example of a conical mound surrounded by "moats." *From — Squier & Davis (1848).*

shape and 3-5 inches in length. The reverse side usually has grooves cut into it. Red ochre has been found staining some of the tablets giving a clue into their use. It is believed they were sacred stamps used to place images — clan images or other sacred symbols — onto skin or clothing. The grooves on the reverse side were formed by the grinding of hematite into red ochre powder. A later chapter will extensively examine the meaning of these enigmatic objects. (See figure 34.)

The Contents of One "Small" Adena Mound

The amount of material from Adena mounds sometimes defies expectation. Dragoo's book, *Mounds for the Dead*, detailed his thorough investigation into the West Virginia Cresap Mound for the Carnegie Museum in 1958.[1] The mound was 15 feet high and 70 feet in diameter — quite small compared to the larger Adena mounds. It took 13 weeks to complete the excavation.

Figure 34
The Cincinnati Tablet discovered in December 1841. *From — Squier & Davis (1848).*

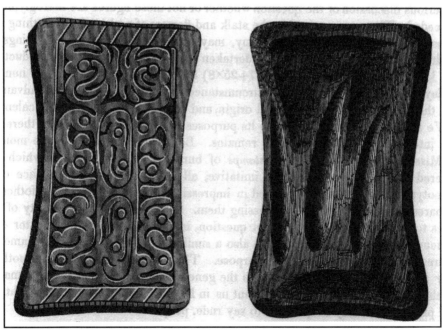

A total of 54 burials were contained in the mound. Associated with the burials were the 22 tablets mentioned earlier along with 10 polished gorgets and pendants, 35 celts, 3 polished stone balls, 12 partial spheres, 4 pipes, 47 stone artifacts (points, hammerstones, and elliptical stone bars), 93 chipped stone artifacts, 9 drills, 39 scrapers, 373 copper artifacts (mostly beads), 23 bone artifacts (including an elk skull head-dress), 115 shell artifacts, and 9 pots.

Cayce & Adena Influences

Cayce's explanation of how the mound building era began in the Ohio area has already been detailed. In brief, the story involved a migration to Ohio from Mexico and the Yucatan of remnants of the Lost Tribes combined with the descendants of the 11 Atlanteans who had gone to the Yucatan before 10,000 B.C. These people eventually reached Ohio and merged with the natives already present in the area. The Cayce readings go on to say that the mounds were a combination of influences from the Lost Tribes, Atlanteans, and others.

In the prior chapter, the chronology of the Cayce story was shown to match the current findings. The first "mound" site at Watson Brake was a circular encampment similar to ancient Israelite camps. It was not used for burials — a finding also consistent with Israelite practices. The site was established in the 3000 B.C. time period, the date Cayce claimed that a group of Lost Tribes arrived in southern America. Less than 200 years later the site was abandoned and the people of Watson Brake "disappeared." Cayce stated that they moved to the Mexico City area.

After an unknown time period, some of the descendants of the Lost Tribes left the Mexico City area as human sacrifice became prevalent. The Lost Tribes then joined with a group of Atlantean descendants and made their way north. It is a logical deduction that they would travel in boats and return to the vast, rich area they first came to when arriving on American shores. Even though 1000 years had passed, it is likely that the story of their 3000 B.C. arrival in America would be passed on from one generation to the next. And the descendants of the Lost Tribes, in trying to escape the brutality of human sacrifice (called the Belial influence by Cayce), might well attempt to return to the safe, abundant lands they had been told about in their legends. The same reasoning could be applied to the descendants of the Atlanteans in the Yucatan. Cayce is silent on how the Lost Tribes joined with these Atlanteans, but it is likely that the Atlantean descendants in the Yucatan would have been appalled and dismayed at the savage turn of events in how their pyramids were used. The original group of Atlanteans who went to the Yucatan sought to preserve the records of Atlantis and humanity — especially the story of the Children of the Law of One. Knowing that many other Atlanteans had fled north at the time of Atlantis' destruction, it is reasonable to surmise that they would migrate north to escape the conflicts in Central America.

Moving up the Mississippi River, the combined groups came to an area very close to the original Watson Brake encampment. They established a large culture at Poverty Point arriving perhaps around 2000 B.C. and even constructed terraces similar to the raised circle at Watson Brake. After perhaps 300 years of building a new culture and established trading sites linked to Poverty Point, a series of migrations traveled north — further up the Mississippi River. It could be speculated that the Atlanteans accompanying the Lost Tribes wanted to join with some of their Atlantean brethren whom they knew were further north. As they reached the Ohio Valley, they met people who were clearly descendants of the early Atlanteans.

The archaeological record shows that the Ohio Adena culture was a coming together of several influences. A clear "Mexican" influence is obvious in the development of Adena as shown by the appearance of gourd and squash in 1300 B.C. and maize in 500 B.C. The implication is simple: people from Mexico carried the crops with them when they migrated to the area.

The sudden appearance of pottery and highly refined artifacts in Adena times indicates that a rapid advancement in culture appeared in the Ohio Valley. In addition, the new form of larger burial mounds and the sacred circles are consistent with a coming together of several influences. The Israelites utilized sub-surface tombs and pits for burials. These were often constructed of stone or logs. The ancient Iroquois tribes (the Red Paint People and the Old Copper Culture) utilized small mounds for burials — using vast amounts of red ochre. The Atlanteans from the Yucatan were accustomed to constructing huge pyramids of stone and earth. However, stone wasn't present at Poverty Point, and their massive structures had to be erected from earth. Combining these three elements describes the archetypal Adena mound. Burials were performed in sub-surface tombs made from logs or stone slabs. They spread large amounts of red ochre in their burials. They heaped an earthen mound over the burials and built a circular mortuary complex atop the mound. The mound was gradually enlarged to a massive size as each new burial was performed.

According to the Cayce readings, the mound-encircling moats and circular earthworks found at many Adena sites would probably be an

Atlantean characteristic. Plato's description of Atlantis detailed alternating rings of water and land encircling a central mountain (or mound) upon which a temple was erected. In a later chapter we will more fully explore the possible Atlantean connection.

In summary, the essence of the archaeological record on the Adena Era centering in Ohio rather astonishingly fits all the details Cayce related about it. It is interesting to note that the modern excavations of Adena outlining the characteristics of the culture were done after Cayce's death. In addition, the time frames that archaeology has established for the arrival of the Mexican crops wasn't known until after Cayce's death. However, the pinnacle of the Cayce story of mound building comes with the culture that developed in the Ohio area as Adena faded. That is the Hopewell Culture to which we now turn our attention.

Chapter 7

The Incredible Hopewell

...a group of seven smaller mounds ...duplicate the arrangement of the
famous Seven Sisters in the constellation Pleiades. Nearby is a [mound]
group that appears to be one of the dippers. And there [in a mound group]
is Orion's Belt, a group familiar to most star gazers.
Ted Bauer (1987) *The Marietta Times*

The transition from the Adena Era to the Hopewell Era is controversial
and poorly understood. Some assert that Hopewell was a natural development from Adena because large mounds and circular earthworks continued to be erected during Hopewell. In addition, the grave goods during
Hopewell were similar to those of Adena — but much, much improved
and finer. Others, however, view Hopewell as a new and different culture
that developed alongside Adena. According to this idea, Hopewell probably emerged from a new cultural group entering the Ohio area in about
500 B.C.

Carbon dating shows that Hopewell began just before 500 B.C. and
reached its peak during the 300 years between 100 B.C. and A.D. 200.
Hopewell seemed to just fade away in about A.D. 750. Adena began in
about 1500 B.C. and disappeared around A.D. 900. Thus, the two cultures
overlapped in time with Adena lasting the entire 1200-year period of the
Hopewell.

Evidence of a Mexican Influence at Hopewell

The sudden appearance of maize in Ohio around 500 B.C. is one clue which seems to indicate that another influx of immigrants came to Ohio from somewhere in Mexico or via Poverty Point. Another clue comes from an impressive mound culture in Florida called the Crystal River Complex. In about 537 B.C., the main site at Crystal River was erected. Crystal River contains two temple mounds, a plaza, burial mounds, and smaller "residential" flat-topped mounds. The flat-topped mounds are generally not typical of Hopewell sites, but they do appear at some complexes. For example, two impressive Ohio Hopewell sites, Marietta and Newark, and one in Tennessee also have them. Crystal River excavations have yielded numerous Hopewell artifacts and a clear trading link has been found between the Florida culture and Ohio Hopewell.

In 1961 West Virginia archaeologist, Edward McMichael, proposed that the Hopewell culture came to Ohio from Mexico via Florida. He theorized that the Olmec site of La Venta, with its mounds and earthen enclosures, was the origin of Hopewell.[1] La Venta, the site of gigantic head sculptures depicting what appear to be African, Chinese, and Polynesian people, flourished by 800 B.C., long after the Olmec Culture began in 2000 B.C. Two stone columns were discovered at Crystal River by the Florida State Museum in 1965. The columns seemingly confirmed McMichael's hypothesis because the columns were clearly Mexican.

In 1967 the Ohio Hopewell Culture was linked to the site of Teotihuacan near Mexico City. Rene Millon found that Teotihuacan had been built on a grid system made up of 187-foot squares. Millon found that the 187-foot grid (and its diagonal measurement) seemed to match more than 100 different Hopewell mound sites.[2] The grid was also found at sites outside the Ohio area. For example, 10 miles south of Jackson, Tennessee is a massive, 1000-acre mound site called Pinson. Pinson was established about 100 B.C. Until 300 A.D., Pinson was the largest ceremonial mound site in all of ancient America. The site contains at least 12 mounds including four truncated (flat-topped) earthen pyramids and the second tallest mound remaining in America today (at 72 feet tall). Various alignments to solar and stellar events are found at the Pinson site. Pinson may have served as gigantic "Medicine Wheel" where specific star sightings were used to serve as markers for ceremonies.[2, 3] (See figures 35, 36, & 37.)

Figure 35 (above) Saul's Mound is at the center of the 1000-acre Pinson site. It stands 72 feet tall and is 330 feet in diameter. It is a truncated pyramid. From its summit, the morning rising of the stars Rigel, Aldebaran, and Orion's Belt could be viewed across other mounds. *Photo — G. Little.*

Figure 36 (above)
Ozier's Mound ramp is aligned to the rising sun at the summer solstice. It is 32 feet tall and has a base of 230 x 240 feet. It has been carbon dated to 1 A.D. From atop Ozier's Mound, the early morning rising of the star Sirius could be viewed across Saul's Mound. *Photo — G. Little.*

Figure 37 (right) Pinson appears to have served as a gigantic "medicine wheel" where the rising of the stars were used to time rituals. It was a ceremonial center. No one ever lived at the site. *Map — Adapted from People of the Web (1990).*

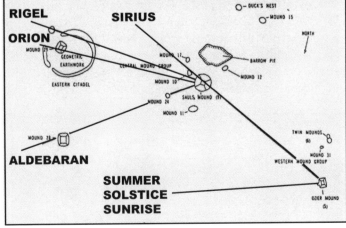

Interestingly, the Crystal River site, mentioned earlier in this chapter, has sighting alignments between mounds and its circular earthworks to the sunrise and sunset of the solstices. Pinson also contains circular earthworks that are based on the 187-foot grid found at Teotihuacan.[4]

The Pinson site has elements of both Hopewell and Adena. While Ohio was the focal point of Hopewell, as well as the location where it reached its zenith, it should be understood that Hopewell and Adena sites have been found dotting the entire eastern half of America.

Engineer James Marshall began studying the layout of Hopewell sites in the 1960s. He subsequently categorized them into 5 basic types.[5] The first type was characterized by a peculiar form of earthworks usually referred to as "hilltop forts." These appear to have been built in late Hopewell times and about 25 of them remain today. Most are in Ohio, but Tennessee, and even Canada, have them. They are found at the top of steep hills and usually consist of high earthen or stone embankments outlining the hilltop. The embankments can reach 33 feet in height. Although there has been disagreement about whether they served a defensive or ceremonial purpose, recent research by Wright State University's Robert Riordan, has shown that at least some of them were used for both purposes. While evidence has long shown that ceremonies took place in the hilltop enclosures, Riordan found that wooden palisades (log walls) were erected in some.[6] Marshall's analysis of the geometry of the hilltop forts showed that there was no mathematical plan utilized in constructing the forts. They were simply built to conform to the hill's topography.

Marshall's second classification of Hopewell sites is based on the 187-foot grid first discovered by Millon. The 3rd, 4th, and 5th types of Hopewell sites are based on cryptographs and the use of pi. Marshall found that the squares, circles, rectangles, octagons, and ellipses formed by many Hopewell earthworks formed right triangles aligned to the Cardinal directions while utilizing the 187-foot grid. He termed these configurations "cryptographs." Some earthworks combined the cryptographs into complex overlays where sites miles apart were connected by long, parallel embankments. Many sites were constructed with obvious knowledge of

Figure 38
Central mound at
Hopewell site in
1891. *Photo —
Museum of
Natural History.*

pi (the relationship of the circumference to the diameter of a circle). Marshall has concluded that the Hopewell had complex mathematical knowledge and that some sites could have been erected as a means of transmitting that knowledge.

Anthropologist William Romain believes the fundamental measuring unit of the Hopewell was 25.3 inches (or 2.1 feet). This unit of measurement, he believes, came from the average length of the arm from the shoulder to wrist.[7] Romain concludes that Hopewell sites contain precise astronomical alignments that were used in the conducting of rituals and ceremonies. We shall return to this idea in a later chapter.

Hopewell's Unusual Characteristics

An 1891-2 excavation of Captain M. C. Hopewell's estate in Ross County, Ohio gave the culture its name. In preparation for a mound exhibition at the Chicago World's Fair in 1893, Warren Moorehead excavated a large, enclosed mound site on Hopewell's estate. (See figure 38.) The site had been briefly excavated by Ephriam Squier and Edwin Davis in 1845. Encouraged by the fine artifacts Squier and Davis found at the site, Moorehead hoped to find more. He was not disappointed. Another excavation at the original Hopewell site, in 1922-25 by Henry Sheltrone, uncovered even more artifacts. These excavations and numerous surveys have provided the diverse Hopewell Culture with a wide range of characteristics. These include the unique artifacts and altars found in mounds, the obvious ritualistic nature of some artifacts, the unusual earthworks and long parallel walls forming walkways, the curious effigy mounds, and the astronomical alignments found at many sites.

Stone Altars

Stone altars have been found in many Hopewell mounds including at the original Hopewell site. (See figure 39.) These altars were usually found at the bottom of mounds. They are often associated with altar hearths and evidence of altar fire offerings have almost always been found in both the hearths and on the stone altars. One such altar was found on the farm of B. Mechen at the base of an 11-foot mound removed by workers from the Baltimore and Ohio Railroad in 1851. Next to the altar was found a well-preserved skeleton covered in a foot of ashes. Radiating out from this skeleton were 12 other skeletons with their heads next to the one by the altar.[5]

Figure 39
Stone altar found at base of excavated mound at Hopewell site in 1891.
Photo —Moorehead (1892).

Artifacts & Trade Network

The number and quality of artifacts placed in Hopewell mounds was astounding. The 1891 excavations at Hopewell recovered over 8,000 polished chert "discs" from a single small mound. Over 100,000 pearls were found at Hopewell. Exquisite sculptures of people, hands, animals, symbols, and effigy pipes were made from copper, stone, obsidian (volcanic glass), and thin polished mica sheets. The mica is often so reflective that it could serve as a mirror. Copper and stone ceremonial axes have been recovered in many Hopewell Era mounds along with other weapons and implements. The quality and number of these incredible artifacts nearly defy description. Not only that, these objects were made from materials imported from nearly all of America. The extent of the Hopewell trading network is mind-boggling. Obsidian was imported from Wyoming and Montana, Grizzly Bear teeth came from South Dakota, copper and silver came from the Great Lakes, quartz came from Arkansas and Georgia, shells, alligator teeth, shark teeth, and fossils came from Florida and Georgia, and mica came from the Carolinas. (See figures 40-43.)

Figures 40 -41 (right)
Full-size mica sheet
of the human torso; &
mica hand.
*Photos —Natl. Park
Service.*

*Figures 42 -43
(below)*
Deer headdress on
skeleton found at
Hopewell.
*From —Moorehead
(1892).*

Hopewell face mask..
Photo — G. Little

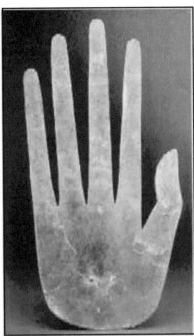

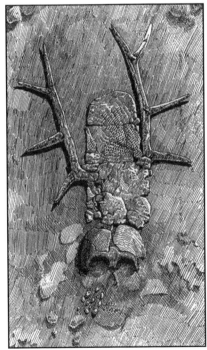

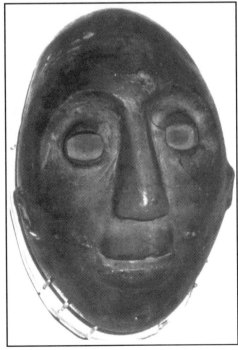

Ritual Artifacts & Hallucinogenic Substances

Clues about the ritualistic habits of the Hopewell started emerging with the first excavations. The many altars and burned sacrificial remains associated with them hinted at a society that conducted elaborate ceremonies for the dead and for other purposes as well. Exquisite stone pipes with effigies of animals and people showed that the Hopewell used tobacco in their rituals and ceremonies. Some of these pipes were so large and exquisite that daily use was probably not practical. In addition, the quantity of the pipes found in Hopewell mounds was large. In 1848 Squier and Davis found 200 pipes piled together in a single mound at the Mound City Group at Chillicothe. Not far away from Mound City, the Tremper Mound yielded 136 pipes buried within a small area.

Artifacts that clearly had only ritualistic purposes have been recovered from Hopewell mounds. During his 1891 excavation of Hopewell, Moorehead found two copper headdresses with copper antlers on the top of two skulls. (See figure 42.) A bear effigy headdress and another deer antler headdress, both made from copper, were later found in Mound City. The Wray figure, found at the Newark earthworks, depicts a shaman inside a bear costume. Hopewell musical instruments, believed to have been used in rituals, have also been found. These include flutes and a host of different types of rattles.

Evidence now shows that the Hopewell's rituals included the use of hallucinogenic substances.[7] This should not be surprising, since the Maya and Aztecs, as well as the Incas, all used hallucinogenics in their rituals. In 1922 Mills reported finding a 13 $1/2$-inch long mushroom effigy made from copper-covered wood at Mound City. Moorehead also found many mushroom effigies made from copper at Hopewell. The mushrooms appear to depict the mushroom *Amanita muscaria* commonly referred to as fly agaric. The name is derived from the observation that flies landing on the mushroom fall into a stupor. The mushroom was used by Siberian nomads in historic times and is found almost everywhere in the world.[9]

The tobacco used by the Hopewell also had mind-altering characteristics. Nicotine is a poison at high doses and is used in the manufacture of some insecticides. At low doses, such as that delivered by a modern cigarette, nicotine leads to a paradoxical effect of both relaxation and energy. At moderate doses, nicotine is a powerful stimulant capable of producing muscle spasms and anxious energy in the user. At higher doses, nicotine causes a physical and mental stupor and even seizures.[9] The particular type of tobacco used by the Hopewell, *Nicotiana rustica*, has a nicotine content so high that it cannot be used in the production of modern tobacco products.

Unusual Earthworks

Squier and Davis commented on the Hopewell earthworks in their monumental 1848 work, *Ancient Monuments of the Mississippi Valley*. They wrote that it is "impossible to give anything like a comprehensive description of them." The Hopewell constructed gigantic geometric earthworks by forming embankments of earth up to 33 feet high. These embankments formed circles, squares, octagons, ellipses, and other shapes. In some cases, the earthworks enclosed areas of 50 or more acres. The earthworks usually contained mounds obviously arranged with a plan. Some of these extended for many miles. The Newark, Ohio Earthworks are probably the most famous. Only a few of these will be described below, but we have described others in picture captions included in this chapter.

The Newark Earthworks. Newark was not a site devoted to mortuary rituals but was used for periodic ceremonies seemingly unrelated to death. Carbon dated to about 200 A.D., the Newark site covered miles. (See figure 44.) Its earthen walls generally vary from 8 to 14 feet high. Now a golf course, the Circle and Octagon site is perhaps the most mysterious. The circle, essentially a perfect circle, encloses 20 acres and is connected by a narrow set of walls to an octagon. The octagon encloses 50 acres and has 8

Figure 44
The main complex of Newark. *From — Squier & Davis (1848).*

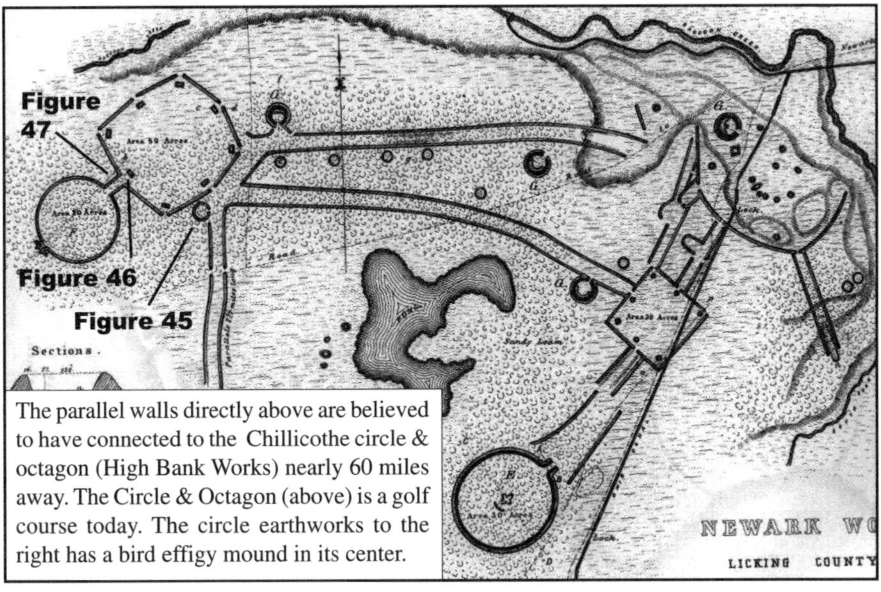

The parallel walls directly above are believed to have connected to the Chillicothe circle & octagon (High Bank Works) nearly 60 miles away. The Circle & Octagon (above) is a golf course today. The circle earthworks to the right has a bird effigy mound in its center.

rectangular mounds at the points where the eight walls forming the octagon come together. Actually, the walls of the octagon do not connect but have small openings blocked by the eight mounds just inside the octagon. Numerous small circles, with lower earthen walls, were located near the octagon as well as at other places in Newark. Each of these circles is a cul-de-sac and has a single opening leading inside.

Although they are now destroyed, three sets of parallel walls led from the octagon. The parallel walls formed "walkways" 175 feet wide with the sides 3 feet tall or more. The northernmost walkway led a mile east to a complex set of mounds, embankments, and circles that defy description. (See figure 44.) The center walkway also extended east to a 20-acre embankment in the form of a square. To the southeast from the square, more embankments led to a gigantic 30-acre circular earthwork with a single opening pointing to the northeast. The circle, generally known as the "Great Fairgrounds Circle," was formed by a uniform outer wall 9 feet tall. A moat, 7 feet deep, ran inside the wall creating a 16-foot, continuous interior wall. The outside of the circle's walls had a dark brown color, however, a bright-yellow loam was layered on the inside of the enclosure. The entire 30-acre floor of the Great Circle was covered with this yellow loam, as was the inside of the walls. It must have been an overwhelming view.

Figure 45
Photo of small circular embankment next to Newark Circle/Octagon. *Photo — G. Little.*

At the center of the circle, several mounds, forming the apparent shape of an eagle, were erected. Excavation of this Eagle Mound produced a stone altar with ashes, charcoal, and animal bone. No human remains have been recovered in the mounds or the circle.[10]

The third set of parallel walls at the octagon lead southwest. The first person to scientifically investigate the site was Caleb Atwater in 1820. Atwater wrote that this set of walls ran over 30 miles to earthworks at the Hocking River. Squier and Davis only walked the first 2 $1/2$ miles of the walls and stopped at Ramp Creek. In 1862 the Salisbury brothers crossed Ramp Creek and followed the walled walkway another six miles. They noted that it ran further, but the brothers turned back. The following section discusses these walls in more detail.

Figure 46 (right)
Squier & Davis' 1848
drawing of gateway
into Octagon.

Figure 47 (below)
Photo of parallel
embankments
connecting Circle &
Octagon.
Photo — G. Little.

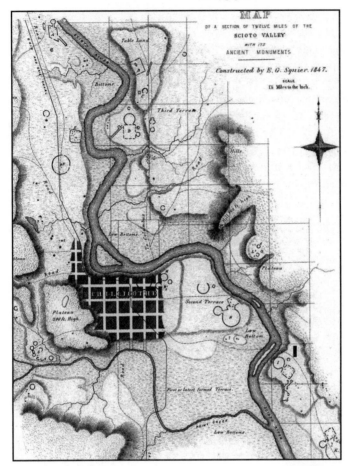

Figure 48
Squier & Davis'
1848 drawing of a
12-mile section of
the Scioto Valley
containing 10
separate sets of
earthworks.

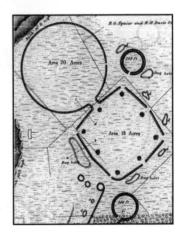

Figure 49
Squier & Davis' 1848 survey of the
High Bank Works.
On figure 48, this circle/octagon is
located near the lower right corner and
labelled as "I."

Scioto Valley/Chillicothe Earthworks. About 60 miles to the southwest of Newark, near modern-day Chillicothe, on a 12-mile long swath of the Scioto River, at least six different sets of complicated earthworks were located. These were found along with countless mounds, smaller earthworks, and sacred circles scattered nearly everywhere along the river as well as near-by Paint Creek. (See figures 48 & 49.) One of these, called the High Bank Works, was a near duplicate of the circle and octagon at Newark. Three others were circle and square variations of the circle and octagon.

The Marietta Earthworks. Another incredible Hopewell complex was found at Marietta at the confluence of the Muskingum River and the Ohio River. A few of the mounds and portions of the earthworks were preserved by the city and remain today. The site was first described in 1791 (see figure 50). It is about a mile long and half a mile in width and consists of two irregular square earthworks. Within one of the squares (50 acres) were four large truncated mounds. A walkway led southwest from that earthwork down to the Muskingum River. The walls of this "graded way" (a broad, flat avenue with a continuous slope down to the river) were originally 33 feet high, but the city sold the dirt to a bricklayer. It is known as the "Sacra Via" or Sacred Way; it is primarily aligned to the winter solstice sunset (in 250 A.D.), but other alignments are present. These will be explored shortly.

The second "square" earthwork encloses 27 acres. It was actually comprised of 8 large, straight embankments and had 8 small conical mounds.

Figure 50
Squier & Davis' 1848 drawing of the Marietta complex.

Figure 51
Conical mound at Marietta; it is surrounded by a moat and aligned to a square embankment.
Photo — G. Little.

Aligned to this square is a 30-foot tall conical mound ringed by a 4-foot deep moat which itself is outlined by a 4-foot tall circular embankment. This mound still exists today. (See figure 51.)

The Portsmouth Earthworks. At the confluence of the Scioto and Ohio Rivers, an amazing set of earthworks was erected by the Hopewell sometime around 100 A.D. (See figure 13; page 40.) On the Ohio side of the river in modern-day Portsmouth, a unique set of mounds and earthen enclosures were found in the early 1800s. Two of these enclosures were horseshoe-shaped. Today, only a single mound and one of the horseshoe embankments remain. (See figures 52 & 53.) The walls of the U-shaped embankment were 12-feet tall in 1848 when Squier and Davis published their book, but are about 10-feet tall now. Three sets of parallel walls lead from this site. The walkways enclosed by the walls were 160 feet wide. Farming had greatly lowered the walls by 1848, but even then they were 4 feet tall and 20 feet thick. One walkway led to the southeast for over 5 miles. It crossed the Ohio River and ended at an amazing set of circular embankments 1200 feet in diameter in Kentucky. A 22-foot tall truncated mound stood in the center of this complex.

A second walkway led about 7 miles from the Portsmouth horseshoe embankments southwest to the Ohio River. On the other side of the river in Kentucky was a 15-acre square enclosure with two extensions created by huge parallel walls. A third set of walls went to the northwest, however, farming had obliterated all but a half-mile of this road. Squier and

Figure 52
Mound/hill formation in center of Portsmouth group next to the horseshoe formations.
Photo — G. Little.

Figure 53
Side/rear view of the only remaining horseshoe earthwork at Portsmouth.
Photo — G. Little.

Portsmouth central group survey with lines indicating
the location of figures 52 and 53.

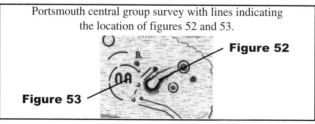

Figure 54
Drawing of Circleville, Ohio in 1836 showing how the town began with intentions of preserving the ancient circular earthworks. A few years later the town decided to obliterate the earthworks and conform to the typical block pattern. *Drawing — F. Heer (1900).*

Davis noted that the road had at one time extended further and that numerous other earthworks had been present in the Portsmouth area prior to 1848. However, farming and other construction had obliterated them.

The circular, ringed earthwork in Kentucky has similarities to one originally forming the layout of Circleville, Ohio. (See figure 54.) Caleb Atwater was the postmaster of Circleville and sought to preserve the circular embankment and its attached square with eight mounds — which was later destroyed by the town when it decided that conforming to the circle was "silly." Virtually nothing remains of the Circleville earthworks today. The outer circle was originally less than 1000 feet in diameter.

The Milford Earthworks. About a mile east of Milford, Ohio at the junction of the Little Miami River with the East Fork of the Little Miami River, (and extending north for 20 miles) a controversial set of mounds and earthworks once existed. Squier and Davis published an early survey they obtained of these earthworks, but in Cyrus Thomas (1890) report to the Bureau of Ethnology, he stated that they were "imaginary." Thomas was unable to verify the existence of these earthworks in the late 1880s, and the implications of their shapes were disturbing. One of the shapes was at the end of a parallel walkway extending from a circle and square. A circular embankment at that point opens to a long, radiating series of lines reminiscent of sun rays. While this would not be unusual for a sun worshipping culture, the form resembles part of an ancient carving depicting the Egyptian pharaoh Akhenaten. (See figures 55 and 56.) Akhenaten briefly brought monotheism to Egypt in 1348 B.C. believing that the sun represented god.

Figure 55 (left)
Akhenaten in the rays of the sun disc. *From — Art Today.*

Figure 56 (below)
Portion of the Milford Earthworks drawn by *Squier & Davis (1848)* showing a circular embankment with rays extending.

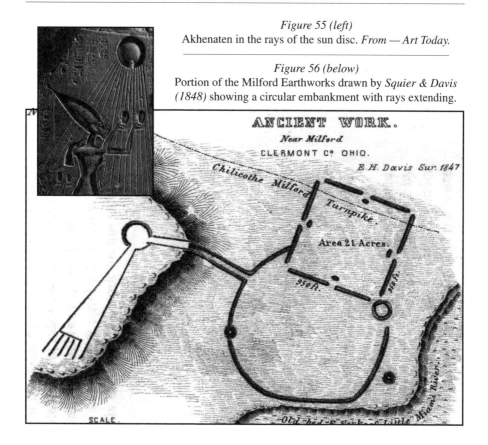

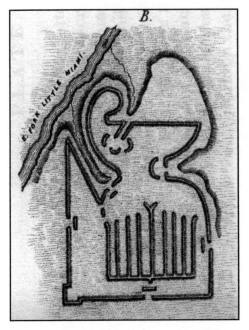

Figure 57
Portion of the Milford (Hannukiah [sic])
Earthworks drawn by *Squier & Davis*
(1848) showing what clearly resembles a
9-pointed menorah surrounded by an
earthwork in the shape of an ancient
Hebrew oil lamp.

The most disturbing earthwork at Milford seemed to indicate an ancient Israelite presence in Ohio. A 9-pointed menorah appeared to be outlined by the form of an ancient oil lamp (see figure 57). Squier and Davis wrote, "we may be permitted to say that there can be no doubt of the existence of a work of this general and extraordinary outline." The initial publication of the survey caused a stir and archaeologists responded by asserting that the works were fictional and never existed. One archaeologist even published the original survey on its side sarcastically writing that the lines might have been an ancient football field. We shall return to this earthwork in a later chapter.

Long Parallel Walls (Roads)

The road walkways formed by the parallel embankments at Hopewell sites must have been awesome. (See figure 58.) Portions of these remain today and indications are that they were enclosed by walls up to 33 feet tall. These ancient "roads" ran uninterrupted over the terrain with the enclosed walkway cleared, smoothed, and often hardened. They are reminiscent of the *sacbe*, the sacred white roads of the Maya that extended hundreds of miles throughout the Yucatan. The Maya believed that the sacbe represented the Milky Way, a great river of souls. In 1890, anthropologist Daniel Brinton wrote about a legend of the Delaware Indians, the Lenni

Figure 58
The "Graded Way" about one mile south of Piketon, Ohio as drawn by *Squier & Davis (1848)*. The parallel walls were 200-300 feet wide and up to 22 feet high. In 1848 the "Chillicothe-Portsmouth Turnpike" ran within the walls because it provided an excellent level roadway between hills.

Lenape. In their legend, the Lenni Lenape said that in ancient times they had a system of white roads that extended across America. While inside this road, travelers could move without fear of being attacked.[11] The Lenape used the term "Beautiful White Path" to describe the journey of a soul through life before it passes to the Milky Way after death.[11]

It should be kept in mind that the Hopewell roads were not narrow; they were 160-170 feet wide. Obviously, they were used to channel and control the movements of many people. The linear length of the known Portsmouth roads was about 20 miles. At Newark, the roads depicted by Squier and Davis' published survey extended several miles, but, as mentioned previously, in 1820 Caleb Atwater stated that one of these roads extended for 30 miles. In 1930, a flier looking for evidence of the roads noticed that a faint outline of them still existed nearly all the way to Millersport (30 miles). He also saw numerous cul-de-sac earthwork circles that appeared to be built next to the road every mile and a half. Archaeologist Bradley Lepper, head of the Ohio Historical Society Museum, has spent years tracing the final destination of this road. Using both infrared aerial photographs and archival aerial photographs, Lepper has found clear evidence that the road extended far further than anyone suspected. The "Great Hopewell Road," as Lepper terms it, ran from Newark to Chillicothe in a straight line for 56 miles.[10] The circle and octagon at Newark was linked to a nearly identical circle and octagon at Chillicothe by this road. Astronomical evidence (discussed shortly) shows a definite link between these two sites.

Hilltop Forts

About 25 or so of these irregularly shaped earthworks remain. They are all generally dated to the first three hundred years A.D. They exist in Ohio, Tennessee, New York, and in other states. They are all built on the

---

Figures 59, 60, & 61

Below left: Fort Ancient in Warren County, Ohio encloses 100 acres and has an outer wall varying in height from 4 to 34 feet tall. *From — Squier & Davis* (1848).

Right top: "Old Fort Hill" at Ellington in Chautauqua County, New York. The "fort" was erected on the top of a steep, 100-foot tall hill overlooking a valley. The elliptical diameters were 270 x 170 feet with walls at least 3 feet tall when examined in the 1800s. Several other similar hilltop forts were nearby. *From — Thomas (1890).*

Right bottom: The "Old Stone Fort" near Manchester, Tennessee encloses 32 acres and has earthen and stone walls encircling it. *From — Squier & Davis* (1848).

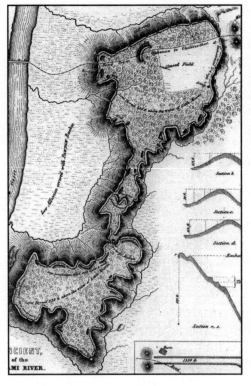

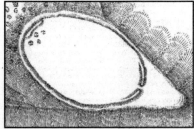

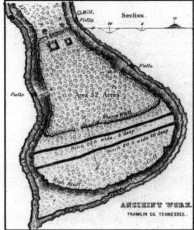

top of steep hills overlooking rivers or streams. Most of them have one or more sides where sheer cliffs make entry nearly impossible. Along the outlines of the cliffs and hilltop, huge earthen or stone embankments were formed. Some of these embankments supported a tall, wooden stockade essentially making them into fortresses. The area enclosed by them varies with the size of the hilltop they are constructed upon. Mounds and other earthworks are commonly located inside and around the irregular sites. The most famous is Fort Ancient in Warren County, Ohio. (See figure 59.) Stone and earthen walls between 4 to 34 feet tall wind around the site for 3.5 miles enclosing 100 acres. The 33-acre Fort Hill site in Highland County, Ohio is enclosed by 1.6 miles of walls 6-15 feet high. (See figure 62.)

Excavations show that the hilltop forts were, indeed, used for defense. Many of them show evidence that the wooden walls were repeatedly burnt and then rebuilt. Some appear to have been constructed quickly and were used only for a brief time. Others show evidence of long-term habitation. They are known to be a Hopewell phenomenon, but their exact significance isn't understood. All that is known is that, from time to time, the Hopewells had to defend themselves against dangerous foes.

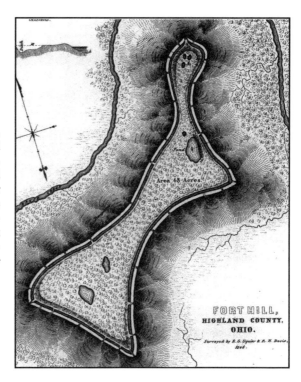

Figure 62
Fort Hill in Highland County, Ohio encloses 48 acres and had an outer wall up to 23-feet tall. It is built on top of an isolated and conspicuous hill with sheer cliffs up to 500 feet above the Brush Creek running at the bottom of the hill. This earthwork would have made an easily-defensible fortress. *From — Squier & Davis* (1848).

Effigy Mounds

Another distinctive trait of the Hopewells was the erection of mounds symbolizing animals and even human shapes. This Effigy Mound Culture appeared toward the end of the Hopewell period (A.D. 500-650). Effigy mounds are found in Georgia, Tennessee, Louisiana, Ohio, and other areas. But the most prodigious erection of effigy mounds occurred in Iowa, Minnesota, Wisconsin, and Illinois. A series of studies in Iowa beginning in the 1970s discovered 54 different effigy mound groups mainly along the Mississippi River. These 54 groups had once contained at least 1,438 separate mounds.[12] Effigies of 9 different animals were represented in 375 of these. Hopkins wrote that, "at one time, an estimated 10,000 mounds existed in northeast Iowa alone."[13] Today, Effigy Mounds National Park in Iowa has 191 mounds preserved with 29 of these in the shape of animals. The largest known was a quarter-mile long flying bird, however, it was destroyed long ago.

Figure 63 (top)
Bird mounds at the Chantry Hollow Group in Iowa. *Photo — National Park Service.*

Figure 64 (bottom)
Part of the "Marching Bear" Mound Group in Iowa. *Photo — National Park Service.*

Many effigy mounds remain on private property and are subject to destruction. The Ghost Eagle site near Muscoda, Wisconsin is an example. More than 24 bird or "eagle mounds" were originally found at this amazing site but almost all have been destroyed. James Scherz of Madison has evaluated the astronomical significance of these mounds and concluded that they were used to predict the solstices and equinoxes.[14] The rate of destruction of effigy mounds is rapid. More than 80% of effigy mounds known in 1890 were destroyed by 1973.[12]

Birds, bears, turtles, lizards, and panthers are the most common form of effigy mounds. However mounds depicting men and women exist. Some of the effigies are believed to represent clan and family symbols.

While the north-central region has the greatest number of effigy mounds, the largest ones in existence today are found further south. In Putnam County, Georgia, an eagle is represented in a mound made entirely of milky quartz boulders. (See figure 65.) The body is 10 feet thick and extends 120 feet from head to tail and 120 feet from wing tip to wing tip. Several other eagle effigy mounds made from milky quartz once existed in Georgia. Tennessee's Pinson site also contains an earthen effigy mound depicting an eagle.

Without doubt, the most famous effigy mound is the Serpent Mound in Adams County, Ohio. It coils on the ground for 1,348 feet depicting a

Figure 65
Rock Eagle Mound in Putnam County, Georgia. *Photo — G. Little.*

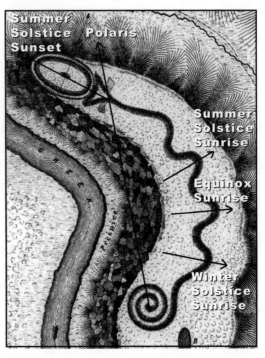

Figure 66
Ohio's Serpent Mound as shown by *Squier & Davis (1848)*. The alignments from the 1993 investigation are indicated.

snake apparently swallowing an egg. It is 20 feet wide and has a height between 2-6 feet. (See figure 66.) Several small mounds are associated with the site. While the mound has long been thought to date to 200 A.D. to 500 A.D., a 1991 excavation dated charcoal samples to 1070 A.D. It is believed to be directly linked to the Fort Ancient Culture (a Hopewell Culture discussed earlier in this chapter). A 1993 investigation showed that the serpent is oriented to Polaris. Its head points to the Summer Solstice sunset and the coils are aligned to the sunrises of the solstices and equinox.

Astronomical Alignments

The area of archaeology investigating astronomical alignments of sites is called archaeoastronomy. Emerging computer technology able to precisely compute the positions of the sun, moon, and stars at any given time and place has made their work extremely scientific and credible. As described earlier in this chapter, the Hopewell erected many sites as a means to predict the solstices and equinoxes.

The Newark Circle and Octagon is certainly one of the most mysterious earthworks in the world. In the 1980s, "amateur" archaeoastronomers began unraveling its astronomical significance. Perhaps the most significant contribution to Hopewell astronomy was made by two professors from Indiana's Earlham College who spent a decade studying the site. Ray Hively and Robert Horn, professors of Physics and Philosophy, found something incredible at the Newark site. The Circle and Octagon was used to precisely chart the 18.61-year cycle of the moon. (See figure 67.)

Figure 67
Newark Circle/Octagon Earthworks alignments to moonrise and moonsets. The geometry of
the alignments allows precise calculations of the 18.61 year cycle of the moon.
After Hively & Horn, 1982 (*Archaeoastronomy*, 13).

Geometry & Alignments of the
Octagon Works at Newark, Ohio

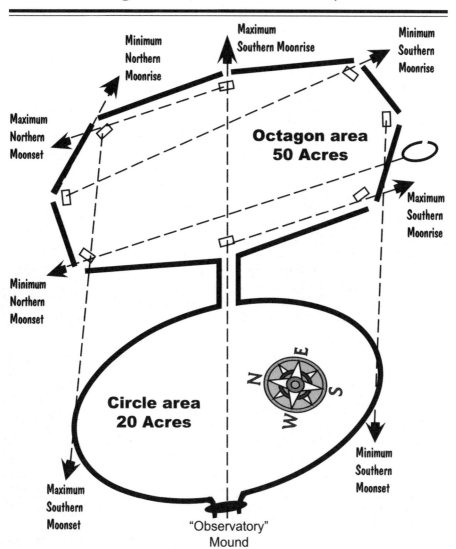

During its 28-day cycle, the moon's rising and setting points vary between two extreme northern and southern points of the visible horizon. However, over several year's time, the extreme rising and setting points change little-by-little until they gradually move backward. After a period of 18.61 years, the extreme rising and setting points return to where they began. The rising and setting of the moon cannot be viewed each night because of cloud cover and the two researchers estimated that it probably took a hundred years of careful observation prior to constructing the earthwork. Encouraged and fascinated by this result, after publishing their findings on Newark, Hively and Horn turned their attention to the circle and octagon at Chillicothe. The Chillicothe circle and octagon has long been known as the High Banks Works.

High Banks is nearly a duplicate to Newark's Circle and Octagon. However, the High Banks' circle and octagon is oriented 90 degrees off the Circle and Octagon at Newark. Not only did the High Banks Works show the expected lunar alignments, it also showed the sun's rising and setting points at the solstices. (See figure 68.) Commenting on their work, Bradley Lepper wrote: "the substantial earthen walls and a height that corresponds, more or less, to eye level are massive (and therefore long-lived and tamper proof) fixed instruments for making astronomical observations."[10]

In a prior section of this chapter, the "Great Hopewell Road," which runs from the Newark Circle and Octagon to Chillicothe, was mentioned. It is now believed that this road connected the High Banks Works with the Newark earthworks. Joseph Knapp has carefully plotted the surrounding topography of both the Newark and High Banks' circle and octagon and come to a startling conclusion. The High Banks Works was utilized for moon observations January through June of each year. During that time period, the horizon at Newark blocked the best views of the moon. However, in July through December of each year, the Circle and Octagon at Newark was the best place to view the movements of the moon. That, he believes, partially explains the road between Newark and Chillicothe.[15]

While charting the moon's movements over an 18 year period can be viewed as a sort of long-term calendar, it has another advantage. Every 18.61 years a major lunar standstill occurs. This event was significant at Stonehenge as well as at many other European stone circle sites. Perhaps more importantly, solar eclipses could be predicted by knowing the *saros cycle*, a related 18 year, 11 $1/3$ day cycle. The ancient Babylonians successfully predicted eclipses through the *saros cycle*. A *saros series*, is a series of eclipses every 18 years 11+ days over a span of 1,200 years. During that time, 68-75 solar eclipses would occur. Only a few of these would be full eclipses. A full eclipse will occur on the same spot on earth, on average,

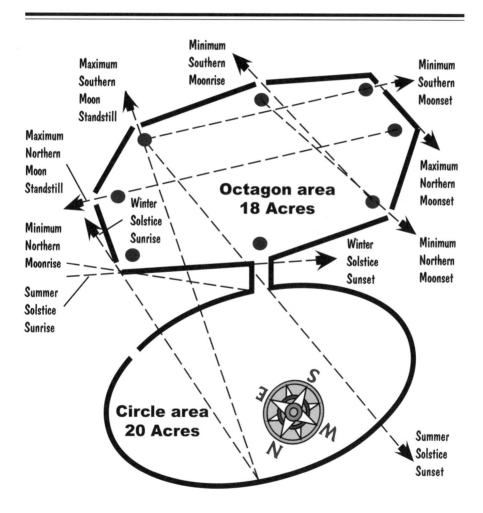

Figure 68
High Bank Circle/Octagon Earthworks alignments to moonrise and moonsets.
The geometry of the alignments allows precise calculations of the
18.61 year cycle of the moon.
After Hively & Horn, 1984 (*Archaeoastronomy*, 7).

Geometry & Alignments of the
High Bank Works at Chillicothe, Ohio

Minimum
Southern
Moonrise

Maximum
Southern
Moon
Standstill

Minimum
Southern
Moonset

Maximum
Northern
Moon
Standstill

Maximum
Northern
Moonset

Octagon area
18 Acres

Winter
Solstice
Sunrise

Minimum
Northern
Moonrise

Winter
Solstice
Sunset

Minimum
Northern
Moonset

Summer
Solstice
Sunrise

Circle area
20 Acres

Summer
Solstice
Sunset

about once every 360 years. However, partial eclipses occur about every 2.5 years.

William Romain[7], found solar alignments present at many Hopewell sites with circle and square earthworks. The Seal site is aligned to the equinoxes, the Dunlap works is aligned to the summer solstice sunrise, the Hopeton site is aligned to both the summer and winter solstice sunsets, the Anderson site is aligned to the summer solstice sunset, Mound City is aligned to the summer solstice sunset, and the original Hopewell site is aligned to the winter solstice sunrise.

Romain also found many alignments at the Marietta Works. Three different alignments were found at Marietta to the winter solstice sunset. In addition, the moon's maximum rising and setting points were present. However, some of the most interesting work at Marietta has come from David Berry, a retired chemist, and former *Marietta Times* Editor Ted Bauer. In 1983 Bauer suggested that the Marietta works was made to display the important sunrises.[16] Joining with Berry, the two made preliminary calculations showing that Marietta not only showed the important sunrises and

Figure 69

Daytime photo looking down the "Sacred Way" at Marietta toward the Muskingum River. On the tall bluffs on the other side of the river, four stone mounds once stood. These mounds served as visual alignments to lunar events as well as stellar risings. We noticed the full moon hovering just above the horizon formed by the bluff. The trees were not present during prehistoric times and 33-foot tall parallel walls on each side of the "Sacred Way" framed the view.

Photo — G. Little.

sunsets, but also the rising and setting points of the moon. A set of seven stone mounds on a ridge on the other side of the Muskingum River — directly across from the Sacre Via — served as important sighting points. In September 2000, authors Greg and Lora Little observed a spectacular full moon hovering on the horizon as viewed down the Sacred Way at Marietta. (See figure 69.)

Berry and Bauer also discovered that the gaps in the circular cul-de-sac earthworks at Newark and Chillicothe were oriented toward something unexpected — prominent stars, especially the star Sirius. In 1987 the two proposed that many mound sites were arranged to depict constellations. They specifically identified the Pleiades and the three stars comprising Orion's Belt in mound groupings.[17] This was a profoundly interesting and notable achievement by the two. The best-selling book that is widely credited as the first to propose that the ancients built structures on Earth to mimic Orion's three main stars, *The Orion Mystery*, was published in 1994 — more than 6 years after Berry and Bauer proposed the idea. It seems certain that the Hopewell Culture carefully watched the movements and risings and settings of the sun, moon, stars and planets. As mentioned previously, there is strong evidence that the Pinson site in Tennessee was utilized to observe the rising of the stars Sirius, Rigel, and Aldebaran.

Cayce & Hopewell

The Edgar Cayce readings never mentioned "Adena" or "Hopewell" by name. This should not be surprising since the terms had nothing to do with either Native Americans or ancient America. As we have outlined several times, however, the Cayce readings do provide an overview of the mound builders. Cayce's assertions essentially agree with the Hopewell characteristics identified by archaeologists. The existence of stone altars in many Hopewell mounds lends support to Cayce's statement that the Lost Tribes influenced the culture. In addition, the evidence that Hopewell was influenced by Mexican cultures is overwhelming, despite the rejection of this idea by the majority of academic archaeologists. The 187-foot grid at Teotihuacan and Hopewell sites appears to fully support Cayce's assertion that, prior to moving into America to become mound builders, the Lost Tribes lived near Mexico City and became involved with the pyramid-building culture there. The stone columns at the Crystal River Complex, the appearance of corn in Ohio in 500 B.C., and even the shape of some earthworks support Cayce's idea of the Lost Tribes migrating north. In addition, the similarities between the sacred roads of the Maya and the embanked walkways in America appear to indicate that their construction could have originated from related groups.

Cayce stated that the mound builder era began with a fusion of the Lost Tribes with the Atlantean culture. The incredible Hopewell earthworks were, therefore, from the Cayce viewpoint, an outgrowth of Atlantean influences. The use of altars and burials in sub-mound tombs lined with logs and stones was an adaptation from the Lost Tribes.

The presence of lunar and solar alignments at Hopewell sites is fascinating. Cayce gave long readings on the influence of astrology on human life, and both the sun and moon played prominent roles in these readings. The influence of the Pleiades and Orion were also mentioned several times by Cayce. In addition, Cayce mentioned that temples dedicated to the sun and moon had been built in ancient America by Atlanteans. The Circle and Octagon works, as well as many of the circle/square works, may be representations of these temples. It is possible that a form of lunar initiation occurred at some of these sites.

We shall fully examine the possibility of an Atlantean influence on mound building in a later chapter. However, the history of American mound building must be completed first. For the largest mounds were not built until the Hopewell era ended. This cultural group, collectively called the Mississippians, not only built the largest mounds, but also built them to resemble pyramids.

Chapter 8

The Mississippians

Mississippian towns rank among the largest and most archaeologically
complex prehistoric cultural spaces in the eastern United States. Although
surface collected, looted, excavated, and mapped by generations of archaeologists,
interested citizens, and pot hunters, surprisingly little is known about them...
R, B. Lewis & C. Stout (1998) *Mississippian Towns and Sacred Spaces*

As the Hopewell Era waned in 500 A.D. and Adena ended in 900 A.D.,
a new form of mound building emerged that came to dominate the
entire Eastern Woodlands. The strange earthworks of the Hopewell sites
were abandoned and construction of large pyramid-shaped mounds in
the midst of gigantic housing complexes was undertaken. Some of the most
important factors contributing to this change were the development of advanced agriculture, better pottery, improved food storage capability, and
an increasingly stratified society.

The Mississippian Era began as early as 300 A.D. and continued to
about 1600 A.D. It reached its pinnacle in 1400 and amazingly, a few reliable accounts of these mound builders exist. From these accounts it is
known that the Mississippians were sun worshipers and had absolute rulers who lived atop the mounds dominating their cities.

In 1539, Hernando DeSoto and a group of 622 men, mostly Spanish
soldiers, landed near Tampa, Florida. Seeking a "city of gold," DeSoto's
troops marched through Georgia, South Carolina, and then into North
Carolina. They turned west moving through Tennessee's Blue Ridge Mountains before marching south. After reaching central Alabama, the group
moved to the northwest through Mississippi until they came to the Mississippi River near Memphis. It took them a month to build barges big enough
to cross the 2-mile wide river. Moving north through Arkansas, they may

have gone as far as New Madrid, Missouri before they went west through the Ozarks eventually reaching Oklahoma. Exhausted, frustrated by not finding any gold, and facing constant battles, they finally decided to return to the Gulf of Mexico and leave. While passing through Louisiana, DeSoto died and another officer ordered the group to change course and go west. His order led the troops to the deserts of Texas. He then ordered a march to the southeast. By July of 1543, the 311 survivors of DeSoto's ill-fated search for gold floated down the Mississippi River and found their way to Mexico.

As soon as he landed in Florida, DeSoto encountered mound builders who were constructing temple mounds 40 feet in height. But there wasn't any gold. Undaunted, DeSoto and his men were spurred on, moving from village to village by the sage Chiefs who told him that a golden city could be found — but it was always located far in the distance. In Georgia, DeSoto was met by a "fat queen" who ruled the entire area from a large mound complex. DeSoto questioned her about gold and silver and she replied that she did, in fact, have a great supply of it. DeSoto was brought piles of "gold" and "silver" artifacts, but all of them were made from copper and mica. Frustrated, the Spaniards looted 500 pounds of pearls found in coffins atop a temple mound. At another nearby mound site, they looted a 100-foot long temple atop a huge pyramid-shaped mound. In nearly every area DeSoto visited, he encountered huge temples built atop high, earthen mounds forming truncated pyramids. The temples were filled with the beautiful artifacts from the Mississippian period — but contained no gold.[1]

DeSoto's ill-fated quest for gold led him on a zigzagged march through the heart of Mississippian mound building country. His trek ensured that the diseases he and his men carried were spread throughout the entire land. The natives had no resistance to common European diseases, and within only a decade, 90% of the native population died. Sadly, the 4,500-year span of the great ancient American mound building era had ended. By the time the first settlers reached the mounds, all that remained in tribal memories were misty recollections of their ancient ancestors who built them.

Mississippian Characteristics

The Mississippian Era derives its name from the huge valley formed by the Mississippi River and the temple mound complexes built there beginning in about 300 A.D. Similar mounds outside the area are also known as "Mississippian." Mississippian sites extended from the Atlantic coast to Texas and Oklahoma and from Wisconsin to the Gulf. Numerous regional names are used to describe different variations of the culture. Classic Mississippian sites typically have multiple temple mounds, conical burial mounds, and a plaza. This mound complex served as the center of a busy "city." A high wooden wall plastered with mud was usually erected around the entire city or at least around the most important temple mounds in the central city. Surrounding the city were large agricultural areas where corn, beans, and squash were cultivated. (See figure 70.)

The flat plaza at the bottom of the gigantic temple mounds served as both the primary meeting place and as a game area. Just as the Maya and later Aztecs did, the Mississippians used the plazas to play several games where much more than pride was at stake.

In recent years archaeoastronomers have found that many Mississippian Era mounds have alignments to the solstices, equinox, and star risings. It is believed that ceremonies were planned around celestial events like the solstices, but the significance of the star alignments remains puzzling.

Atop the most important temple mound at each site, a sacred fire was burning at all times. Religious, political, and day-to-day life was centered on the great mounds. The ruling chief was sometimes called the "Great Sun" and was revered as a deity. The title was bestowed upon him based upon his lineage. The bones of the great chiefs were usually stored in a temple atop a sacred mound, housed with a multitude of artifacts. Cults

Figure 70
Typical layout of Mississippian Era mound complex. This painting represents Marksville, Louisiana. Note the plaza area in the center, the housing in the bottom right corner, and temples on the pyramidal-mounds. Several conical burial mounds can be seen.
From — Southeastern Archaeological Center, National Park Service.

based on animal identification and ancestor worship were practiced. Fantastic images depicting feathered snakes, men in "bird" costumes, and effigies were found on stone, pottery, and ceremonial objects. Some images, like the "eye-in-the-hand" symbol, the cross, and the "flying snake" appeared at many sites.

Mississippian Sites

Only a few of the larger Mississippian sites will be discussed. A few pictures from additional locations are included and the captions provide some detail about these sites. Thousands of Mississippian mounds remain in existence; however, many continue to be destroyed by farming. The smallest sites usually consist of a single mound only a few feet in height. The largest site, Cahokia, has 106 mounds. A fair number of Mississippian sites are preserved as parks today and serve as reminders of an ancient past in America. Earthen pyramids are not as impressive as the stone pyramids of Egypt, but a simple comparison shows the great extent of the mound building civilization in ancient America. The entire country of Egypt has less than 100 pyramids and the majority of them are fairly small in comparison to the Great Pyramid at Giza. In contrast, the site of Cahokia, near Collinsville, Illinois, once had 120 mounds (106 remain there today). Not only that, but the largest mound at Cahokia has a base of over 14 acres — just larger than the base of Giza's Great Pyramid.

Spiro Mounds, Oklahoma

Near the small town of Spiro, Oklahoma, the Mississippians built an unusual mound complex by the Arkansas River that was apparently used only by priests. The site, containing 12 mounds, was constructed in about 800 A.D. The mounds yielded an incredible array of huge pipes and exquisite ceremonial objects to farmers and others who found the time to dig into them. (See figure 71.) In the 1930s, an eager market of buyers was ready to absorb any artifacts from mounds, and the Spiro mounds' goods were among the very best. Consequently, the Pocola Mining Company decided to turn the site into a commercial operation. They brought in dynamite and huge road equipment and leveled the mounds destroying more artifacts than they removed intact. Years later two amateur archaeologists managed to track down many of the best artifacts collectors had bought from the Pocola Company. They repurchased them and donated them to the state.

Figure 71
The feathered serpent was an
important symbol found on many
artifacts at Spiro.

Cahokia, Collinsville, Illinois

Cahokia lies 5 miles east of the Mississippi River at St. Louis. The 2,200-acre mound complex, designated as a World Heritage Site, contains 68 of the 106 known remaining mounds.(See figure 72.) In A.D. 1200, the central city of Cahokia was home to at least 20,000 people — some archaeologists argue that 50,000 residents may have lived there. Expansive agricultural fields encircling the city supported the residents. It is likely that nearly every tree was used for firewood or construction within many miles of the city.

Cahokia was carefully arranged in rows of houses surrounding various plazas which were subdivided into residential sections. Mounds were erected to house leaders in elevated temples and were laid out based on specific solar and other astronomical events. Around the central city was a tall wooden stockade plastered with hardened clay. Bastions were erected at regular intervals to make defense of the walls easier. Cahokia was a gigantic fortress, but excavations show that the walls were rebuilt at least four times. Attacks on the city left thousands of arrowheads in lines following the walls. The walls had burned and the ash from the wood formed a deep cover for the points as they fell to the ground. Exactly who it was who had sufficient numbers of warriors to attack the site so many times is unknown.

The largest mound is called "Monk's Mound," named for a group of French monks who lived there in the 1800s. (See figure 73.) The mound has 22 million cubic feet of dirt forming four terraces on its 14-acre base. At its summit, 100 feet high, a huge temple once stood. The temple had walls 50 feet high. It was 105 feet long and 48 feet wide. The size of the

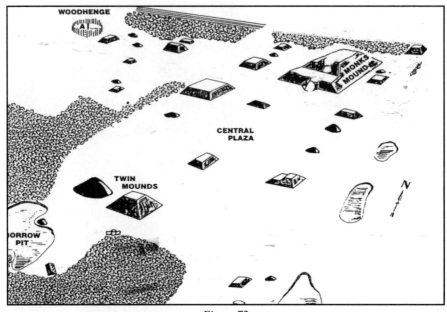

Figure 72
Map of Cahokia today showing Monk's Mound, Woodhenge (upper left side), and other mounds. *Adapted from — Illinois Historic Preservation Agency.*

mound is easy to misjudge in pictures. In 1987, over 4,000 people stood on top of the mound for a Harmonic Convergence celebration.

Burial mounds are included in the city center. A small mound, called Mound 72, was completely excavated. Almost 300 burials were found in it. The main burial in the mound was a male ruler who had been about 45 years old. His body was placed on 20,000 shell beads. Next to his burial were found four men with their heads and hands missing. Also found were the skeletons of 53 women between the ages of 15 and 25 who were sacrificed with the ruler. Over the years, tens of thousands of artifacts have been uncovered in Cahokia burials. Figure 74 shows the Cahokia "Birdman" tablet recovered from Monks' Mound.

In 1964, Warren Wittry conducted a hasty excavation prior to the construction of Interstates 70 and 55 that cut through the site. Wittry found huge cedar post holes carbon dated to A.D. 815. More post holes were subsequently found. These post holes formed several overlapping circles which were subsequently dubbed "woodhenge" because they were used to make alignments with solar events and stars.

In the summer of 1998 a mystery began to unfold at Cahokia as Southern Illinois University at Edwardsville conducted a few test excavations

Figure 73
Monk's Mound from the air. *From — Illinois Historic Preservation Agency.*

on Monk's Mound in preparation for the installation of drainage pipes on the mound. As a drilling rig was boring a horizontal hole 140 feet into the mound, at 40 feet under the 2nd terrace it encountered stone. The drill was forced through 32 feet of stone when the bit suddenly broke off. In July of 1999 efforts at determining the size and shape of the stone structure took place. Remote sensing equipment found three "anomalies." The stone structure appears to be 19 to 30 feet tall, but its extent couldn't be calculated. Just above the stone structure another densely packed earthen structure exists (it is 5 feet wide and 7-17 feet tall). A similar anomalous earthen structure was identified 70 feet deeper into the center of the mound. What these structures are is completely unknown. They do not fit any known type of tomb or style of stone construction utilized by the Mississippians.[1, 2, 3]

Figure 74
Cahokia's emblem comes from this "Birdman" tablet recovered from Monk's Mound (actual size). *Photo — G. Little.*

Moundville, Alabama

About 13 miles south of Tuscaloosa, Alabama a 300-acre area contains 20 truncated earthen pyramids roughly arranged in a huge circle. They range from 3 to 60 feet in height and served as temple mounds. Another 20 burial mounds were erected near the site. Moundville was a major ceremonial center between the years 1200-1400 A.D. and up to 3,000 people lived in the central area that was enclosed by a wooden stockade. Another 10,000 people lived around the stockade. The site was a center for what has been described as "The Southern Death Cult." Complex rituals were held during mortuary celebrations and involved the use of particular symbols found on artifacts uncovered at the site. These include the eye in the hand symbol, the sun circle, the cross, and the feathered serpent.[4] (See figures 75-77.)

Figure 75 (left)
Effigy pipe (cat?) from Moundville, 5.75 inches in length; it contained traces of tobacco. *From — Moore* (1905).

Figure 76 (below)
Moundville from the air. Note the many flat-topped mounds. *From — Alabama Museum of Natural History.*

Figure 77
Eighteen inch, thin sandstone disc found at Moundville depicting knotted snakes and the eye in hand symbol. Dozens of artifacts at Moundville depict this symbol as do artifacts at many other Mississippian sites. *From — Alabama Museum of Natural History.*

Etowah, Georgia

The Etowah site, 3 miles from Cartersville, Georgia, is a classic example of a stockaded Mississippian town centered around three large, flat-topped mounds. (See figures 78 & 79.) The 56 acres of the town was enclosed by a 12-foot deep, 24-foot wide moat with the wooden walls built inside the moat. The largest temple mound is 60 feet high and has a base of 335 x 395

Figure 78
The largest mound at Etowah is 60 feet tall. The group walking up the ramp of the mound depicts how immense this mound truly is. Its base is 335 x 395 feet. The smallest mound can be seen to the left. *Photo — G. Little.*

feet. From 1954 to 1958 a series of excavations uncovered two spectacular marble statues (figure 80). The first was a two-foot high female wearing a backpack-like object. A deep green stain (paint) was found on the breast and face areas. A second statue, a 120-pound male over 2 feet high, also had the same green stain. The male statue was broken in several places and other indications showed that both statues had been hastily and carelessly placed in a burial. Both statues are on display at the well maintained site.[5, 6]

Figure 79 (above)
The second largest mound at Etowah; 22 feet tall as seen from atop the large mound. *Photo — G. Little.*

Figure 80 (left)
The marble statues at Etowah are 2-feet tall. The breastplate stain on the male can be seen. Note the "backpack" on the female. *Photo — G. Little.*

Aztalan, Wisconsin

Sometime around the year 1100 A.D., a small group abandoned Cahokia and fled north up the Mississippi River. They diverted up the Rock River and then took the Crawfish River where they established a new mound site near what is today Lake Mills, Wisconsin. It became the northernmost outpost of the Mississippians. The site, now called Aztalan, originally had 74 conical mounds carefully placed in a double row within wooden walls 12-19 feet high. Two truncated pyramids were also built; the largest is 24 feet tall. Evidence of cannibalism has been found at Aztalan.[7]

Other Mississippian Sites of Interest

Many Mississippian Era mound complexes are maintained as parks and archaeological centers. Each gives a fascinating look at the particular type of practices that were conducted within a regional variation of the Mississippian Era mounds. Among these are Kolomoki Mounds (near Blakely, Georgia), Ocmulgee (Macon, Georgia), Rock Creek Mounds (south of Cusseta. Georgia), Marksville (Louisiana), Caddo Mounds (near Alto, Texas), Indian Mound (Florence, Alabama), Parkin (known to be a site visited by DeSoto in 1541; in Arkansas), Toltec Mounds (southeast of Little Rock, Arkansas), Lake Jackson Mounds (north of Tallahassee, Florida), Temple Mound (Fort Walton Beach, Florida), Emerald Mound, Mangum Mound, Boyd Mounds, Bynum Mounds, Pharr Mounds, and Bear Creek Mound (all on the Natchez Trace in Mississippi), Winterville Mounds (near Greenville, Mississippi), Town Creek (near Mount Gilead, North Carolina),

Figure 81
Aztalan's largest truncated pyramid. *Photo — G. Little.*

Chucalissa and DeSoto Mounds (both in Memphis, Tennessee), Shiloh Mounds (near Savannah, Tennessee), Mississippi Palisades Park (Savanna, Illinois), Angel Mounds (Evansville, Indiana), Wickliffe Mounds (Kentucky), Lilbourn Mounds (New Madrid, Missouri), and Towosahgy Mounds (near East Prairie, Missouri). (See figures 82-85.)

Figure 82
Truncated pyramid at Winterville, Mississippi (55 feet tall). *Photo — G. Little.*

Figure 83
Emerald Mound is actually three mounds. The base mound covers 8 acres and is 770 x 435 feet. A huge truncated pyramid was then erected on one end (upper right of photo) and a smaller pyramid was built on the other end. *Photo — National Park Service.*

Figure 84
One of the best restored sites is Town Creek, North Carolina (below). *Photo — G. Little.*

Figure 85
Huge temple mound at Ocmulgee in Georgia. *Photo — National Park Service.*

Astronomical Significance of Mississippian Sites

It has only been within the past decade that researchers have seriously looked at the possibility that all Mississippian sites were arranged in a pattern aligned with solar and stellar events. Maureen Korp[8] evaluated 57 different Mississippian mound complexes. Eighty-nine percent of contained earthworks oriented to the east. This seems to indicate a strong emphasis on sun worship. Korp asserts that the arrangement of the mounds is very similar to Stonehenge as well as other Neolithic sites in the Old World.

After finding stellar, lunar, and solar significance at the 18-mound site of Toltec in Arkansas, researchers analyzed 31 other Mississippian sites for possible alignments.[9] Seventy-one percent of these sites showed alignments to the solstices. Alignments to the rising of the stars Vega, Sirius, Arcturus, Aldebaran, Rigel, Fomalhaut, and Capella were found at several sites. Lunar alignments were also found. For example, at Toltec the extreme southern setting point of the moon is indicated.

The majority of the mound sites were oriented around three large mounds, sometimes in a line, but more often in a triangle. A survey of 536 Mississippian mound centers found that the most common number of mounds found at these sites is three.[9] The typical site has three mounds with a plaza area between them. (See figure 86.) Secondary mounds are usually found in groups of three off the sides of the plaza area between the two largest mounds.

Figure 86
Drawing of the most frequent Mississippian mound arrangement. Three truncated pyramids are arranged into a triangle with a plaza in the center. Smaller secondary burial mounds are sometimes located outside of the main plaza area. *Illustration — Southeastern Archaeological Center, National Park Service.*

Cayce's Assertions About The Mound Builders

In one of his most interesting readings on the mound builders (in 1936), Cayce stated that the Native American Indian mounds were replicas of the Yucatan, Atlantis, and Gobi experiences. In the next chapter, the Atlantis connection to the mounds will be discussed. The parallels between the mounds and the Maya sites in the Yucatan will be briefly outlined in the following section. But what could Cayce have meant when he spoke of the Gobi experience?

The word "Gobi" appears 199 times on the Cayce CD ROM. It appears in well under 100 life readings. Several Cayce readings call the Gobi the "Sun Land" and indicate that sun worship was their primary religion (2067-4; 2091-1). In March of 1935 Cayce referred to a lost city buried under the sands of the Gobi (873-1), and, in 1936 he called this city the "City of Gold" and the "Golden City." He also stated that this city would probably be discovered in the future (877-12; 1554-3; 2402-2).

According to Cayce, one important characteristic of the Gobi civilization was the implementation of a rigid social structure he likened to a "caste system." The rulers were held in awe and were seen as gods themselves (2067-4; 1505-1). They lived in temples and, in a 1940 reading, Cayce referred to "terraced buildings" with temples in the Gobi (2067-4).

Cayce's descriptions of the caste system in the Gobi fit the Mississippian Era mound builders quite well. It is known that the King (or Queen) was called the "Great Sun" and was seen as a deity. (See figure 87.) The Great Sun ruler was carried around on a platform seated on a throne. Their rule was absolute. In addition, they lived atop the high, flat-top mounds in huge temples — matching Cayce's descriptions of "the Gobi experience."

Most of Cayce's readings on the Gobi occurred in the 1930s with the last one occurring in 1944. From the readings it appears that he was speaking about several different locations in the huge area of the Gobi Desert. For example, the Gobi City of Gold is described in detail in some readings. In other readings, Cayce describes a plain with many terraced buildings and temples — and these descriptions are different from the City of Gold.

According to religious historians, the primary spiritual ideas of the ancient Chinese were "concerned with the structure and form of the world in which they lived and with the mysterious forces that operated within the geometric framework of that world. That framework consisted of a flat platform of earth...surmounted by the canopy of Heaven studded with the fiery stars that controlled human destiny."[10] Recorded Chinese history goes back nearly 5,000 years but, in historic times, China has, for the most part, always been a land closed to Westerners. The presence of huge mounds ("flat platforms of earth") in China was essentially unknown to the outside world until 1945, and even then, only a handful of people were aware of their presence.

In 1947, it was revealed that a military aircraft from the United States had flown over an area to the southwest of the city of Xi'an in 1945. The crew photographed a huge earthen pyramid that they spotted from the air and a picture of it was published in 1947. (See figure 88.) The accompanying article suggested that the mound was perhaps 1000 feet high and that other mounds were spotted by the pilots.

Figure 87
The "Great Sun" of the Natchez was carried everywhere and was seen as a deity. *Illustration — DuPratz (1758).*

Author Hartwig Hausdorf became interested in the topic in the late 1980s and subsequently managed to visit central China and photograph (at a distance) some of these mounds. His book, *The Chinese Roswell*, depicts them. Near "the forbidden zones" Hausdorf managed to use a zoom on a videocamera and counted over 100 pyramidal mounds on the plains. A number of governmental satellite reconnaissance photos of the central China plains have subsequently been examined revealing the presence of hundreds of mounds shaped like pyramids. (See figure 89.) They vary in size with some of them being immense. Not all of the satellite photos are from the area Hausdorf visited; most of them lie further to the north. However, their exact location is unclear. It is likely that the location of some of the reconnaissance photos will turn out to be in the southern Gobi.

Figure 88
1947 U.S. military aircraft photo of huge earthen pyramid near Xi'an in China. Although the sides show evidence of erosion, the shape of this mound is strikingly similar to Mississippian Era mounds in America.

Figure 89
Force 9, a British web site, obtained military reconnaissance photos of several areas of China. This photo is believed to be to the north and east of Xi'an near the Gobi. While the resolution of the photo is poor, about 20 earthen pyramids are visible.

The pyramids near Xi'an are not in the Gobi itself, but in the plains just south of it. It is in the Shensi Province bordering the Gobi and the Great Wall. This was the heart of ancient Chinese civilization; an area that extended well into the Gobi prior to the construction of the Great Wall by Ch'in Shih in 200 B.C.

Edgar Cayce's simple assertion linking the American mounds to similar terraced temples in the Gobi were preposterous at the time he made it. And his idea that envoys and small groups of people moved between the Gobi, Egypt, and Atlantis was preposterous. The 2001 finding of a trace of the X haplotype in the northern area of the Gobi seems to establish a firm link between the areas Cayce identified. Once again, it appears Cayce's "impossible" ideas turn out to be credible.

Heaven On Earth?
The Yucatan, Egypt,
and the Mound Builders

In *The Lost Hall of Records* the "Cosmic Hearth" of the Maya was discussed at length. The Cosmic Hearth is a triangle formed by three stars of the constellation of Orion. (See figure 90.) The stars are Alnitak (the outer star of the three stars comprising the "belt"), Saiph, and Rigel. The triangle of the Cosmic Hearth is a key concept in the Maya myth of the coming of the Great Father god Itzamna and the beginning of the 4th world in 3114 B.C. There is no doubt in Maya archaeology that the Cosmic Hearth was Orion. In addition, the probable site of the Yucatan Hall of Records (as told by Cayce) at Piedras Negras has several pyramid formations that appear to symbolize this triangle. In fact, Piedras Negras has a pyramid aligned to the rising of Orion's Belt on August 14, 3114 B.C. and another pyramid aligned to the setting of Orion on December 22, 2012. (That is the Maya date for the end of the current world and the beginning of the new one.) Itzamna may have been a representation of Iltar who Cayce said left Atlantis and went to the Yucatan to establish the temple to house the ancient Atlantean records.

Mythology provides a number of details about Orion. He was a great hunter and a warrior. The Hebrews saw him as Nimrod, the builder of the Tower of Babel. There are several versions of Orion's origin in Greek mythology, but all of them involve Poseidon in one way or another. The least complex and most "plausible" of these tales casts Orion as the son of

Poseidon and Euryale 2.[11] According to Plato, Poseidon is the god who established ancient Atlantis. Since Orion was the son of Poseidon, it would appear, at least on the surface level, that a link between Orion to the mythology of Atlantis may be present.

The underlying realities of mythology tend to be obscured not only by time but also by inconsistent and unclear symbols. In Egypt, Orion was associated with the god Osiris. Edgar Cayce's readings indicated that the great civilization of ancient Egypt developed when some Atlanteans escaped the final destruction of their islands sometime before 10,000 B.C. Robert Bauval and Adrian Gilbert's 1994 book, *The Orion Mystery*, made a well-received connection between Orion and ancient Egypt. They asserted that the alignment of the pyramids at Giza symbolized Orion's Belt and were an effort to represent heaven on earth. Bauval and Gilbert date this event to 10,400 B.C. and term it "the first time." Edgar Cayce may have foreshadowed this finding in a 1932 reading when he stated that the Great Pyramid was formed by the position of various stars.[12]

In the prior chapter, the story of David Berry, a retired chemist, and former *Marietta Times* Editor Ted Bauer was related. In 1987 the two proposed that many mound sites were arranged to depict constellations —

Figure 90

The Maya "Cosmic Hearth" — the site of creation and humanity's entrance into the world. A crack appeared on the top of a turtle's back. From this triangular spot, life emerged. The triangle was formed within the Constellation of Orion. Many Maya sites depict this sacred triangular orientation including Piedras Negras, the probable site of the Yucatan Hall of Records. *From — The Lost Hall of Records (2000).*

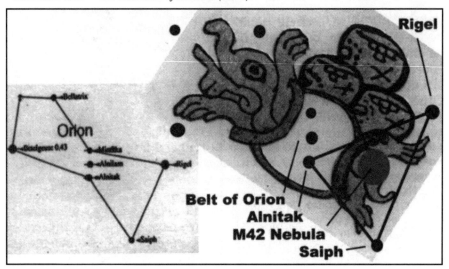

especially Orion's Belt and the Pleiades. The triangle formed by the stereotypical Mississippian mound site is clearly reminiscent of the Orion-based Maya Cosmic Hearth. (See figure 91.) Therefore, it appears we have found a common link between the many sites in Central America to those in North America — and Egypt. All three geographic locations, it appears, had ancient sites depicting Orion and the Cosmic Hearth of creation.

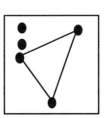

Figure 91
The triangular Hearth shape and the 3-star pattern (with the top star slightly offset) is the Orion configuration.

Figure 92
Etowah, Georgia shows the classic "Cosmic Hearth" triangle formation. *From — Thomas (1891).*

Figure 93
The Schlimpert Mounds in Jackson County, Illinois had the typical "Belt of Orion" pattern. *From — Thomas (1891).*

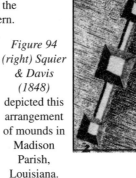

Figure 94 (right) Squier & Davis (1848) depicted this arrangement of mounds in Madison Parish, Louisiana.

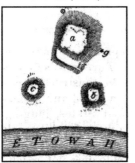

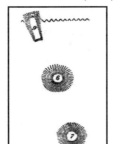

Figure 95
The original "Hopewell" site appears to depict both Orion's Belt as well as the Pleiades. From *Squier & Davis (1848).*

Figure 96
Powter's Fort mounds in Butler County, Missouri. *From — Thomas (1891).*

Figure 97
Orion's Belt appears to be represented at this Alabama complex. Nearby is a site with a hexagonal mound. *From Squier & Davis (1848).*

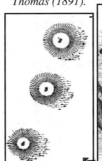

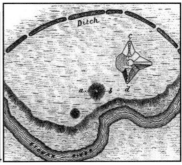

Many Mississippian Era mound sites show the triangular arrangement of the "Cosmic Hearth" as well as an arrangement of mounds that fits Orion's Belt. The Etowah, Georgia site, the Schlimpert Mounds (Jackson County, Illinois), Powter's Fort (Butler County, Missouri), the Dublin Earthworks (Franklin County, Ohio), the Hopewell site, and the Ancient Works (on the Etowah River in Alabama) are only a few of many (see figures 92-96).

In *Fingerprints of the Gods* Graham Hancock hypothesized that a great civilization existed in the world prior to 10,500 B.C. At the end of the last Ice Age, a worldwide cataclysm occurred that caused a great flood and the sudden destruction of this great civilization.[13] Survivors of this cataclysm went to different areas of the world and established a "wisdom cult" designed to impart a spiritual knowledge through astronomy and the construction of structures based on astronomical alignments. Their descendants sought to continue, using a phrase Hancock used in an earlier book[14], "a tradition of secret wisdom started by the survivors of a flood." This is, of course, one of Cayce's main contentions. He stated that the American mounds were a representation of the experiences in ancient Atlantis. It is to this incredible idea that we now turn our attention.

Chapter 9

Atlantis —
Plato, Cayce, and
the Mound Builders

That fancies flourish where facts are few
Is true of Atlantis and also of Mu.
Folsom & Folsom (1993) *America's Ancient Treasures*

A man who has once looked with the archaeological eye will never see quite normally.
Loren Eiseley (1971) *Night Country*

It seems as if cable television runs a "documentary" on Atlantis nearly every day. Most seem to focus on eager seekers who look for the remains of the lost continent in South America, Central America, islands in the Mediterranean, islands in the Atlantic, Antarctica, Europe, and even Wisconsin. Atlantis is widely derided by professional archaeologists in America. So too, is Mu. Yet, in other countries, these two "mythical" lands are taken seriously. The problem with professional acceptance of Atlantis is twofold. First, the possibility of an enormous sunken continent in the middle of the Atlantic is slim — at best. Secondly, it has long been argued that migrants from an advanced civilization did not suddenly appear in the Americas — or elsewhere — in 10,000 B.C. The Cayce story of Atlantis poses an additional problem. That is, Cayce's story of Atlantis was derived from a "psychic" source. Few archaeologists would ever seriously consider "evidence" coming from such a source.

None-the-less, there is evidence that an "advanced" civilization suddenly appeared in ancient America. Sometime around 10,000 B.C., a great migration occurred into America. The culture that came, called Clovis, migrated everywhere into the Americas bringing their weaponry, toolkits, improved home-building techniques, and other advancements with them. Until 1997, it was thought that Clovis was first in America. Now we know that, prior to Clovis, there were a lot of other people in the Americas — and they were not nearly as advanced as the Clovis people. The fact is simple — there is solid evidence that an "advanced" culture appeared in America in 10,000 B.C.

Another argument given against Atlantis' existence is that the pyramids in Egypt and those in Central and South America were built well after 10,000 B.C. "If the Atlanteans went to these two locations, why," it is asked, "weren't the pyramids we found in the world built in 10,000 B.C?"

The answer is astonishingly simple. *Building pyramids wasn't their priority.*

The "Forgotten" Plato Account

In the hopes of keeping this discussion easy to understand, we will not retell Plato's entire story of Atlantis. We will only touch upon a few relevant details and give a brief overview of the story.

Plato (427 B.C.-347 B.C.) told the story of Atlantis in two of his dialogues and attributed it to one of his relatives, Solon (615 B.C.-535 B.C.). Solon traveled extensively throughout the Mediterranean area and was given the account by Egyptian priests in the city of Sais. Plato prefaced the story by telling that many long-forgotten civilizations had been destroyed in the past. Just prior to telling the story, he told of three "disastrous floods" that culminated with the "deluge in the time of Deucalion." Greek historians date the Deucalion deluge to the end of the last Ice Age — about 10,000 B.C.

The Atlantis story that follows is from the *Critias*. It begins by stating that 9,000 years before that time (circa 9,600 B.C.) a war had occurred between Atlantis and the countries in the Mediterranean area.

According to the story, *long* ago the ancient gods divided up the earth among themselves. Poseidon took the island of Atlantis and soon married a mortal woman named Cleito. "…and to make the hill whereon she dwelt impregnable he broke it off all round about; and he made circular belts of sea and land enclosing one another alternately, some greater, some smaller, two being of land and three of sea…for at that time neither ships nor sailing were yet in existence…"

The fact that Plato mentioned that this event took place at a time before any ships existed is important. The very word "Atlantis" conjures up a vision of an advanced civilization. Few people keep in mind that the Atlantis account is one describing the gradual, long-term advance of a civilization before its sudden demise. Atlantis did not suddenly appear; it was a gradually developing civilization.

Poseidon and Cleito had five pairs of twin sons, and they subsequently divided the island into 10 parts for them. The first-born was Atlas and the Atlantic Ocean was named for him. Plato's account goes on to say that Atlas had many sons and a vast trading network was eventually established with the rest of the world. From imports and from the land of Atlantis itself, the list of riches Atlantis had was long: metals, timber, animals of all kinds, elephants, roots, herbs, gums, fruits, vegetables, and flowers. (And even here the story is a plausible description of a civilization making gradual advances.) Various temples and docks were eventually built, and a bridge was constructed over the rings of water and land leading to the "royal palace" that had been established on the central hill. The population of Atlantis increased quickly and many lived on the land rings surrounding the central palace. Eventually, a wide canal was dug from the sea leading to the central hill. The rings of land were heightened and given stone sides to resist the forces of the sea, which now ran all the way to the city. Brass and tin were used to cover the stonewalls on two of the rings. This work took some time as Plato described the passing of the central palace from one generation to the next: "and as each king received it from his predecessors, he added to its adornment and did all he could to surpass the king before him, until finally they made of it an abode amazing to behold for the magnitude and beauty of the workmanship."

Plato provided a detailed description of the magnificent central temple to Poseidon and Cleito. Tree plantations, reservoirs, baths for men and women, and gardens were placed around the temple as well as on the rings of land. Guardhouses with *"spearmen"* are also detailed.

After describing the surrounding plain of Atlantis, Plato goes on to tell how the military of Atlantis was formed. "War-chariots," "horses," "shields," "archers," and "javelins" are specifically mentioned. A blood sacrifice ritual with a bull on the top of a "pillar" is then explained. Plato continues, "For many generations, so long as the inherited nature of the God remained strong in them, they were submissive to the laws and kindly disposed to their divine kindred. For the intents of their hearts were true and in all ways noble, and they showed gentleness joined with wisdom in dealing with the changes and chances of life and in their dealings with one another." But, over time, as their riches increased to massive proportions, "the portion of divinity within them was now becoming faint and weak" and their tempers were increasing. Zeus, the God of gods, "marked how this race was in an evil plight, and desired to inflict punishment upon them..."

Plato never finished his account of Atlantis. But in the *Timaeus*, Plato told of the sudden ending of the land. He related that, Atlantis "made an attempt one time to enslave by one single onslaught both your country and ours and the whole of the territory within the Straits" (of Gibraltar — the Mediterranean). "...But at a later time there occurred portentous earthquakes and floods, and one grievous day and night befell them...and the island of Atlantis...was swallowed up by the sea and vanished."

New Archaeological Evidence & Plato's Atlantis Account

It is true that world history prior to 3500 B.C. is essentially a near-complete mystery. All we have are artifacts to analyze and a few stories like Plato's with which to reflect upon. Plato's story describes a civilization with spears, shields, archers, and javelins, perhaps well advanced for 10,000 B.C., but not to the point of stretching credulity. According to Plato, at some time well before 9600 B.C., Atlanteans attempted to colonize parts of Iberia as well as the entire Mediterranean. Thus, some evidence of an Atlantean presence in those areas should be expected — but it would have to be from a time period well before 9600 B.C.

In addition, around 9600 B.C., the entire island of Atlantis was destroyed. If there were survivors from Atlantis, some evidence of their presence, dating to around 9600 B.C. should be expected — but where? Where would the surviving Atlanteans flee?

Since the Atlanteans presumably knew that the lands to the east were hostile to them, a rational conclusion is that they would flee west — toward the Americas. Thus, there should be some evidence of their presence in the Americas exactly around 9600 B.C. And, because their culture also went to Iberia and the Mediterranean (some time well before 9600 B.C.), there should be a strong similarity between some cultural remains in ancient America and Iberia. Does such evidence exist? The answer is an absolute yes!

In Chapter 4, two types of evidence were detailed that directly bear on this issue. First, the American Clovis Culture made a sudden appearance around 10,000 B.C. nearly everywhere in both North and South America. This date coincides with Plato's date for the destruction of Atlantis. A virtually identical culture, called the Solutrean, appeared suddenly in Spain and parts of France in 15,000 B.C. If the war between Atlantis and the Mediterranean countries occurred some time around 15,000 B.C., the implication appears obvious. But a true confirmation of a link between 10,000 B.C. America and an earlier civilization in the Mediterranean may lie in the most "scientific" of scientific evidence — genetics.

The second piece of evidence detailed in Chapter 4 is the genetic evidence from mitochondrial DNA testing (mtDNA). Recapping those findings in brief, Native Americans show 5 types of mtDNA. These are A, B, C, D, and X. Types A, C, and D appear to have definitely come from Siberian Asia via the Bering Straits. The B type comes from Polynesia, China, and Japan. But the origin of the X type is unknown. The X type is found in three percent of Native Americans. But it is also found in Spain and Portugal (Iberia), Italy, the northern Gobi, and parts of the Middle East — especially in Israel. The X type appeared in America in 10,000 B.C. — matching the appearance of Clovis. In short, Plato's account of Atlantis is clearly in line with the newest evidence. His date for the sinking of Atlantis (9600 B.C.) is close to Clovis, but we are, of course, only speculating about the possible date of the Atlantean War and its relationship to the Solutrean Culture.

Cayce's Story of Atlantis

Cayce's readings on Atlantis total 700. Edgar Evans Cayce's two books, *Edgar Cayce on Atlantis* (1968) and *Mysteries of Atlantis Revisited* (1988), present a great amount of detail and information on Cayce's history of Atlantis pieced together from these readings. Those interested in a complete description are referred to these excellent books. For those encountering Cayce for the first time, take note that Edgar Evans Cayce, the author of these books, *is not Edgar Cayce the "psychic."* He is his son.

Cayce's Atlantis readings do not directly contradict Plato. The date Cayce gives for Atlantis' destruction is 10,014 B.C. rather than Plato's 9600 B.C. date, but that doesn't seem to be a major discrepancy. Cayce's readings appear to extend Plato's story and provide detail in areas Plato avoided.

Cayce's account of Atlantis came in readings where he was often commenting on the spiritual development of individuals. Thus, he often discussed specific issues of a personal nature describing a gradual evolution of the people in Atlantis. While this evolution was primarily a technological one, Cayce's primary focus was on spiritual development. His readings tended to give information about an individual's personal spiritual development over many lifetimes. However, because his Atlantis' material came in the form of specific events for specific people, there are long periods in the story of Atlantis that were unaddressed by Cayce.

Like Plato, Cayce placed Atlantis in the Atlantic Ocean. However, unlike Plato, Cayce provided a date for the appearance of man on Atlantis — 210,000 B.C. In addition, Cayce stated that Atlantis went through a series of three destructions. The first was in 50,700 B.C. when the continent broke into many islands. The second occurred in 28,000 B.C., after which the once huge continent was comprised of five large islands. The final destruction of Atlantis occurred in 10,014 B.C. This destruction was the one Plato's story described.

With the three different destructive events, Atlantis went through long periods of advancement followed by sudden disaster that apparently took them back to a more primitive way of life before they recovered. Prior to the first destruction in 50,700 B.C., Cayce stated that the Atlantean civilization had developed "machines of destruction that sailed both through the air or under the water" (1735-2). He described the making of hot air balloons from sewing animal skins together as well as how these were used for travel. He mentioned that some had an appearance like the Graf (Zeppelin). Prior to 50,700 B.C., the Atlanteans had also discovered a form of radio communication. In addition, a never-ending conflict began between two spiritually opposed groups. As discussed earlier, these were the Sons of Belial and the Children of the Law of One. Their disagreements were magnified at a meeting where the huge animals overrunning the Earth were discussed. The Belial group wanted to use the most destructive means available to kill the animals. Ultimately, the Belial group misused the explosives setting off a chain reaction causing the first destruction in 50,700 B.C.

Between 50,700 B.C. and 28,000 B.C. the Atlanteans not only recovered, but developed a much more advanced technology. A form of nuclear power was alluded to, as were forms of radio, television, and advanced means of travel. Cayce stated that a laser-like firestone crystal was used to produce power. Several of these crystal power-producing devices had been set up in many places in Atlantis. They were mistakenly "tuned" too high resulting in a series of violent explosions. These explosions set off a chain reaction of volcanoes and earthquakes reducing Atlantis to five islands. This was a major disaster.

Prior to this destruction, Cayce stated that some Atlanteans migrated to various parts of the world. These people, of the peaceful faction (The Children of the Law of One), went to South America and America, but some presumably fled elsewhere. Their philosophy rejected the blatant satisfaction of physical desires and the emphasis on ease and pleasure in the physical world. They sought a simpler way of life that brought them into better harmony with their spiritual source.

The second destruction of Atlantis was apparently severe and violent. Nearly half of all of Cayce's Atlantean life readings concern the time between the second destruction (28,000 B.C.) and the final destruction in 10,014 B.C. Prior to the final destruction, Cayce describes a migration of Atlanteans to other lands in sailing ships — and descriptions of advanced technology are few. In fact, one reading (315-4) describes a large group sailing for Egypt who (perhaps inadvertently) wound up in Portugal, France, and Spain. Others fled to America, South America, Egypt, the Gobi, and the Yucatan. One reading (1710-3) describes a sole person fleeing to the Yucatan in an "air machine." However, this could refer to the earlier destruction. Another reading describes an important person who traveled in a "flying boat" between Atlantis and Iberia and Egypt to help in the establishment of the record's hall (3184-1).

Cayce's readings tell us that many of those who fled Atlantis prior to the final destruction, attempted to continue their way of life. His descriptions of this time, however, do not include a technology of many aircraft, nuclear energy, radios, television, and submarines. Instead, they are simpler: "worked with adorning buildings with gems and precious stones" (955-1); "explored [Egypt] along waterways" (797-1); "aided in the development of mechanical appliances for cutting stone" (1177-1); "aided in replenishing and rebuilding of the temple service" (439-1); "aided in making the Nile more productive" (1842-1); "aided in preparations for vocational guidance" (2916-1); "persuaded many to make for activities that would preserve to the people what would be recipes, placards, drawings" (516-2); "became what today would be an instructor in psychological tests" (1751-1); "aided in styling for dress and conveniences for home" (1120-1).

The migration of Atlanteans to Egypt is described in more detail in the readings. This migration was better planned and was designed to preserve the Atlantean records as well as establish a center for the Children of the Law of One. The descriptions indicate that many of the people who went to Egypt had great mental powers as well as healing ability. A conscious attempt was made in Egypt to "build for the people...an understanding of the relationship...of man to the creative forces" (2031-1). In Cayce's story of Atlantis, the destruction of Atlantis eventually contributed to the great civilization of ancient Egypt.

In Cayce's chronology, the last islands of Atlantis sunk in 10,014 B.C. It was a gradual, but still violent series of events. A shifting of the earth's poles may have been a causal factor, but Cayce was apparently never asked the exact cause.

New Archaeological Evidence Supporting Cayce's Account

Cayce's chronology of Atlantis does not include a war between Greece and the Atlanteans. It could have occurred, however, it appears no one ever asked Cayce about it during a reading. His story contains three fairly large migrations of Atlanteans. Prior to 50,700 B.C. some Atlanteans went to America, South America, and elsewhere. Before the second destruction in 28,000 B.C., some Atlanteans fled to America and South America. After the second destruction in 28,000 B.C., he relates that large groups of Atlanteans went to Iberia (Spain, Portugal, and France). In addition, in the 500 or so years prior to 10,014 B.C., many Atlanteans migrated to the Americas, Spain, Portugal, France, and Egypt. The readings are clear in stating that the Atlanteans had to merge with the people already present.

The ubiquitous Clovis Culture appeared nearly everywhere in both North and South America in 10,000 B.C. It replaced the more primitive cultures that archaeologists have uncovered since the collapse of the Clovis barrier in 1997. As mentioned in Chapter 4, when Cayce gave his readings, this was totally unknown. Thus, what an astonishing coincidence it would be if Cayce had "guessed" or made up the 10,000 B.C. date! In fact, Cayce's date for the final destruction of Atlantis (10,014 B.C.) matches the appearance of Clovis even better than does Plato's date (9600 B.C.) As to the appearance of the identical Solutrean Culture in Spain and France in 15,000 B.C., Cayce made it plain that some Atlanteans fled to that very land after the second destruction of Atlantis. This would account for the presence of the Clovis-like culture in Iberia before its appearance in America. In addition, as mentioned in Chapter 4, the X haplotype of mitochondrial DNA showed its appearance in America prior to 10,000 B.C., but the main migration of people carrying that DNA type entered at that exact time — completely in line with the Cayce readings. And, of course, the presence of the X type in Spain, Italy, the Gobi, and Israel also supports Cayce's contentions. If all of these facts aligning to Cayce's statements are coincidences, they are remarkable ones, indeed.

Blind To The Truth

It is not our intention to attempt to prove that Atlantis once existed in the middle of the Atlantic Ocean. Many others have attempted this — and nothing but a host of disputed clues has emerged. But from the material presented thus far, it is obvious that either Edgar Cayce was an astonishingly lucky "guesser" of obscure dates — or he was something else. His "guesses" (as some might refer to them) include the dates (and even the existence) of Clovis, the Solutrean Culture, and the several dates of large migrations into America now confirmed through mtDNA analysis. Another lucky "guess" by Cayce is his timing of the mound building culture in America as well as the combination of influences that seem to have led to the culture itself. His lucky "guesses" also include the specific migration to America by Chinese, Polynesian, and other people. Of course, as discussed in prior chapters, it appears all of these "guesses" were correct. And it is interesting to ponder that all of Cayce's "lucky guesses" about ancient America were diametrically opposed to the established view of the time. Thus, we might conclude that *Cayce was something other than a lucky guesser.* Consequently, although we can't prove Atlantis existed, based on Cayce's remarkable "insights," we'll assume that the story of Atlantis has at least some truth to it and pursue the issue further.

The many people who search the Atlantic for Atlantis are often looking for the remains of a great and powerful advanced civilization. Some of them apparently believe they will eventually find vast areas with temples, planes, automobiles, televisions, nuclear reactors, gigantic crystal lasers, elevators, and a host of other technological remains. But Plato gave us the absolute dimensions of the great city of Atlantis. The city center, which contained the greatest splendor of the advanced civilization, had a diameter *of only one-half mile.* The diameter of the entire water and land-ringed city was two miles. The plain surrounding it was 335 miles by 223 miles.[1] Plato told us that the surrounding plain was primarily agricultural. The remainder of the vast continent was populated but was essentially rural in nature — comprised of mountains, valleys, and agricultural and grazing lands. The North Atlantic Ocean, extending down to the equator— both Plato's and Cayce's location for Atlantis — consists of over *40 million square miles.* Unless an explorer hit the 80 million-to-one chance of landing on top of the center city, what, if anything, could we expect to find if we chanced upon any of the other areas of Atlantis? After 12,000 years at the bottom of the ocean, with millennia of silt accumulation, the corrosion of ocean water, and the actions of organisms and other sea creatures, the chances are great that little of the technological splendor of Atlantis would remain.

One more observation is relevant here. From the Cayce readings, it is apparent that the technological advances made in Atlantis prior to the second destruction — which Cayce described as being widely available to the population — were nearly destroyed in 28,000 B.C. His descriptions of most of the advanced technology appear primarily in readings covering the pre-28,000 B.C. period. Only a few post-28,000 B.C. readings come close to describing the technology typically attributed to Atlantis. It is quite likely that the cataclysm, which split Atlantis into five islands in 28,000 B.C., destroyed a great deal of Atlantis' glory. Perhaps Atlantis blasted itself back to the Stone Age just as experts fear a nuclear war would do to whatever remained of our current civilization. It could have taken thousands of years for Atlantis to regain its technological splendor — if it ever did. That may well explain why the readings describing the Atlantean migrations just prior to 10,000 B.C. are so mundane. In short, the Atlantis that explorers have been searching for may have been largely destroyed in 28,000 B.C. What remains of that lost land may be far less than imagined. Our preconceived notions about Atlantis may be driving us to look for something that is perhaps less grand than we want to believe. An example of this could be in the Atlantean's application of mysterious forces to lift the huge stones that were used in pyramids and other massive stone structures. Cayce was asked several times how these huge stones (in Egypt) could have been lifted so high? His reply indicated that there were lifting forces in gases and nature that were not yet completely understood by modern science (5750-1). Some Atlantis proponents have suggested levitation, a harmonic "tuning" of the stones, and other esoteric explanations. But the answer may be exactly what Cayce told us — but something so unexpected that it almost seems embarrassing to a culture that has sent people to the moon, uses huge helicopters to lift objects, and finds it difficult to lift an ancient obelisk with a crane.

On Saturday, June 23, 2001, it took only two people to raise a 6,900-pound concrete obelisk upright in well under 5 minutes in the Mohave Desert. The idea for this astonishingly simple feat came from a business consultant who served as one of the two people who lifted the obelisk. Using only rope, a primitive pulley system, a wooden scaffold, and a 30-foot parachute modified to work as a kite, they demonstrated how a 14 mile-per-hour wind easily and quickly lifted the huge obelisk. The technique resulted in the obelisk standing straight up — something modern engineers have had great trouble doing in Egypt today when an obelisk is moved. The *Associated Press* story announcing the startling results took Egyptologists by surprise. Without any genuine reflection on the significance, New York Egyptologists described it as "highly unlikely." But scientists at the California Institute of Technology who were recruited into the project by the business consultant said they had already proven that stones of almost any size could be easily moved.[2]

It is interesting that Cayce told us a natural lifting force was used by the ancients to move huge stones. Perhaps even more interesting is that, just as Cayce told us, modern civilization hadn't discovered it yet. The method described above is certainly an application of mental powers rather than technological prowess — just as Cayce described. We aren't saying that this is exactly what Cayce was referring to, but it certainly fits his descriptions. Many people have been expecting to eventually find a much more advanced technology involved in the movement of the huge stones, and this finding could prove disappointing to them. But it points out how perceptual bias can blind us to simple truths.

It would perhaps be wise to keep in mind the essential motivation behind Cayce's readings: that was in helping to promote spiritual growth and service to others. Cayce's moral of Atlantis shows us that the Atlanteans created their own demise because they lost touch with their source and purpose. They experienced a moral struggle between a self-serving, self-aggrandizing faction that embraced the physical world and a faction that sought to continually maintain a connection to their spiritual source.

Edgar Evans Cayce observed in his books that advanced civilizations are the easiest to destroy. He also asserted that when the Atlanteans migrated from the islands prior to the final destruction, their primary concern was safety and adapting to the people already present. In short, survival was their immediate concern. It isn't likely that the Law of One Atlanteans described by Cayce would try to build pyramids, planes, and elevators as soon as they arrived. What they would do is try to make peace and survive. They would adapt or die. Gradually, over time, their culture would appear by blending with the previously existing cultures. And that is exactly what the evidence seems to show.

The quote beginning this chapter, "A man who has once looked with the archaeological eye will never see quite normally," was intended to imply several things. It was cited in a debunking book on "cult archaeology." It means that archaeologists are trained to see things in a more rational and factual way than nonarchaeologists. But it also means archaeologists may be so indoctrinated in their beliefs that, they can't perceive anything outside their belief system. They may be perceptually blind — just as the Preface of this book describes.

Atlantis In The Mounds

In prior chapters, we have discussed Cayce's assertion that the mounds were a representation of the Yucatan and Gobi experiences. In that same reading he also said the mounds were a representation of the "Atlantean" experience. So, is there any evidence that Atlantis is somehow represented in the mounds?

As we have shown, mounds often have alignments to Orion, the lunar cycle, solar cycles, and various other star risings. These are tenuous, indirect "threads" to Atlantis but mainly connect the mounds to the Yucatan as well as Egypt. Cayce stated that the Great Pyramid of Giza was built to have a relationship to certain stars and, in a similar fashion, many mounds display the same alignments. But is there something more? Is there a way we can directly link Atlantis to the mounds?

Perhaps the evidence of "Atlantis in the mounds" has been there all along and it is far simpler than we expect. Instead of looking for high technology artifacts buried in the mounds, perhaps applying Cayce's actual statement about the mounds would show the answer?

On May 15, 1943 (3004-1) Cayce used this statement to describe the mounds: "the mounds that were called the *replica or representative* of the Yucatan experiences, as well as the Atlantean and in Gobi land." As shown in the last chapter, there is indisputable evidence that the Gobi land has earthen mounds the shape and form of which are identical to the American ones. In addition, the arrangements and alignments of mounds in America match many of those in the Yucatan. The "replication or representation" of Atlantis in the mounds does seem to occur in many circular mounds and earthworks.

Moat-Encircled Mounds & Circular Earthworks — Atlantis Representations

Archaeologist William Romain[3] has theorized that the circular earthworks symbolized the earth to the Hopewell. When they enclose a central conical mound, the mound represents the "mountain at the center of the earth." He cites a long list of evidence showing that some civilizations, did in fact, create mounds to symbolize actual mountains or volcanoes. Romain also mentions the Iroquois' creation myth: the world formed on the back of a huge turtle (a conical shaped mound), which emerged from the center of the oceans. From the Cayce perspective, the implication is that a large hill or mountain in the center of the ocean served as the beginning point — or homeland — of the Iroquois. And, according to Cayce, the Iroquois were originally Atlantean. Romain adds that other Iroquois tribes, including the Seneca, believed the same thing.

The idea that the mound builders saw their original home as a circular island is reflected in many myths. Indians who lived in the heart of the Mississippian Era mounds believed the earth started as a huge circle of land surrounded by water.[4] Mound building descendants described the world as a great island which they depicted as one or more circles with a cross in the center.[5] (See figure 98.)

Atlantis was, of course, described as an island. The central hill of the main city was conical and supported a temple. Surrounding this city were huge circles, alternating between earth and water. The bands of water were interconnected by four canals forming what is essentially a cross. The main canal extended to the sea. (See figure 99.)

There are many earthworks that fit this simple description. The simplest explanation of Cayce's statement that, the mounds were a "replication or representation" of Atlantis may have meant that some mounds were constructed in the basic shape of Atlantis.

While there are many other examples of these "Atlantean-like" mound representations, the most striking example was found across the Ohio River at Portsmouth. Figure 100 is adapted from a mural painting on the floodwalls of modern Portsmouth. It shows how a long embanked walkway extended from Portsmouth down to the Ohio River. Immediately on the

Figure 98
Pottery from Missouri mound depicting the cross in the circle. *From — Bureau of American Ethnology (1881).*

Figure 99

Illustration of the main city in Atlantis based on Plato's description. Although the city was the focal point of the culture, it was small in comparison to the overall size given the continent by Plato. The central city of Atlantis was about one-half mile in diameter. Plato describes the total diameter of the city with its water and land rings at about 2 miles. Note the cross pattern formed by the bridges and canals. The center of the city was a high hill, shaped much like a conical mound with a truncated (flat) top. A temple was built on this central hill — just as ancient Americans erected temples atop similar structures.

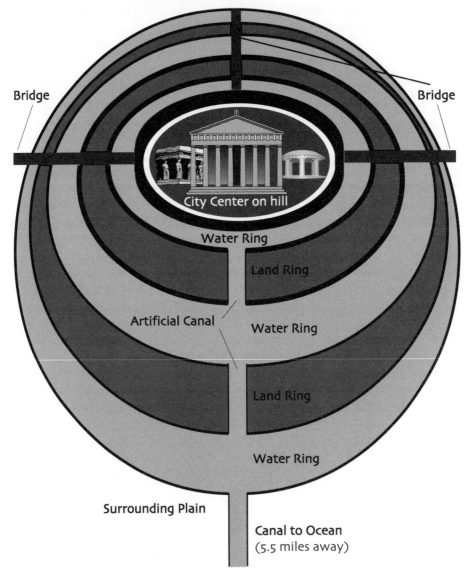

Bridge

Bridge

City Center on hill

Water Ring

Land Ring

Artificial Canal

Water Ring

Land Ring

Water Ring

Surrounding Plain

Canal to Ocean
(5.5 miles away)

other side of the Ohio River the embankment picks up again and leads to the center of a multi-ringed series of embankments and moats a quarter-mile in diameter. In the center of the earthen rings a large flat-topped mound was erected.

The "cross-shaped" pattern of the rings (see figure 101) is identical to the description of the connecting canals in Atlantis, and the "embanked walkway" leads from the central mound to the Ohio River 1.5 miles away. This walkway could represent the canal leading to the ocean. The similarity of this earthwork to Atlantis is even more striking because the number

Figure 100
Illustration of a portion of the Portsmouth earthworks adapted from the city's floodwall murals — by permission. Note the circular shaped earthworks on the other side of the Ohio River and the parallel walls leading from that complex to the area with the "horseshoe-shaped" earthworks. The distance between these sets of earthworks is about 5 miles.

of rings depicted in it — and even their distance apart — closely parallels Plato's description. This drawing comes from Squier & Davis' 1848 survey.

Many other mound sites show this structure. The Great Fairgrounds Circle in Newark is one such example. It had an outer band of raised earth and an inner band of water. In the center was a mound complex. Circular earthworks in Marietta, Chillicothe, and Circleville all depict this arrangement. (See figure 102.)

More Cayce Coincidences?

The striking similarity between the description of Atlantis given by Plato to the actual physical construction of some ancient American earthworks and mounds may be a coincidence. Of course, that will be the

---

Figure 101

Enlargement of *Squier & Davis (1848)* survey of the circular earthworks in Kentucky across the Ohio River from Portsmouth. The central mound appears to form an island surrounded by a series of rings. This complex, now destroyed, may have been the best representation of Atlantis in all of the Americas. The rings have been labelled in accordance with Plato's description of Atlantis.

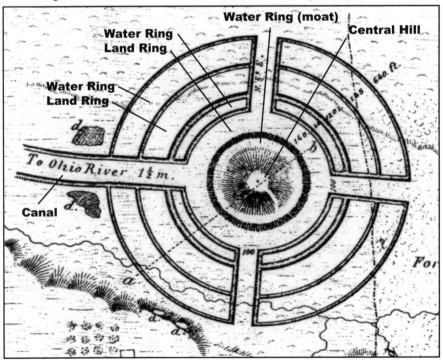

Figure 102
The great conical mound at Marietta has a deep moat encircling it. Some archaeologists believe that the moat-encircled mounds represent the ancient myths of humanity beginning on a circular island. These myths could be a remembrance of Atlantis. *From — Squier & Davis (1848).*

major argument posed against this idea. It will probably be derided as being nonscientific and baseless. Some people will say we *wanted* to find Atlantis in the mounds — so we did. In truth, as the saying goes, "we let the cards fall where they fell." And where these "evidence cards" have landed is surprising even to us. Squier and Davis described the Portsmouth earthworks and published a survey of them in 1848. It's been there all along. Anyone could have noted the similarity between the Portsmouth earthworks and Plato's Atlantis description. Perhaps perceptual blindness and devotion to a belief system kept the obvious from being seen.

Another curious "coincidence" in the Cayce readings may link the Portsmouth Group to Stonehenge and Avebury. Several readings indicate that Stonehenge was established as a temple by some of the "Lost Tribes." As we have seen, Cayce dated this event at 3000 B.C. — a date closely matching the time archaeologists believe the initial Stonehenge was actually built. Two interesting aspects of Stonehenge bear a curious resemblance to Portsmouth. The center of Stonehenge consists of a "horseshoe" arrangement — similar to the "horseshoe" earthworks at Portsmouth. In addition, the "ceremonial causeway" leading from the center of Stonehenge is similar to that found at Portsmouth as well as at many other American sites. (See figure 103.) In addition, the overall layout of Avebury (see figure 104) bears a great resemblance to Portsmouth. Cayce stated that the American mounds, Avebury, and Stonehenge were all influenced by the Lost Tribes. Thus, if the Cayce readings are correct, some similarity between American mound sites and the sites of Stonehenge and Avebury (associated with Stonehenge) would be expected.

Evaluated in the perspective of Cayce's other correct "guesses" about the mound builders, the evidence strongly suggests that a representation of Atlantis is, in fact, found in the mounds. Related to this finding is that the Native American legends have long asserted that their ancient homes were across the oceans on islands. But Cayce related that several migrations came into ancient America from both the east and the west. What do the ancient legends tell us about this assertion? And how do the legends of Native Americans match the genetic evidence that has emerged since 1997?

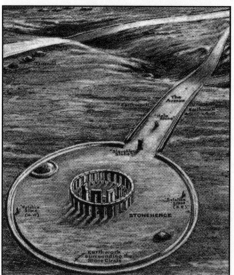

Figure 103
The layout of Stonehenge included a large circular earthwork and a long causeway with parallel earthen embankments. The inside of Stonehenge was a horseshoe-shaped arrangements of trilithons. *From — London Illustrated News (1922).*

Figure 104
The Avebury stone rings and causeways bear an uncanny resemblance to Portsmouth. *From — Stuckeley (1700s).*

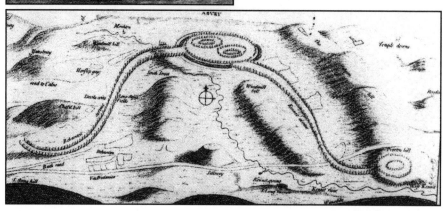

Chapter 10

Legends About The Ancient Ones

The time has long since passed, at least among thinking men, when the religious legends of [other] races were looked upon as trivial fables, or as the inventions of the Father of Lies. They are neither the one nor the other. They express, in image and incident, the opinions of these races on the mightiest topics of human thought, on the origin and destiny of man...
Daniel Brinton (1882) *American Hero-Myths*

As revealed in the prior chapters, evidence from archaeology, genetics, and an examination of the mounds supports the main contentions of Cayce's story of ancient America. Another area of possible evidence lies in the history Native Americans reveal about themselves in their legends.

Despite the noble intent of the quote above, the "truth" of the legends of most Native American tribes has been discounted. This has occurred often, but especially when the time frame the legends discuss is older than Clovis. In addition, when the legends tell of transoceanic migrations, archaeologists have consistently ignored them as misrepresentations.

The term "Ancient Ones" has often been applied to the mythical Anasazi, a mysterious "lost" tribe who lived in the southwest of America. The beginnings of the Anasazi Culture have typically been dated to about 5000 B.C. in the general area of the Four Corners. The Hopi Indians of today assert that they are the progeny of the Ancient Ones — the Anasazi. Hopi legends relate a nearly complete tale of their entry into America. Before looking at the Hopi legends though, it will be helpful if we first review Cayce's story of humanity. In Cayce's readings, the Ancient Ones were diverse migrating peoples from the legendary continents of Mu and Atlantis, and from the biblical calamity we call the Tower of Babel incident. Babel was a significant turning point for ancient humans. It divided them into many tongues and subsequently into many tribes. The Babel incident caused some tribes to migrate great distances in search of new hope, new opportunities. Some of these groups were pre-Abraham Semitic tribes who were seeking shelter from groups in the old country that had become conquest-driven, violent, and vile. Let's briefly outline this story here and then show how the Hopi Indian legend fits right into this view of ancient life and the Ancient Ones.

Cayce's Genesis

Cayce tells of a Genesis in which there was an original descent of pre-human beings from out of an unseen spirit world into the physical world. These powerful prehumans were composed of minds and souls with free will and independent consciousnesses. Some of these beings pushed their way into matter to gratify desires and urges, with no thought for the consequences of such an act. Others did not intend to completely come into matter, but gradually lost their way, eventually becoming trapped in matter.

These beings were powerful but consisted of more mind than body. Their power was so great that they were able to control weather, animals, and move massive, megalithic stones with ease. Some were powerful in a low-tech manner, controlling the elements and animals by thought, while others expressed their powers through high-tech devices, such as lasers, crystals, and machines that affected magnetic fields. Examples of the low-tech people would be the inhabitants of Mu as described in Chapter 2. According to the Cayce readings, the high-tech ones were the Atlanteans. Over time they built temples, pyramids, and mounds. Many of their structures are underneath the current ones we see today, especially in Central and North America. This idea was explained fully in *The Lost Hall of Records*; in fact, the Mayan centers were built one on top of another with the visible structure being the more recent one. But, according to Cayce, many of the megalithic structures we find around the world today are remnants of their temples and shelters.

According to Cayce, these Ancient Ones, for all their power and wisdom, were vulnerable to many temptations and weaknesses. Because of this, they gradually devolved, losing much of their power and control over the elements and animals, relying increasingly on physical ways of surviving. This was due to their gradual loss of attunement to the Source of Life. Within their collective group they developed two distinct factions. One proclaimed that there was no one single Source of Life to which they need maintain connection and cooperation – no God, no Supreme Being, no Great Spirit. The other group claimed that, despite the outward appearance of multiplicity and separateness, there was indeed one Source for all life. They believed that if they lost a connection to it they'd become subordinate to the powers and laws of Nature. Great battles developed between these two groups. Some battles were subtle shifts in political, social, and artistic movements, others were open physical combat. Eventually, the battles caused both groups to lose their level of connection with the Life Force, with the Great Spirit.

The effect of this loss was devastating. Wars, earthquakes, storms, and giant animals began to gain control over these beings. Their celestial, non-physical nature gradually crystallized into matter and form. Their minds became incased in bodies. What was celestial was now terrestrial, and subject to the Earth's evolution and circumstances. Cayce says that these early beings went through four major changes in form. The earlier forms were more ethereal and closer to the vibrations and consciousness of the Creator. The later forms were denser and more separated from the oneness, the collective.

He said that the first two forms appeared in the ancient continent of Mu. The third was in Atlantis. And the fourth was begun in Eden, which today is thought to have been located between the Tigris and Euphrates rivers. These changes coincided with four Ages, or, as the Maya and Aztecs called them, four "Suns."

Mu and Atlantis eventually broke into large islands, then into smaller and smaller ones, until it was obvious to all that these lands were no longer inhabitable. This occurred in three primary stages correlating with the first three Ages – two in Mu and the third in Atlantis. A great migration to find new lands was begun after each Age ended, and continued for many thousands of years. The first Age was about twelve million years ago, the second about ten million years ago. During this time "human" beings were not as physical as we are today. The third Age only lasted about 200,000 years and included the migrations to the Americas we have been discussing in this book.

Migrants from each of these Ages were only a shadow of their former selves, having lost much of their supernatural powers and consciousness. As a result, they became much more terrestrial and physical. Some of those who traveled to the Americas found new shelter in the mountains (the Andes, Monte Alban, Chaco Canyon, the Rockies). Others moved into the jungles and dense woods. Some established their lives out on the plains of Argentina and North America, and still others lived along the shores of the great rivers and oceans.

If Cayce's story of ancient history, with its four Ages and great migration, is true, then some of this truth should be reflected in the North American Indian legends — because these people would be the descendants of the ancient ones. As we shall see, this is definitely the case.

The Amazing Hopi Legend

Of all the North American Indians, the Hopi have a truly amazing legend, and it fits so well with Cayce's story that we must retell it here. The story, it should be mentioned, was first published in 1963, 18 years after Cayce's death.

Figure 105
Hopi shaman "Wiki" at Mishongnovi during snake ceremony. *Photo — Bureau of American Ethnology (1897).*

Figure 106
Hopi Antelope Priest "Kakapti" about to enter kiva at Walpi. *Photo — Bureau of American Ethnology (1897).*

Thirty elders of the Hopi Indian tribe in northern Arizona recounted their legend to Frank Waters who wrote it in his excellent book, *The Book of the Hopi*.[1] According to these elders, the Hopi are the first inhabitants of America. Their village of Oraibi is indisputably the oldest continuously occupied settlement in the United States. It, and most of the other Hopi villages, clings to six-hundred-foot-high escarpments of three rocky mesas rising abruptly out of the desert plain. (See figures 105 & 106.) Here's the story these elders tell with our comments on parts of it enclosed by [brackets]:

In the Beginning...

First there was the Creator, *Taiowa*, then there was *Tokpela*, literally, "Endless Space." There was and is no beginning, no end. There is no time, no space. All is in the mind of the Creator. The Infinite conceived the finite. The Creator is considered to be "the great Uncle," who created *Sotuknang*, the Logos, "the great Nephew." The Nephew was created to carry out a plan for all of life in the Endless Space. The Nephew, or what we might think of as the Logos[2], created nine universal kingdoms: one for the Creator, one for himself, and seven for all of life to come. All life was created according to universal laws or ways naturally reflected in the Creator. Life rotates around the central essence of the Creator. When beings were created, an axis was formed around which the forces of their life rotates. In our physical body that axis is the spine. Along the spine the great Nephew created five centers. The first one is on the top of the head, the soft spot at birth, called *kopavi* by the Hopis. This spot is considered to be the open door through which each individual receives his life and communication with the Creator. The second center is the brain, which is used to think. The third is the throat through which passes the breath of life and the sound of speech. The fourth is the heart, the place of feelings. The fifth is just below the navel and is considered to be the location of the Creator within each body, from which all the functions of the body are controlled.

[Cayce called this area the "abdominal brain." As you may know, most Eastern mystical philosophies identify seven spiritual centers or chakras in the body, the additional two being the solar plexus and the gonads. Cayce identified these with the seven endocrine glands of the body.]

The First People – The First World

According to the Hopi, the great Nephew created the First People, who were always healthy and in attunement with the Creator and the ways of the universe. The First People lived in Endless Space. Gradually there were those among the First People who forgot the original commandments and began to gratify themselves with less and less thought for the ways and laws of the Creator. Among them arose "The Talker" (*Lavaihoya*). He came in the form of the mockingbird; and the more he talked, the more he convinced the First People of their differences and the separateness of all life. It was then that the animals drew away from the people, and then people drew away from one another, noting differences among themselves. The Talker was followed by "The Handsome One," a snake, who beguiled the people still further away from one another. He created suspicion and fault-finding among them eventually leading to fierce fights. The First World became an unhappy, disruptive place.

[As the Maya and Aztec myths tell of the First World's wondrous potential and yet its unfortunate destiny, so the Hopi tell how the Great Nephew discussed with other godly forces the need to end the First World and begin a new one.]

Fortunately, among the First People were many who held to the ideal of the oneness of all life within the Creator. This group was not disruptive or self-seeking, and maintained a communication with the Creator through the tops of their heads. To these people the great Nephew appeared, telling them that they were to be the Chosen Ones. They would inhabit a new world that he was about to create. He told them that the center on the tops of their heads would guide them to this new world. This inner wisdom, he said, will give you the sight to see a certain cloud, which you will follow by day, and a certain star, which you will follow by night.

[It is fascinating how similar this story is to that of the Israelites. Recall how the Lord told them that they were a Chosen People, and led them out from among the others to a promised land, instructing them that the Lord would be with them in a cloud by day and a column of fire by night.]

When the great Nephew had finished instructing the Chosen Ones, all over the First World the Chosen Ones disappeared. Their villages became empty houses, temples, and fields. Many of those left behind called out to them, "Where are you going?" To which the Chosen Ones replied, "We are following the cloud and the star." The others laughed and said, "We see no cloud or star." This was because they had lost the inner vision that came from the tops of their heads.

When the Chosen Ones reached the new place, they were met by others who had traveled there from different lands. These others were also called by the great Nephew and instructed to follow the cloud and the star. Even though they were from different tribes, all the Chosen Ones welcomed the others because they were of the same mind. When all had arrived the Nephew appeared and led them to the hill of the Ant People.

The Nephew instructed them to enter the anthill and learn from the Ant People because, "They obey the plan of the Creator." When they were safely in the anthill, the Nephew destroyed the First World.

[It is interesting how this legend is both physical and non-physical. Remember that this First World is in Endless Space, but the imagery includes an *anthill*. Does this describe some kind of underground shelter for the Chosen Ones until the surface of the planet was cleansed of evil? Or is it some kind of unconscious shelter for their minds while all unsheltered consciousness was absorbed back into the mind of the Nephew who created the peoples? According to Cayce, *events happen first in the mind* and *later they manifest in matter*, often repeatedly, cycling through the mental and the physical over and over until a harmony is reached. Whatever the case may have been in this Hopi legend, there are numerous massive cave and underground passage systems around this planet, and they are of great antiquity. Could these be the physical anthills?]

The Second World

When the Second World was ready, the Nephew returned and brought the Chosen Ones out of the anthill and into the Second World. It was not as beautiful as the First World. The Nephew instructed them to obey the Creator's plan. He explains that when he hears them singing a joyful praise, then he will be in their hearts and they will know they are close to him. The Chosen Ones could travel throughout both the manifested and unmanifested worlds because the door was left open between the spirit world and the physical one. But in the material world they could not live with the animals any longer because the animals had separated themselves from humans and were now wild and dangerous.

Everything the Chosen People needed was in the Second World. Nevertheless, as human nature continued to reveal its weaknesses, the Chosen Ones eventually began desiring things they did not need. Trouble began again.

Consciously, they did not realize that they were drawing away from the good life. But they did forget to sing joyful praises. And they focused more on one another's faults and weaknesses rather than their strengths and virtues. Soon they began to quarrel. Fights broke out. Ultimately, wars broke out. As before, some still sang praises and maintained their hearts and minds in attunement with the Creator and in harmony with the plan. But the wicked laughed at them until they could only sing their songs quietly in their hearts.

The Nephew appeared again, upset and explaining that the "thread is running out on the world." The meaning of this statement was that life was no longer eternal and death was appearing for the first time. There-fore, he led the loyal ones to the safety of the anthill once again while he destroyed the Second World and those who were wicked. Then, he created the Third World.

[Interestingly, the Hopi say that the Nephew destroyed the Second World by drastically shifting the poles of the Earth, a tale that Cayce also tells. In Cayce's version, the axis poles of the Earth were reversed in an-cient times. The planet actually rolled over!]

The Third World

When the Third World was finished, the people spread out and re-populated it, continuing their progress along the great journey of life. In the First World they had lived simply and in harmony with Nature and the animals. In the Second World they had developed handicrafts, tools, homes, and villages. In this Third World they multiplied in such numbers and advanced so fast that they built huge cities, countries, and whole civi-lizations.[3]

This development made it even more difficult for them to stay in har-mony with the Creator and the Nephew. They became wholly occupied with their own earthly plans. Especially notable was an increasing misuse and abuse of their reproductive powers. The Hopis tell of one renown woman who boasted of having so many turquoise necklaces from her sexual favors that she could wind them around a ladder that reached to the end of the world's axis.[4]

Of course, as always, some among the masses maintained harmony with the Creator and sang songs in their hearts. But amid the rising cor-ruption, the people could hardly hear the songs of praise. One curious part of this Hopi story is about how evil tribes used their creative powers to make flying "shields" (*patuwvota*). They used these shields to fly into big cities, attack, and leave so fast that no one could figure out where they came from. War was becoming a focus of thought, energy, and creative power.

[In Cayce's story of Atlantis, during the time between the first and second destruction, the Atlanteans devised implements of war that included flying "ships." Atlantis was also torn between two factions — those desir-ous of satisfying physical urges, and those true to their Creator's plan. The Hopi description of other "evil tribes" using their powers to create a flying weapon could refer to this part of the Atlantis story.]

Spider Woman, created by the Nephew, exclaimed that there is no use waiting until the "thread runs out this time," or until the life force dimin-ishes any further. Something had to be done lest the people with the song in their hearts become corrupted and killed off, too. The Nephew agreed and instructed Spider Woman to cut down hollow reeds and put people who still had the song in their hearts inside these reeds with a little water and cornmeal. When she had completed this, he loosed the great waters upon the Earth and cleansed the Third World with a massive flood. [The Great Flood legend is found in cultures around the world — including virtually all Native American tribes.]

The Fourth World

Once the world was cleansed and calm was restored, Spider Woman took the saved people by the tops of their heads and led them out of the reeds to the top of what had been a great mountain in the Third World. All that was left of it was its "top," now a little island in the midst of a vast sea. All around the saved people was water.

To their surprise they each discovered they had the same amount of water and cornmeal that they had when they first entered the reeds. This was a wondrous thing for it had been a very long time in the reeds and they had eaten each day.

The saved people began to send out birds to find new land to which they could travel and make their new homes [just as Noah and his people did in the Western legend]. But all the birds returned tired without finding land. So they planted a reed and it grew high into the sky. They climbed up and viewed as far as their eyes could see, but still, there was no land anywhere. Then Spider Woman, instructed by the Nephew, told the people, "You must continue traveling on. Your inner wisdom will guide you. The door at the top of your head is open." Spider Woman directed the people to make boats from the reeds. Then, trusting their inner guidance, they sailed away from the old mountaintop in search of the new Fourth World. They sailed toward the rising sun, toward the east.

They found an island that they wanted to stay on but Spider Woman instructed them to sail on. They continued to sail, eastward and a little northward this time. Again, they found a wonderful island filled with vegetation and beauty. But Spider Woman told them that they must travel on further. So again they set sail. She explained to them that these islands were too easy and pleasant for them, and that they would soon fall into evil ways again. They must go on.

[The Hopi hold to an ancient saying attributed to the great Nephew: *"The farther you go, the harder it gets."* This saying reflects their belief that life becomes harder the further you stray from the original oneness and harmony with the Creator. Yet, the more easy and pleasurable life is, the more likely one is to fall into wickedness. Therefore, a hard life is better.]

After setting sail from the second beautiful island, Spider Woman informed them that she had done all she was commanded to do for them. Now they must find their *Place of Emergence*. She instructed them to, "Keep your doors open, and your spirits will guide you."

[The "Place of Emergence" is another fascinating concept expressed in this ancient legend. Again the people seem to be experiencing both a physical journey and a mental-spiritual one. Where they emerge is up to them based on what they are seeking. Furthermore, notice just how far from the original state of life the people have come. Now, the tops of their heads don't bring them inner guidance and the sight to see the cloud and the star, but only the whisperings of their spirit guides. Now, they are no longer directly guided by Spider Woman, or, as before, by the great Nephew of the Creator. They are losing more and more of their initial oneness with and consciousness of the Creator. Yet, each time they appear to be lost, an opportunity comes for them to make a new place, a fresh start. And so it is in this story.]

At this point in the story an argument breaks out among the people as to which direction is the right one to travel. Some say south, some north. In both directions the people journeyed but found only high mountains and no passageways. Not knowing what to do, the people stopped, opened their heads and let themselves be guided. The waters suddenly smoothed over and they felt a current grab hold of their boats and rafts. Before long they landed. They jumped up and down and joyfully celebrated the finding of the Fourth World.

As before, other saved people — remnants of the previous Third World — also arrived in the same place with the Hopi. And, as before, the great Nephew appeared to them. He showed them the direction from which they had come, from the west, and the many islands that they "hopped" along their way to this new world. "They are the footprints of your journey," said the Nephew, "the tops of the high mountains of the Third World, which I destroyed. Now watch."

As the people watched, the closest island sank under the water, then the next, until all were gone. "I have washed away even the footprints of your Emergence; the stepping-stones which I left for you." the Nephew explained, "Down on the bottom of the seas lie all the proud cities, the flying shields, and the worldly treasures corrupted by evil, and those people who found no time to sing praises to the Creator. But the day will come, if you preserve the memory and the meaning of your Emergence, when these stepping-stones will emerge again to prove the truth you speak."[5]

[This legend of island hopping to get to a new world is also found in the sacred book of the Maya, the *Popol Vuh*. In this book, the Maya tell how the waters parted and the tribes crossed on "stones in a row, sand under the sea" to a new world. Another interesting parallel in the Hopi legend is with Cayce's Atlantis story. Atlantis underwent three different destructions. The second destruction, occurring in 28,000 B.C., appears to have struck a severe blow to the technological wonders of Atlantis. The Hopi statement, "Down on the bottom of the seas lie all the proud cities, the flying shields, and the worldly treasures corrupted by evil," could be a reference to Atlantis. If this is the case, it would date the Hopi's entry into ancient America to sometime just after 28,000 B.C. This date would support the new finds in archaeology that have shown migrations did, in fact, occur around that time.]

The Fourth World of the Hopi is called *Tuwaqachi*, meaning "World Complete." The Nephew explains that it is not as beautiful as the previous worlds but it has everything the people need. The people must now use their free wills to choose. How they choose will determine if they are carrying out the Creator's plan, and whether this world needs to be destroyed as the others.

After the great Nephew disappears from them, they begin to enter the new land. They hear a noise and see a handsome man. To their surprise this was the head caretaker of the former Third World who became a little self-important, losing his humility, and the Creator had thus demoted him to caretaker of death and the underworld. He was not a person but a spirit. After the Third World was destroyed, the Creator decided to give him another chance, and appointed him caretaker of the Fourth World. He was the first spirit the people met in this new land and they asked his permission to live here. His name was and is *Masaw*.

Masaw gave them permission but required them to first migrate to the four directions of the great land. They would go north as far as they could, then east to the next shore, then south to the tip of the land, then west. Once these migrations were complete, they could settle between the Colorado and Rio Grande rivers.

The Serpent Mound

Interestingly, the Hopi legend tells of a time during their eastern migration when one of the clans, the Snake Clan, desired to "leave their footprint." But since there were no cliffs to mark with picture writings, they shaped the ground into a gigantic serpent. The Hopi believe that their ancestors were the builders of the great Serpent Mound in Locust Grove, Ohio. It is in the shape of a serpent whose body is extended in seven deep curves with its head facing west and its mouth open holding an egg. In

Figure 107
Serpent Mound as seen from the observation tower at the site.
Page 118 shows a drawing of the whole site. *Photo — G. Little.*

front of the egg is a projection, and on both sides of the head are small mounds. (See figure 107.)

Frank Waters wrote that one of the Hopi Snake Clan's people interpreted the Serpent Mound's shape from a photograph and a drawing Frank showed him. The Hopi said that the egg was symbolic of the people's village placed in the jaws of the snake for protection. The projection in front of the mouth indicated that the snake had the power to "draw light." The two small mounds on each side of the head represent eyes. The snake is facing west because the people were traveling west when they built this mound. The snake's name is *Tokchi'i,* which means "Guardian of the East."

The "Back Door" — Beringia?

Before we move on to another Indian legend, it is interesting to note that the Hopi say that Masaw told them that the northern area would be the "back door" to this new world, this new continent, and that in the future many people would come into this new land via this back door. But they would do so without Masaw's permission. Could this back door be

Beringia, the Bering Straits? If the time frame of the Hopis' entrance into America was circa 28,000 B.C., then this could well be the case.

The Hopi Legend Correlates with the Mayan & Aztec

Like the Hopi legend, in Nahua (Aztec and Toltec), Maya, Mixtec, Zapotec, and Otomi legends there are also four creations, or "World Ages," or "Suns." We find the same number among the Navaho and Pueblo of North America and the Quechua in Peru. But to the original four worlds the Maya and Aztec add a fifth: this current age we live in, in which the previous four play a role. This current world or age is the age of "Movement." This legend is carved in the magnificent Aztec Sun Stone currently on exhibit in the National Museum of Anthropology in Mexico City. It is a 25-ton, basalt, circular monolith, almost 12 feet in diameter, called the *Cuauhxicalli* or "Eagle Bowl" (See figure 108).

On this magnificent stone these Ages go in clockwise order around the Sun Stone beginning in the upper right. The order of the Suns or Worlds is: 1) Jaguar Sun (*Nahui Ocelot*), 2) Water Sun (*Nahui Atl*), 3) Firey Rain Sun (*Nahui Quiahuitl*), and 4) Wind Sun (*Nahui Ehecatl*). In each world age humans assumed a different form. According to the Aztecs, who are retelling

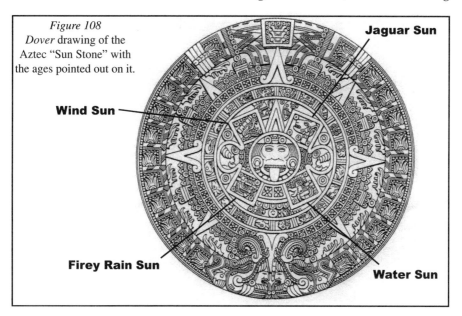

Figure 108
Dover drawing of the Aztec "Sun Stone" with the ages pointed out on it.

Jaguar Sun

Wind Sun

Firey Rain Sun

Water Sun

a legend they heard from the Maya, in the Jaguar Age people were giants with great power who became hard-hearted and stopped listening to the heavens, to the gods, and began pursuing their own interests despite the laws of the universe and Nature. These people would correlate well with the Bible's giants, the "Nephilim," whom God regretted having made. This age was destroyed and new attempt began with the Age of Water in which the people were made of mud (Aztec version) or clay (Mayan version). This correlates well the Bible's Genesis in which God first created people in God's image in chapter one of Genesis but then in chapter two created them from the dust of the Earth. According to the Mayan-Aztec legend, the earthy people became lost, like fish in the sea they could no longer see the horizon. Therefore, the great god Kukulcan (Mayan) and Quetzalcoatl (Aztec) divided the waters above from the waters below and created a firmament upon which the people could discern which direction to continue in. The Mayan *Popol Vuh* tells that this was the age when animals were created. This age ends with the division of the waters and the third age, the Age of Fire, begins. During this age the people were like birds, but not high-flying birds, more like turkeys. They could fly a little but also needed to run along the ground. This was the age of testing. It was the time when the Lords of the Underworld attempted to capture and possess the people, while the forces or gods of the heavens attempted to save them. It was also the time when the most perfect people were created, the maize (corn) people. But even these perfect people stumbled in their efforts to live a good life in harmony with the heavenly forces. Eventually, this age ends by volcanoes and earthquakes (so like the corresponding Hopi age), and the fourth age begins. In the fourth age, the Age of Air or Wind, people are made like the monkeys or simians. According to the legend carved into the Sun Stone, a fifth age, the Age of Movement, began August 13, 3114 B.C. and ends this coming December 23, 2012 A.D. After the fifth world the legend indicates that the original state prior to the creations returns. Whether this is gradual or cataclysmic is unclear in the legend, but Cayce states that it will be gradual.

The Algonquin Legend
Walam Olum (literally, *"Painted Record"*)

The chronicles of the Algonquin Indians are recorded in pictographs and words using the Delaware Indian language. It is unclear who first painted and wrote the *Walam Olum*. Some anthropologists doubt it is of ancient origin, however, it is clear that this is a legend from antiquity, probably carried down through the ages orally and in pictographs, then written down by someone using the Delaware language. It begins with the Great Spirit creating all of life and continues until the arrival of the white people. ("Great Spirit" is an English translation of *Kitanitowit-essop* in Delaware, the language of the *Walam Olum*. But *Kitshi Manitou* are the words of the original Algonquin language which mean "Great Spirit.") Not surprisingly, the *Walam Olum* coincides quite well with aspects of the Hopi legend, Cayce's readings, and even some of our current scientific evidence. It is of a different style than the Hopi legend, written in brief, image-rich lines or stanzas. Here it is[6] with the headings added for clarity:

The First Age – The Great Spirit Creates Life

"In the beginning and for all time, the first place was above the earth. On the earth was a vast mist, and there the Great Spirit was. In the beginning and for all time, the Great Spirit was unseen in space. The Great Spirit made the vast land and sky. It made the sun, moon, and stars. It made them all to move evenly. This was the first state of things."

The Second Age – Wind of Change

"Then the wind blew violently, blowing things out of their course and the water flowed strong and far. Groups of islands rose newly and remained." [This could be symbolic of a new influence within the consciousness of the Creator – most likely something rising up in the minds and spirits of the free-willed pre-human beings who always start the trouble in these ancient legends.]

"The Great Spirit spoke anew, as a Spirit speaking to spirits, and speaking to beings, mortals, souls, and all." [*Speaking anew* could be an indicator that a new relationship had developed between the Creator and the created, similar to the second chapter of Genesis where God's name is changed from Elohim to Yahweh Elohim and he creates man again, but this time out of the dust of the earth and breathes the breath of life into him. Instead of man being one with God, as in the first verse of *Walam Olum* and the first chapter of Genesis, he is now separated. This is indicated in the line, "as a Spirit speaking to spirits," rather than one Spirit together.]

"Forever he was and will be a spirit to men. Forever he will be their grandfather. He brought forth the first mother, the mother of all beings." This is like the creation of Eve in Genesis, called "the mother of all."

"He brought forth the fish, the turtles, the beasts, and the birds."

The Third Age – A Serpent in Paradise

"But then, an evil Spirit made evil beings, monsters, flies, and gnats. But all beings were still friendly. Truly the spirits were active and kindly. Those first men and first mothers took spouses. They took food when they desired it. All had cheerful knowledge, leisure, and thought in gladness. But very secretly an evil being, a mighty magician, came upon the earth. With him he brought badness, quarreling, unhappiness, bad weather, sickness, and death." [This fits well with the Hopi's tale of the slippery evil of The Talker and The Handsome One, which led the people into quarrels, fights, and unhappiness.]

"All of this took place of old on the earth, beyond the great tide-water, in the beginning."

"Long ago rose a mighty snake and beings evil to man. This mighty snake hated those who were in the beginning and disquieted those whom he hated. In the struggle between the snake and man, they both did harm, injured each other, and were not at peace. Driven from their original homes the people fought with this murderer. The mighty snake firmly resolved to harm men." [In this depiction, the Algonquin snake is much more aggressive than the Genesis serpent, but both bring the loss of Paradise.]

The Great Flood

"The mighty snake brought a monster and rushing water. Between the hills the water rushed and rushed, dashing through and through, destroying much."

Turtle Island

"*Nanabush*, the "Strong White One," grandfather of beings, grandfather of men, was on Turtle Island. There he was walking and creating. As he passed by he created the turtle. Beings and men all go forth, walking in the floods and shallows down stream to Turtle Island. Along the way there were many monster fishes which ate some of them. The Great Spirit's daughter came in her canoe to help all, as they came and came.

"Now the men were together on the turtle, like turtles. Frightened on the turtle they prayed that what was spoiled may be restored. So the waters ran off, the earth dried, the lakes became calm, all was silent and the mighty snake departed."

[This part of the legend is similar to an Iroquois legend: "The Supreme Being in the form of a female descended from heaven, landed on the back of a turtle stuck in mud." We might interpret this part of the story as Mother God coming out of the spirit worlds to help evolving material life rise to a new level of consciousness after it had become stuck. The Maya legend relating that the World Tree and the Maize God sprang from a crack in a turtle's back is also similar. This event, as recorded in Maya chronology, took place in 3114 B.C.] "She gives birth to a daughter conceived with the turtle." [This passage may reflect the marriage of heavenly forces (Mother God) with earthly ones (the turtle) in a great effort to save life.] "Their daughter then conceived two sons: the first was good, the second was born through his mother's side and killed her. However, the sons grew up and helped the Grandmother, the feminine Supreme Being, finish the formation of earth plan."

[It's helpful to remember that the Iroquois were matriarchal, as were all peoples prior to the fourth Age. According to Cayce, the feminine spirit was dominant in the ancient times. Since then, the masculine has ruled, but eventually both will unite in an era of balance.]

Searching for the Fourth Age – Migration from Turtle Island

"After the waters had subsided, the Lenape [the Algonquins] of the turtle were close together, living together in hollow houses [similar to the Hopi's hollow reeds that they had to live in for so long].

"They lived in a land that freezes, where snow and storms and cold is [probably Siberia, prior to their migration eastward]. At this northern place they talked of milder places with many deer and buffaloes. As they sojourned they separated into rich house-builders and strong hunters. The strongest, most united and purest among them were the hunters. In that ancient country, that northern country, the best of the Lenape were the people of the Turtle totem.

"But for them, change came again. All the cabin fires of the Turtle land were disquieted and all the priests said, 'Let us go.' Grieving, they set off to the east, to the Snake land. Their land was split apart. It was trembling [earthquakes?], burned, and broken. So they headed to the Snake Island in the east." [This part is reminiscent of the Hopi's Snake Mound in the east, intended to guard the east from western invaders.]

"The tribes of the north land, being free, went forth from the land of snow, in many directions. The tribes of the Bald Eagle and the White Wolf remained along the sea, rich in fish and muscles. Our fathers were rich and in the light when they were at those islands, floating up the streams in their canoes.

"But now, the tribes of the Head Beaver and Big Bird said, 'Let us go to Snake Island.' They say they will go along to destroy all the land. Those of the north and east agree.

"Over the water, the frozen sea, they went to enjoy the new land. On the wonderful slippery water, on the stone-hard water, all went, on the great Tidal Sea, the muscle-bearing sea. They walked and walked, all of them. Ten thousand at night. All in one night, to Snake Island, to east, at night. They walked and walked, all of them." [Is this migration over the frozen sea, on stone-hard water, a reference to Beringia, the Bering Strait's land bridge? Also, their comments about coming "to destroy all the land" may indicate their negative intentions and that they are those who the Hopi were told would come into this new land from the northwest through "the back door," the Bering Straits, and were not invited.]

Land of the Spruce Pines

"They tarry at the land of the spruce pines. [This could be a description of western Canada and Washington State.] They think highly of their old home at Turtle Land [Siberia?]. Now they were in the land of the spruce trees. Long ago the fathers of the Lenape were in the land of the spruce pines."

"Moving east, there was no rain, and no corn [perhaps western Washington state or Wyoming?], so they moved farther seaward. At the place of caves, in the Buffalo land, they at last had food, on a pleasant plain." [This could well be the Dakotas with the caves in the Black Hills and the plains of buffalo below them.]

[In the following verses their hunters venture out searching for the Snake lands. Apparently, one hunting party came upon the Snake tribe and there was a slaughter, which left the Snake tribe weakened and hiding from the Lenape hunters. The Snake tribe could well be the Iroquois, who originally possessed the eastern lands of modern-day U.S.A. (northeast and central) and whose name literally means "real snakes."]

"In these days the Bald Eagle tribe carried the sacred pipe and Beautiful Head was chief. After him Keeping-Guard was chief, then Snow Bird (who spoke of the south, and that our fathers should possess it). Continuing their search for Snake Island, the hunters, about to depart, met together. Then, they journeyed out in search of Snake Island. Coming to the Snakes there was a slaughter at Snake Hill, and they had to leave. The Snake tribe was weak, and hid themselves in Marshy Vale." [This is possibly the marshlands of northern New Jersey.]

Snake Lands – First War, then Peace

"It was decided that the tribes would divide and travel in several directions. During the next many generations there were many wars, especially in the south and the east. The east land [of North America] was a wide and great land – a land without snakes [uncertain of this meaning, it certainly cannot mean that the whole eastern area was without Iroquois], rich and pleasant. All the hunters made wampum again at the great shore of the rising sun [the east coast, especially in the area of modern-day Virginia where the Algonquin had major corn fields and fishing camps; making 'wampum' refers to collecting rare shells for trade]. After a long period of wars, a chief named *Affable*, the first of this name, made peace with all. All were friends, all united, under this new chief."

"Then came the whites on the Eastern sea in great boats. From the north and the south came the whites. They were peaceful. They had great things. Who are they?"

And here the *Walam Olum* ends.

Whites in Ancient America?

Many of the Indians in Central and Northern America have legends about ancient "white people" (often bearded) who helped them and would return in the future to help them again. In many of these tales, the whites originally came from and would return from the east. Therefore, you can see how this created confusion among the Indians when the Spanish landed on the eastern shores of Central and Northern America in 1500s. Though the legends maintained that these people were good, the whites carried diseases that were deadly, and attitudes that were self-serving. They certainly did not fit the legend's hopeful promises.

By all accounts, northeastern Algonquins were the first groups of Indians north of Mexico to have extended contact with white people. Their eastern tribes were so greatly influenced by the whites, that historians found only their western tribes to be more connected with Algonquin traditions and myths. The western Algonquins maintained the "Grand Medicine Society" (as did the Eastern Sioux) whose activities revolved around the quest for a vision that would bring them into direct contact with the Supreme Being, the Great Spirit. During this vision the Great Spirit would instruct them in all aspects of life, especially in healing ceremonies. The members of this society were not shamans, claimed no individual powers, and were only effective when they acted in a group and the Great Spirit came upon them.

Migrations From the East

Strangely, little has been uncovered about the legends surrounding the origin of the Iroquois. Like other Native American tribes, the Iroquois believed that the world was once destroyed by water and that only a few people survived. They also have many other myths and legends, but none directly bear on their origin. It is known that the Algonquins and the Iroquois were bitter enemies and saw each other as completely "different." Also known is that several tribes in the Great Lakes area, as well as in the Ohio Valley, related stories to Catholic priests in the 1700s that asserted they came from the east following a great flood. These tribes were not Algonquin. From the priests' descriptions, they appear to be Iroquois. The mystery of the lack of an origin legend in tribes occupying the areas of the mound builders was summed up by Charles Hudson in his book, *The Southeastern Indians*. Hudson writes, "the Southeastern Indians are the victims of a virtual amnesia…"

The World Tree and the Four Worlds Connecting the Adena Mound Builders to the Maya

The most definite ancient American "migration from the east" story comes from the Maya. The Maya story contains elements that are highly similar to both the Hopi and Algonquin legends. This story is carved on the Aztec Sun Stone mentioned earlier. The Aztecs, descendants from earlier cultures including the Maya, related that their origin was Atlan, an island to the *east* of Central America. *The Lost Hall of Records* details this story.

Amazingly, Edgar Cayce tells the story of two Atlanteans who were in charge of preserving the records of Atlantis: Atlan and Iltar. According to Cayce, Atlan remained on the Atlantean island of Posiedia, storing his collection of the records in a temple that sank off the coast of modern-day Bimini Island in the Bahamas. Iltar sailed westward bringing his collection of the records to the modern-day Yucatan peninsula just before the final destruction of Atlantis. Cayce explained that Iltar first established his temples on the peninsula but during the Atlantean destruction, they were so damaged that Iltar moved his people and records deeper into the heart of Central America.

In brief, the Maya-Aztec legend tells how the world has gone through four creations. According to this tale, the fourth creation occurred in a specific spot on earth where an image of heaven was impressed on the Earth. Part of the image was of three stones on the back of a turtle. The three stones represent the three stars in the Belt of Orion. In Chapter 9 the triangle formed by the three stones — the "Cosmic Hearth" of creation — was discussed. The triangular arrangement of some mound sites is believed to represent the cosmic hearth of Orion. The Mayan and Aztecs believed that life on Earth today came out of the Cosmic Hearth.

An important part of this story involves a fascinating character named *Itzamna* who divided the sky into the four Cardinal directions and four semi-Cardinal directions. This was done by "raising the sky." The act of raising the sky, or separating the heavens from Earth, left an impression of the heavens upon the surface of the earth and created "The World Tree" (see figure 109). It is said that Itzamna traveled from the east to the west over a large body of water to establish the fourth world. The "turtle's back" is believed to represent an island appearing in the midst of floodwaters with an expanding landmass building up on it. It was there that Itzamna established the new civilization.

The World Tree is usually depicted as an "upward movement" emerging from water, like a great tree trunk whose branches reach into heaven (representing the future). Its roots reach into the underworld or the primordial age. It often depicts the four Cardinal directions and the four creations, as well as the "yin" and the "yang" duality of Earth.

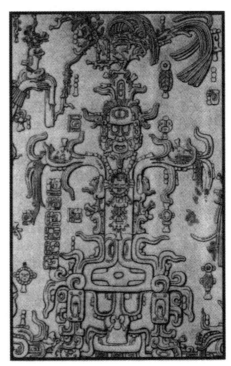

Figure 109
The "World Tree" as depicted on one of the panels at the Temple of the Foliated Cross at Palenque. *From — Maudsley (1902).*

Adena Tablets & The World Tree

The Adena Era was the first true mound building era in the Ohio Valley area. As related in Chapter 6, one of the curious characteristics of the Adena mound culture was the making of the "Adena Tablet." These were typically small, rectangular flat sandstone tablets with curious carvings. The engraved figures are usually described as zoomorphic or geometric designs. Don Dragoo's *Mounds for the Dead* (1963), states that most of the tablets show raptorial birds, however, a few show a turtle. In fact, an Adena Tablet carved into the shape of a turtle was recovered at the Cresap Mound. Dragoo believes that the tablets were used in mortuary rituals or as "clan" totems. They were sometimes covered in red hematite paint and used as "stamps." Dean Snow's 1976 text, *The Archaeology of North America*, calls the Adena Tablets "abstract zoomorphic motifs" and admits they are not understood. Others have called them "whetstones" used to sharpen implements. In short, no one has ever deciphered exactly what these tablets represent. For example, in figure 110, the "Wilmington Tablet" is shown at actual size. Archaeologists relate that it depicts a "conventionalized bird of prey," but it is difficult to recognize the bird.

When we examined this tablet carefully, we noticed that along the tablet's edge is a symbol identical to the Egyptian hieroglyph for the god Ra, a circle with a dot in the center. Descending from this circle is an arrow. This seems to represent the manifestation of Ra into the realms of Earth, the physical world. It also indicates how the tablet should be held in order to decipher the images on front of the tablet. When held in this manner the tablet shows the World Tree and the four ages or "suns" of the Maya and Aztec legend. When we view other Adena tablets, the pattern of the World Tree and the four ages is seen again and again.

Viewing the Wilmington Tablet in figure 110, notice the watery pattern at the bottom of the tablet. Notice the "notched" pattern below the water on the right side and the reversed notches on the left side – these could symbolize land below oceans that eventually rose above the primordial waters (the left hand "land" actually goes up the left side of the tablet, perhaps depicting it rising out of the sea). From the middle of the sea rises the stylized trunk of the World Tree, spreading its branches to the right and the left at the top of the tablet. The trunk is serpentine with a labyrinth-like pattern perhaps depicting the winding path of life. At the top of the tree following its branches are two spirit-like figures, one going to the right with a singular serpent-like body and the other going to the left with a feminine-like passageway leading to a uterine-like triangle in its body. These appear to represent the yang and the yin spirits so prominent in ancient Eastern philosophies. Below the branches are four distinct areas depicting the four ages. If the ages follow the pattern on the Aztec Sun Stone, then we would begin with the upper right hand image, just below the right branch of the Tree. This would be the first age or sun, the "Jaguar Age" (Nahui Ocelot). Below this symbol would then be the symbol of the age of water (Nahui Atl). On the lower left side of the World Tree trunk, would be the age of fire, or fiery rain as the Aztecs called it (Nahui Quiahuitl). And just above it would be the age of wind (Nahui Ehecatl). Notice how the four elements correspond with the four ages: earth, water, fire, and air.

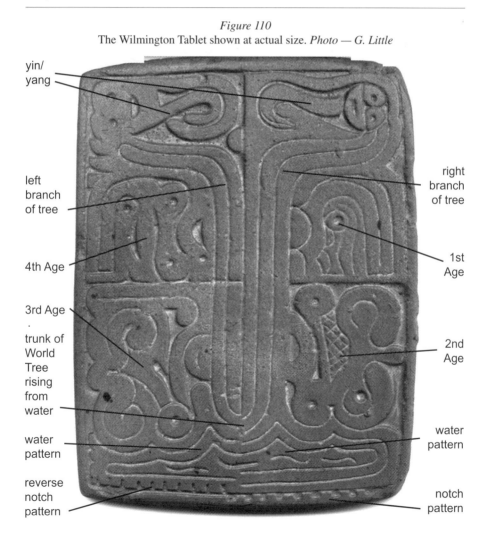

Figure 110
The Wilmington Tablet shown at actual size. *Photo — G. Little*

yin/
yang

left
branch
of tree

4th Age

3rd Age

trunk of
World
Tree
rising
from
water

water
pattern

reverse
notch
pattern

right
branch
of tree

1st
Age

2nd
Age

water
pattern

notch
pattern

The Wilmington Tablet's four ages are abstract, stylized images, just like the Aztec Sun Stone. Unfortunately, we do not have as yet any corroborating text for the Adena tablet as have for the Sun Stone. Perhaps future excavations will discover this.

Other tablets have similar patterns to the Wilmington. Some examples are the Meigs Country tablet, Kiefer tablet, Cincinnati tablet, Gaitskill clay tablet, and some of the images (the four ages, two branches, and primordial waters) are found on the Lakin B tablet.

Interestingly, the Berlin tablet (figure 111) has an image of the seven "caves" of the Toltec *Chicomoztoc* (see figure 112). In addition, a large sandstone disc found at Moundville, Alabama may have two representations

Figure 111 (right)
Drawing of he Berlin Tablet after *Webb and Baby (1957).*

Figure 112 (below)
The Seven Caves. *From — The Lost Hall of Records (2000).*

Figure 113 (below right)
Carving on stone disc from Moundville. *From — Moore (1905).*

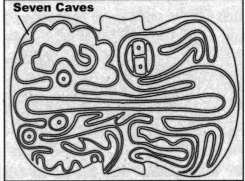

of the seven caves (see figure 113). The "7 Caves" image depicts an event that happened in the third age. According to the Maya/Aztec legend, after the perfect maize people of the third age stumbled and lost their perfect vision, they went into seven caves (sometimes told as seven canyons) from which they eventually emerged as a new human race, divided into five nations, five races, five tribes. Each of these tribes journeyed to different parts of the world and began the fourth age. This fits exactly with Cayce's statement that at some point in the creation of life and the challenges of this world, the children of God decided that this realm was more difficult than first imagined. They therefore divided into five races and nations, each accentuating one of the five senses. Over time they hoped to learn how to subdue its power over our minds and spirit, and, when reunited again, each group would benefit from the other groups' victory.

Atlantis, Mu, & Cayce

In Cayce's history of ancient America, several different migrations occurred at several different times. He told of people coming "from across the Pacific," from Mu, Atlantis, as well as from the South Pacific and elsewhere. He also related that many of these people blended culturally as well as through intermarriage. Thus, a mixture of racial groups would be seen in modern Native American tribes.

The depiction of the Maya World Tree, the Suns (ages), and the Seven Caves on Adena Tablets certainly seems to confirm the link between the Yucatan and the Ohio mound builders. Cayce stated that the Ohio mound culture was begun by people migrating from the Yucatan. Since Adena was the first mound culture in the area, it should be expected that some Maya-like symbols would be found.

Cayce's story also meshes well with what little we know from Native American tribal legends. The Hopi tale of the "Place of Emergence" as being the Pacific Coast would show that they are, indeed, "The Ancient Ones." From their descriptions, they originated from Mu, the land where life first appeared.

The "back door" into the New World described by the Hopi seems to definitely describe Beringia. The images used in the Algonquin legends clearly lead us to surmise they describe a migration from Siberia across Beringia. Interestingly, the Algonquins tell of meeting other people in the New World; including the dreaded "snake people" — known to be the Iroquois (see figure 114). Based on Cayce's migration story, the Algonquins could fit his statement about "people coming from across the Pacific." Cayce did not mention the Bering Straits or Beringia as a migratory path, but he did not say that this particular group crossed on water. All we know is that they came "from across the Pacific."

According to Cayce, some of the Iroquois, especially "those of noble birth," were Atlanteans. The key word here is *some*. It is interesting that there is no definitive legend relating the Iroquois' origin. Their "creation myth" involves a turtle's back becoming an island in the center of the ocean, but their ancient migrations are nor recorded in their legends. They were apparently already here when the Algonquins arrived and were a fierce enemy. The Iroquois also battled among themselves leading to a massive split into nearly 20 tribes. These tribes migrated throughout the majority of America. Many of them became mound builders. It is known that some tribes in the Great Lakes (an area occupied by the Iroquois) as well as in Ohio (also occupied by the Iroquois) believed that their ancestors came from the east following a great flood. This nearly mirrors the Iroquois flood legend, although this legend leaves out the direction of the flooded land. It could be speculated that the Iroquois were a mixture of several different groups, and, of course, this is what Cayce asserted. Since they represented a mixture, perhaps with some coming from the east and others from the west, no legend of a "true" origin was possible. On the other hand, the Aztec legend of Atlan is a near mirror of Cayce's story of Atlantis and how Iltar with a group of 10 others migrated to the Yucatan prior to 10,014 B.C.

Figure 114
Atotarho, believed to be the ruler of the Iroquois confederation. He was said to be a sorcerer. The Algonquins feared the Iroquois and called them the "snake people." Atotarho could control animals with his will and rattlesnakes were drawn to him to protect him. He smoked tobacco frequently as did all of the natives. *From Schoolcraft (1851).*

In sum, we can say that the few origin legends of the Native Americans harmonize well with Cayce's story.

The archaeological evidence that has emerged since 1997 places the long-discounted Hopi legend in a different light. America was occupied prior to 28,000 B.C., in fact, the evidence shows that it extends to at least 50,000 B.C. — if not much, much further. The Hopi legend appears to indicate that they arrived around 28,000 B.C., at the time of the second breakup of Atlantis. This date coincides with the destruction of some of Atlantis' technology, which seems to be described in the Hopi account.

A confirmation of the chronology and origins of these groups could come with mtDNA analysis. To our knowledge, the Hopi have not been subjected to mtDNA tests. (At least there are no results published in the scientific literature on it.) Some Navaho, however, have been tested. The mtDNA tests on Navaho have shown that they primarily come from Siberian Asia. However, haplotype X has been found in a small percentage of them. We hypothesize that the X type represents an Atlantean migration. This would imply that a few Atlanteans merged with the ancestors of the Navaho. This, of course, matches the story that Cayce told. A Hopi legend about the Navaho being "latecomers" into the southwest lends some support to this idea.

The X type has also been found in ancient remains buried in Iroquois' lands as well in tribes having Iroquois descent. As we have shown, the X type also appears in France, Spain, and the Gobi as well as in the Mediterranean. Cayce's story fits these findings perfectly. It asserts that the people who originally had the X haplotype migrated to both America as well as to the Mediterranean and the Gobi from a central location.

Legends of Lost Tribes, the Norse, & Other Possibilities

One of the most curious possibilities from the Cayce readings on the Americas relates to the "Lost Tribes" and the origin of the Hebrews themselves. As stated several times, the X haplotype has been found in Israel as well as in a few places in the general area of the Mediterranean. Cayce placed the presence of some of these people in the Americas starting in 3000 B.C.

As related in Chapter 4, mtDNA analysis allows a timeframe to be established indicating the general date when a particular haplotype migrated from their primary source group. (This is a major advantage with mtDNA analysis and one reason it is preferred for such research.) For example, the mutation of the X haplotype in America indicates that the primary entry of people with the X type occurred right at 10,000 B.C. This date, of course, goes much further back in time than "known history" — including the biblical history that can be traced backward. As we have stated, this date also coincides with Cayce's date for the final destruction of Atlantis.

Since Cayce states that the Lost Tribe remnants arrived here in 3000 B.C., but we know the X type arrived in 10,000 B.C., it means the Lost Tribes were not the first "carriers" of the X type to America. Yet the X type is found in Israel today. In addition, there are numerous legends from both North and Central American groups telling of bearded "white people" coming to America prior to the 1492 era. A host of other legends and stories told about seemingly "white" tribes (the Mandans in the north and the moon-eyes in the south) in ancient America.

The Cayce readings did contain material showing that the Norse explored deeply into America and that "some" of them merged with mound builders. Thus, the Norse could be an explanation for the legends of whites in ancient America. However, the issue of the Lost Tribes raises possibilities with much broader implications. The fundamental underpinning of the Mormon religion is based upon several migrations of Semitic and pre-Hebrew groups to ancient America. But the dates of these migrations are well after 10,000 B.C. The X haplotype could be a thread that traces the Hebrews back to ancient Atlantis. Thus, it is to the Norse, Lost Tribes, and Mormon beliefs where we now turn our attention.

Chapter 11

Diffusion
To Ancient America:
Norse, Egyptians, Lost Tribes,
and Other Possible Migrations

> …the simple fact is that, with the exception of the Norse settlement at L'anse
> Meadows *(sic)*, no convincing evidence for such occurrences has ever
> been found or recognized by professional researchers.
> Robert Mainfort & Mary Kwas (1991) *Tennessee Anthropologist*

The idea that pre-Columbian visitors came to the New World is known as "diffusion theory." Diffusion asserts that one culture can influence another culture through some form of contact. This contact could be through migrations, explorations, trading, or simply a ship being blown to an unknown land in a storm. Since the 1997 discoveries in genetics and archaeology, we now know that the heritage of the Native Americans is far greater and deeper than the academics have led us to believe. Their ancestors were here far earlier than expected and they came from unexpected places. The evidence showing multiple "diffusions" is overwhelming. However, opposition to the idea remains strong.

George Carter, discussed in previous chapters, relates that attacks on people who suggest diffusion to the New World are unfounded. Diffusionists today are not suggesting that the Norse, the Welsh, or the

Hebrews built the mounds. Some people just see overwhelming evidence that visitors came to ancient America many times. These "visitors" exerted some influence on the cultures already present. This isn't racist, Carter asserts, but the vicious attacks on the proponents of diffusion may be racist.[1]

The history outlined in the Cayce story credits the Native Americans as having the most ancient ancestors of all. They descended from Mu, the place where human consciousness first entered the physical world. Some descended from Atlantis, the most advanced ancient civilization of all. And, as happens in almost all melting pots, they blended together creating one of the most unique and rich cultures in the world.

The spiritual beliefs of the Native Americans included a great reverence for all life and for Mother Earth herself. Everything was of the Great Spirit, and everything had to be respected. Their unrecognized astronomical knowledge was truly unsurpassed and their massive earthworks unmatched. Yet few people realize the genuine wonder of ancient Portsmouth, Newark, Chillicothe, Moundville, Pinson, Cahokia, Poverty Point, Etowah, thousands of effigy mounds, and countless other sites.

The Norse Visits to Ancient America

It has long been known that the Norse made visits to North America starting circa 1000 A.D., but everything beyond that statement is controversial. Contributing to this controversy are speculations about a seemingly "white" Indian tribe living in widely scattered villages along the upper Missouri River.

Several 1700s and 1800s expeditions traveled up the Missouri River into Montana and reported that along the way they had encountered the *Ouachipounnes* (Mandans), a white tribe. La Verendrye's 1720 expedition described them as "tall of stature, white in colour, with hair light, chestnut, and red..." Subsequent expeditions provided descriptions of the Mandans that were more in line with the traditional Native American appearance. However, theories about the origin of this "white" tribe emerged immediately. The most widely held idea was that the tribe was descended from a 12th century Welsh expedition to America led by Prince Madoc. But others believed they were Norse descendants.

Irish monks may, in fact, have visited America as early as A.D. 800. By that time, a small colony of the monks had been established in Iceland. The monks sought both solitude and a stoic way of life. They frequently traveled from Ireland to Iceland in small leather boats (*curraghs*). There are scattered inferences that a few may have gone further west, but there is virtually no evidence of their presence in America. However, there have been many ancient manuscripts that have been found over the years — including in the Vatican's library — that told of a 500-year history of Norse excursions and settlements in America.

The Norse first reached Iceland in 860 A.D. and found communities of monks who periodically "went away." Within their dwellings they left behind religious books and artifacts. The first Norse simply moved into these small shelters. Between 870 and 930, approximately 30,000 Norse colonized Iceland.

In 982 a Norse "outlaw," Eric the Red, was banned from Iceland for three years. During that time he explored west and found Greenland. Eric quickly established a colony of 700 people there where their descendants remained for over 500 years before mysteriously vanishing. In 1961, the ruins of the first church that had been established in Greenland was discovered and excavated. A 36 x 12 foot wide wooden structure with earthen walls was found surrounded by a cemetery of 16 graves.

In 986 Bjarni Herjolfsson sailed from Iceland to Greenland to find his father who had gone there with Eric. A storm drove Bjarni's ship south where he encountered a flat, wooded land — far different from Greenland. Moving north, he found another flat, forested shore. Before reaching Greenland he encountered another coast, but this one was covered with stones and a "mountain of ice."

According to the Sagas, Eric the Red's first son, Leif Ericsson, sailed south from Greenland in 1002 with 34 companions in search of the land spotted by Bjarni. Just as Bjarni had reported, Leif found a mountain of ice before he encountered the flat, forested shore. He named this land "Markland" (Woodland). After sailing south for two more days, he came to a cape where he ran aground in a shallow bay. He and his men carried their boat up a creek to a small lake and they immediately constructed houses. The town was named "Leifsbudir."

Because he found the surrounding land to be filled with pastures, meadows, and a vast area of grapes, he called it "Vinland." They spent the winter there and saw no snow. In 1004 Leif's brother Thorvald went to Leifsbudir and explored west and then to the south and east. The first encounters with the natives occurred during these explorations and were violent. The *"Skraelings"* (the natives; in Norse *Skraeling* means "savage") were found to be as efficient at warfare as the Norse. A year later Thorvald was killed by an arrow in a battle with the natives.

Shortly thereafter, Thorfin Karlsefni and his wife went to Leifsbudir in Vinland and lived in Leif's home. They took along livestock, cut timber, and collected other resources. The next summer, Thorfin's group began trading with the friendlier "Skraelings" exchanging milk for furs. The following year, one of Thorfin's men killed a native who supposedly was caught trying to steal weapons. A battle followed the event. A few other voyages to Vinland are mentioned in the Sagas. (See figure 115.) They include a yearlong stay in Vinland by a papal envoy, Bishop Eric Gnupsson, in 1117. The Sagas ended in 1347, but it is now confirmed that the Norse maintained settlements in Greenland until 1500. The Sagas give no information about Vinland from the mid-1100s on.[2]

Archaeological Evidence of the Norse

During the 1800s and early 1900s, a remarkable number of sites scattered across America and Canada showed possible evidence of a Norse presence. All were labeled as a fake, hoax, or misrepresentation. These included numerous runic inscriptions, stone structures, iron artifacts, iron smelting furnaces, coins, and other artifacts. Many history textbooks of the era took the position that Vinland extended from Canada's Newfoundland to Massachusetts and Rhode Island. (See figure 116.)

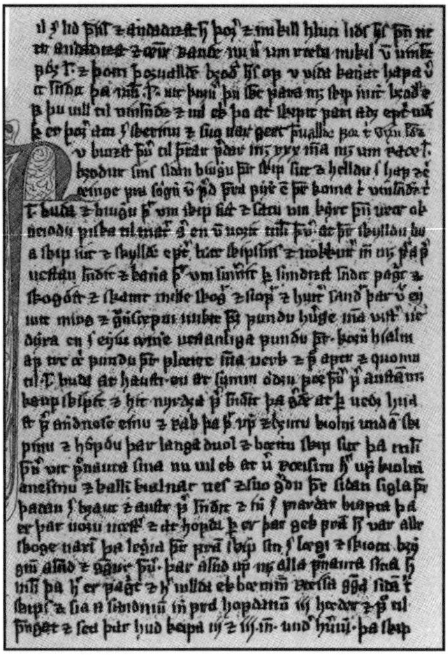

Figure 115

Page from the Flatey Book telling how Leif Ericson sent Thorvald to Vinland with 30 men. The book has several descriptions of the Norse encounters with the Skralings, their term for the indigenous natives present in Vinland. Some of the tales describe violent encounters. The so-called "Vatican Manuscripts of the Norse" were found in 1902 in Vatican Repositories. They tell of numerous trips to the New World beginning in 1000 A.D.

Source: T. H. Smart, The Flatey Book and Recently Discovered Vatican Manuscripts Concerning America as Early as the Tenth Century (1906)

Convinced that the Sagas had to contain genuine stories, Helge Ingstad began studying a 16th century Norse map depicting Iceland and a portion of North America. He and his wife (an archaeologist) began exploring the coastline of the northern peninsula of Newfoundland. In 1960 they found 8 mounds, which turned out to be sod-covered houses. The next seven years of excavations and carbon testing showed that this site had indeed, been a Norse settlement.

L'anse aux Meadows is now a National Historic Park of Canada. It has been excavated and rebuilt into what it probably looked like during Leif Ericson's time. The sod homes are "longhouses" — one of them measures 80 feet in length. Radiocarbon dating yielded dates in the A.D. 1000 range. Over 130 artifacts have been found including iron nails, rivets, a soapstone spindle, a stone lamp, a bronze and bone pin, a birchbark container, the floorboard of a small boat, and various wooden pieces.

Archaeologists typically call this site Vinland. It could be the town of Leifsbudir or even the midway point to Vinland called Markland. The current archaeological thinking about the locations of the Norse settlements is as follows. The "mountain of ice" is cited as being Baffin Island. Markland, the flat land with many trees, is Labrador. Keelness, a small cape found by Thorvald during his fatal 1004 expedition, is supposedly Cape Porcupine. Vinland is cited as L'anse aux Meadows. According to this view, the Norse

Figure 116
Map of Vinland published in Ridpath's authoritative 9-volume *History of the World* (1911). John C. Ridpath states that America was first seen by Herjulfson in 986 and visited by Leif Ericson in 1000. Ridpath goes on to state that Leif remained there for a year visiting Massachusetts, Rhode Island, and even briefly entering New York harbor. Leif's brother Thorwald went to Maine and Massachusetts in 1002. Another brother of Leif went to Vinland in 1005 followed in 1007 by Thorfinn Karlsefne accompanied by 150 men. This group may heve gone as far south as Virginia.

never went further south than Canada's northeastern coast; they never entered the United States.

One acknowledged problem with this view is that Newfoundland lacks grapes; in fact, it lacks many of the descriptive elements of Vinland. The counterargument given is that Leif called wild berries "grapes" and exaggerated the land in the hopes of drawing more settlers. The coastlines of Maine, Massachusetts, and Rhode Island do have many dense grapevines on the coast — as described by Leif.

Disputed Norse Artifact Discoveries

The Newport, Rhode Island Tower. It has been thought that this curious structure was built by Benedict Arnold as a windmill, although there is no convincing evidence supporting that statement. It's as if the town of Newport sprung up around the tower without remembering who built it or why — a collective amnesia. The first mention of it was in 1677 when it seemed that the colonists suddenly noticed it wondered where it came

OLD STONE TOWER AT NEWPORT.

Figure 117
Ridpath's History of the World (1911) stated that the Old Stone Tower in Nweport was built by the Norse visitors.

from. Ridpath's *History of the World* (1911) simply states that it was built by the Norse. (See figure 117.)

Danish scholars and a few archaeologists have claimed that the tower served as a church and lookout for a major Norse settlement. Its construction, shape, size, columns, and even measuring units have been shown to be very similar to Norse towers and churches built in Scandinavia during that time period. However, it is also known that a few colonial windmills were somewhat similar in construction. A more obscure claim is that it is ancient Portuguese.

Modern excavations have proven controversial. The first ones turned up evidence of a colonial presence at the site. A subsequent excavation indicated that, in the 17th century the tower had been strengthened by digging out around the foundation and replacing the soil. This would have resulted in the removal of all evidence of the earliest foundation. The tower has been repaired over the years by replacing mortar and other construction work. A 1993 carbon test of mortar proved inconclusive. It dated to the 1600's; archaeologists stated this proved it was built in the colonial era. But whether the mortar was "original" or from a repair during colonial times is unknown.[3]

Runic Inscriptions Possibly Genuine. By far, the most famous artifact purported to be of Norse origin is the Kensington Runestone. It was found in 1898 among entangled tree roots on a farm near Kensington, Minnesota. A number of scholars looked at the 3-foot-long by 15-inch wide stone's runes and declared it a genuine Norse inscription. (See figure 118.) But another professor declared it a fake because it had incorrect runes for its alleged timeframe. Local citizens dug a few holes on the farm where the stone was found hoping to find buried Norse remains, but nothing else turned up. Many books have been written on it and it makes an impressive display in the Alexandria Museum. Today, it seems there are few mild opinions. In recent years, documents have been found in Europe that showed King Magnus sent Paul Knutson on an expedition into Vinland in 1354. The number of men returning to Scandinavia after the expedition shows that more than half died during the long trip. This closely parallels the story told on the Kensington stone. How far into America did they supposedly get? No one knows, but Cayce stated they went deep into America many times.

Suzanne Carlson reported on 32 probable Norse inscriptions in America in the 1998 book, *Across Before Columbus?* At least seven of these Norse-like inscriptions have turned up in Oklahoma over the years. They have been found by children playing on a hill after a heavy rain, by farmers, Native

American Indians, and Oklahoma resident Gloria Farley, who has devoted decades to finding inscriptions and petroglyphs in the state. The Heavener Runestone near the Arkansas border is located on Poteau Mountain not far from the Mississippian Era mound site of Spiro. The state has made it into a park and publications pronounce it as genuine. It is a date: November 11, 1012. (See figure 119.) One of Farley's finds has been of a petroglyph (rock carving) on Oklahoma's Canadian River. It is a small carving of a ship (see figure 120). It has the appearance of a Norse ship from that early time period. The other runestones

Figure 118 (right)
The Kensington Runestone. *Photo — G. Little.* It says, "8 Goths and 22 Norwegians on discovery - voyage from Vinland over west we had camp by 2 skerries one days journey north from this stone...we were and fished one day after we came home found 10 men red with blood and dead ...Ave Maria preserve from evil...have 10 men by the sea to see after our ships 14 days journey from this island year 1362

Figure 119 (below left)
The size of the Heavener Runestone is apparent in this photo taken before the stone was encased in glass.

Figure 120 (below right)
Drawing made by Gloria Farley of the "Norse ship" carving she found.

found in the state are carved on smaller flat stones. All of them appear to be dates: Dec. 25, 1015; Dec. 30, 1022; Nov. 11, 1017; Dec. 22, 1022; Nov. 24, 1024.[5]

Norse Artifacts. In November 1887, an iron nail and metal buckle was found in a small mound near Washburn, Wisconsin (on Lake Superior).[6] Several Viking swords have been reportedly found: one was "discovered" in 1931 along with an ax and shield handle in Ontario between Hudson Bay and Lake Superior. Known to be authentic, the artifacts were purchased by the Royal Ontario Museum and placed on display. (See figure 121.) Some doubt was later raised about whether the genuine Norse relics were actually found in Ontario or bought by the person who then sold them to the museum at a profit. This is known as the "Beardmore Find." On April 20, 1911 a rusted Viking Sword was found just west of Ulen, Minnesota. It too is genuine and is on display at the Ulen Museum. A controversial set of artifacts was recovered in Wisconsin from the Spencer Lake Mound in 1935-36 by the University of Wisconsin at Milwaukee. A total of 182 burials were uncovered. Birchbark baskets, unusual points, and other artifacts were found. Rumors immediately circulated that Eric the Red had visited the area. These appear to have been based on a prank briefly discussed in the next section.

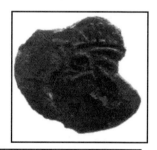

Figure 121 (below)
The "Beardmore Find" on display.
Courtesy of Royal Ontario Museum.

Figure 122 (right)
Norwegian silver penny found in 1957 by Guy Mellgren while excavating the central Maine coast.
Museum photo.

Fig. 1. Viking weapons found at Lake Nipigon near Beardmore, northern Ontario.

Several Norse coins have been recovered in North America. In 1957 Guy Mellgren was finishing his second year of digging into the Goddard site on the central Maine coast. He found a small silver coin. (See figure 122.) It was later identified as a Norwegian penny made between A.D. 1065-1080. It is accepted as genuine but how it came into the United States is disputed. In Minnesota, North Dakota, South Dakota, Montana, and Illinois over 300 unusual stones have been found over the years along streams, lakes, and rivers. The stones have holes drilled in the middle of them and appear to have been used as mooring stones. They are identical to the mooring stones used by the Norse.[7]

Cayce & the Norse

Cayce's readings on the Norse indicated that they had made many trips to ancient America and established a settlement here. Vinland was the coast of Rhode Island, Massachusetts, and Connecticut. Newport was named as a specific location as was Salem and Providence. It is very likely that the Norse reached these areas, and their coasts do have vines with grapes. This was the probable area of Leif's Vinland. The presence of a few artifacts in the area supports this contention.

Cayce's contention that a few Norse eventually merged with the mound builders seems quite probable. The Norse settlements here lasted for at least 100 years, perhaps 400-500 years. The iron nails and metal found in a few mounds could well be Norse. The Native American references to bearded whites, white tribes, and red-haired men and women could well be references to this. Cayce did not state that the Norse built the mounds, came up with the idea, or even influenced the culture. He said that a few Norse merged with mound builders, and, based on the current evidence, that is extremely likely.

Cayce contended that the Norse went deep into America (especially in the 1500s) reaching Minnesota as well as Montana. He stated that a knife belonging to Eric the Red had been recovered in Wisconsin just prior to 1940 and that this find would prove the Norse excursion. While it is probable the Norse went inland, the evidence is not strong enough to make a good judgment as to how far they reached. Some of the runestones are no doubt genuine, but none of these date to 1500 — they purport to be much earlier. The swords, while genuine, are questionable as to their origin. The many mooring stones could be legitimate, but this, too, is unsettled.

Cayce's assertion that the Norse reached Montana in 1500 and that a knife that belonged to Eric the Red was found in Wisconsin just before

1940 appear to be wrong. The Spencer Mound prank, perpetrated on a group of archaeology students by professors, was probably the source of this assertion. In addition, it is known that Eric did not personally explore deep into the continent (as the reading stated).

It's interesting to examine the background of these specific readings. No one has asserted that Cayce was infallible (including Cayce himself). A reading conducted in the Lammer's series indicated that the mindset of the questioners could influence the reply. This appears to be the case with this "Norse" reading as well as the ill-fated oil-prospecting readings. In all of those readings, it seems apparent that the questioners had preconceived wishes and ideas. They wanted something to be there and their questions reflected their hopes. Cayce spoke about how readings could be "shaded" by the mental state of the questioners, and perhaps in this Norse reading and in the oil prospecting readings, the information was "influenced." The individuals receiving the "Norse" information were of Scandanavian background. They had apparently been excited about the evidence being reported about Norse artifacts just being discovered in America and were seeking confirmation.

Egyptians In Ancient America
An Amazing "Coincidence"

The Cayce readings told of several ancient Egyptian excursions to America including to the southwest U.S. as well as several contacts to Central and South America. There is a thread of evidence for this. In 1914, a Mexican archaeologist excavating the Maya ruins at Acajutla found two statues — both were clearly Egyptian. They depicted Isis and Osiris. Little is heard about these today. But the most amazing possible confirmation of Cayce's contention about Egyptians in the Grand Canyon area, comes from what could be seen as a remarkable coincidence.

On April 27, 1991 the Flagstaff *Arizona Daily Sun* published a long article detailing an unusual find in Northern Arizona. At the April meeting of the Society of American Archaeology in New Orleans three archaeologists working for the state announced that they had found a series of catacombs containing ceremonial chambers two miles west of Springerville. They found the catacombs while working to establish the area as a recreational park. They believed the tunnels and chambers were constructed by the Mongollon Indians 700-800 years ago because the site is near a known Mongollon complex. However, no other chambers or tunnels are known to have been built by this culture.

The entrances to the catacombs were hidden and could only be accessed by rappelling down a canyon wall. The entrances were the size of small doorways or narrow crawl spaces. *The interior catacombs were an incredible 3-4 acres in extent with rooms 50 feet high and 100 feet long.* There were no artifacts of note in the catacombs and nothing like this has even been found in North America. The site is known as Casa Malpais. It now is a park but the catacombs are not accessible.

The possible connection of this site to Egypt is a fascinating story. David Hatcher Childress, a prolific author, traveler, and founder of the World Explorers Club, found a forgotten front-page story in the April 5, 1909 issue of the *Phoenix Gazette*. (There is no doubt whatsoever that this story was published.) The article stated that an expedition funded by the Smithsonian and led by S. A. Jordon had found a series of tunnels and chambers in the Grand Canyon. Inside the catacombs a huge number of Egyptian artifacts were found. Mummies, gold and copper artifacts, idols, statues, and hieroglyphic writings were recovered seemingly indicating that it had once been an Egyptian temple. Access could only be gained by rappelling down a steep canyon wall. The artifacts were removed. The descriptions of the catacombs in the 1909 story are essentially identical to the site discovered and reported by archaeologists in 1991. The 1991 group apparently found no artifacts in the catacombs, which would indicate that someone had removed them at a prior time.

Childress recently contacted the Smithsonian, but was told no Egyptian artifacts had ever been recovered in the Americas. The Smithsonian also had no knowledge of S.A. Jordon. Childress suggests that the Smithsonian is involved in covering up the story. But there is a much more plausible possibility.

This is a fascinating story, indeed. The descriptions of the 1909 and 1991 sites seem nearly identical. If the mysterious S. A. Jordon existed and found gold and other Egyptian artifacts in the catacombs, is it possible he gathered them and quietly moved into obscurity for monetary reasons? The 1909 article states that the story came to the attention of reporters after Jordan and his helpers arrived at Phoenix immediately after gathering artifacts at the site. It is conceivable that the individuals involved had looted the valuable remains at the site. While they had no connection to the Smithsonian, they made this claim to the eager reporters when they were questioned. This would have given them an air of authority and removed suspicions. In all probability, fake names were given.

Regardless of the outcome in this story, there are other tantalizing clues that an Egyptian presence may have been in ancient Arizona. Northwest of Tucson, Arizona in the Tortolita Mountains is a site known as Zodiac

Ridge. A 180-foot rock circle with over 800 stones was found several hundred years ago and has been investigated by archaeoastronomers. It contains alignments to the 18.61-year lunar cycle, the solstices, equinox, and several stars including the constellation of Orion. Petroglyphs that have Egyptian-like hieroglyphs have been found nearby.[8]

The possibility of an Egyptian presence in ancient Arizona is preposterous to historians. However, it does seem that the evidence indicates something very much resembling Egyptian artifacts were found there. Cayce stated that a shrine was made in the Arizona area by an Egyptian envoy in 10,000 B.C.

Other Curious Finds

Authentic Roman coins have turned up from time to time in both North and South America. In addition, ancient coins from Syria, Israel, and Sicily have been found. Various ancient inscriptions across America have been cited as being genuine by Harvard epigrapher Barry Fell. These are Celtic, Phoenician, and Egyptian. Fell also cites the many stone chambers dotting New England as genuine evidence of an ancient presence. These include Mystery Hill in New Hampshire. The site is now known as "America's Stonehenge."

In the summer of 1882, a miner in British Columbia found 30 genuine Chinese coins 25 feet below the surface. They are believed to have been produced by the Emperor Huungt around 2637 B.C. Steel blades from supposed Japanese explorers have been found in Alaska. These finds support Cayce's claims that Chinese and Japanese migrations occurred. This is also confirmed by the mtDNA evidence.

In 1933 Mexican archaeologist José García Payón discovered a small, carved head with Roman features in an undisturbed burial site. In 1999, Bulgarian archaeologist Romeo Hristov confirmed that this small figure of a bearded man was a Roman figurine created within a few hundred years of 200 A.D. The Max Planck Institute of Nuclear Physics in Germany determined the date of creation of the small figure. Hristov has identified 13 other artifacts that he believes are significant evidence of pre-Columbian contact.

On August 8, 1999, an extensive interview with Hristov was published in the *Dallas Observer*. Hristov spoke of how numerous American archaeologists tried to stop his research. He called American archaeology "a very dirty game." Nevertheless, there is overwhelming evidence for numerous ancient visitors to America.

Semitic & Hebrew Evidence

The presence of Semitic, Hebrew, or Israelite peoples in the Americas prior to 1492 is highly controversial. The Mormon religion is based on the idea and Joseph Smith was eventually murdered by a mob because of it. Archaeologists are adamant that none of these ancient people migrated to America. Yet, there is very convincing evidence.

The Uxmal " Star of David" or "Adam Kadmon" Star. *The Second Annual Report of the Bureau of Ethnology* (1881) compared a variety of "stone sun disks" found in the Americas. One of these was found in the Yucatan at Uxmal. It depicts the "Star of David" and is unquestionably genuine. (See figure 123.) This six-pointed star has an ancient source. It is the star of Adam Kadmon (the first man) and was used on amulets. (See figure 124.)

Figure 123
Sun disk from Uxmal depicting the Star of David. *From — Bureau of American Ethnology (1881).*

Figure 124
Adam Kadmon is shown on the left side with a 6-pointed star formed. The top right figure is the Shield of David and the bottom figure is an amulet. *From — The Jewish Encyclopedia (1905).*

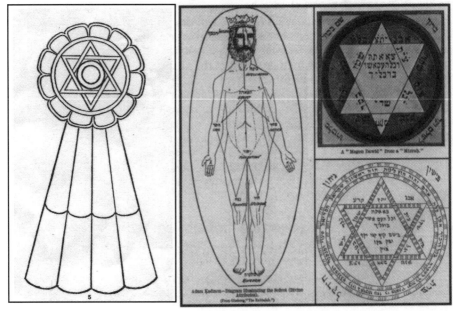

The "Menorah" or "Hanukkiah" Earthworks in Ohio. In an earlier chapter, the "East Fork" earthwork at Milford (about 25 miles east of Cincinnati) was mentioned. When Squier and Davis published a drawing of the earthworks in their monumental Smithsonian publication, *Ancient Monuments of the Mississippi Valley*, the site immediately became known as the "Hanukkiah Earthworks" (sic) because it forms a 9-branched candelabrum — a Jewish menorah. Around the 2000-foot long (each side) menorah earthworks was what exactly depicts an ancient oil lamp. (Tradition tells us that eight of the menorah's candles represent the days an oil lamp miraculously burned during the siege of Jerusalem in 165 B.C.)

The significance of the earthwork's shape is astonishing. Quite simply, it implies some form of ancient Hebrew influence in the Americas — *if the earthwork actually existed.* Until recent developments — it was believed that the Hanukkiah Earthworks never existed.

Cyrus Thomas' (1894) massive, 742-page report on mounds[9] had cryptically little to say about it. Thomas dismissed the site by stating, "Some of the singular works described and figured in *Ancient Monuments* and elsewhere are to a large extent imaginary" (p. 566). Thomas listed the plate number assigned to the Hanukkiah Earthworks as an example.

Squier and Davis did, in fact, copy the earthworks from a surveyor's drawing supplied to them — and never visited the site. The site was believed to have been obliterated by farming. (This may have been a factor in Thomas' dismissal of the site.) Based on these facts, and the obvious "out-of-place" nature of the design, the Hanukkiah Earthworks were believed to be a fantasy or hoax. However, recent investigations into historical events have shown that the earthworks did exist — exactly as depicted in the surveys. (The earthwork is shown on page 112.)

In 1803, President Thomas Jefferson became interested in the early drawings published about the Hanukkiah Earthworks. Because of Jefferson's interest, the US. Army Corp of Engineers sent a team to survey the site in 1823. The group found the site fully intact at that time and drew a survey map. Squier and Davis had used copies of this survey in their report but failed to cite its source. Major Isaac Roberdeau, head of the Bureau of Topographical Engineers for the U.S. Army Corp of Engineers drew the map after surveying the site. The original map has recently been found at the Cartographic and Architectural Branch of the Military Archives Division of the U.S. National Archives in Alexandria. It can be found in Record Group 77; U.S. Army Corp of Engineers, Fortification File; drawer 144, sheet #20.10 J. Huston McCulloch, a professor at Ohio State University is credited with running down the original sources.

The "Bat Creek Stone." In 1988 McCulloch conducted a brilliant series of tests on artifacts associated with "The Bat Creek Stone." The stone tablet was found in an undisturbed mound in east Tennessee during an excavation sponsored by the Smithsonian in 1889. (See figure 125.) Cyrus Thomas, the Project Director, immediately declared the small tablet to be Cherokee. Wooden ear spools and "copper" artifacts found with the unusual burial were also thought to be Cherokee.

By 1894 many, including Thomas, began to believe that the table was not Cherokee. By 1972 several epigraphers and experts in ancient Semitic inscriptions had declared the stone depicted a "Paleo-Hebrew" inscription. (See figure 126.) And here the controversy was stilled until McCulloch had a letter-by-letter comparison made between the tablet, the Cherokee alphabet, and the ancient Semitic script known as Paleo-Hebrew. The tablet is Paleo-Hebrew and reads, "a comet (or star) for the Jews – year (1 or 6). It refers to the "Star Prophecy" (discussed shortly).

McCulloch then proceeded to have the "copper" and wooden artifacts found with the tablet analyzed. Virtually all metal artifacts found in mounds were called "copper" in the 19th century. The Smithsonian's own Analytical Laboratory tested the copper and found it to be a "leaded yellow brass alloy." It contained 27% zinc and 3.3% lead. The British Museum matched the alloy with artifacts found in only one place in the world and only during one time-frame. It had been made in the Middle-East between 45 B.C. and 200 A.D. The wooden ear spools were carbon dated to 437 A.D.; this was 1,400 years before the Cherokee alphabet was invented. McCulloch also found that several authentic coins from the Bar Kokhba rebellion (132-135 A.D.) had been found in Kentucky. (See figure 127.)

The conclusion was inescapable: the Bat Creek Stone was a genuine ancient Hebrew tablet. But how did it get to America? McCulloch believes

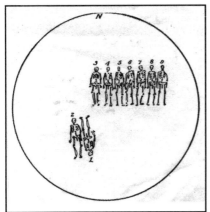

Figure 125
Sketch of the skeletal remains found in the Bat Creek Mound excavated by the Smithsonian in 1889. The tablet, copper, and wooden artifacts were found under the skull of the single individual buried with his head toward the bottom of the page. *From — Thomas (1894).*

Figure 126
The Bat Creek Tablet shown at actual size. *From — Thomas (1894).*

it was a result of the Jewish Wars of 66-73 A.D. In 68 A.D. the Romans smashed the Jewish Navy in a decisive battle that led to the taking of Jerusalem. The Jewish Navy was large but no match for the Romans. The last holdouts of the war were at Masada and their choice to commit suicide rather than submit to the Romans is well-known. There is no dispute among historians about the naval battle or Masada.

McCulloch believes that a few Jewish ships escaped the battle and sailed into the Mediterranean. They made their way through the "Pillars of Hercules" (Gibraltar) and eventually reached North America. The tablet was a reference to the year as well as the prophecy of the coming of a messiah. They brought along artifacts including the brass and eventually found their way to the Tennessee River. The tablet and brass became heirlooms and were passed along through the generations until they were buried with someone important in 437 A.D. McCulloch's results were published in 1988.[11]

Figure 127
Bar Kokhba coin. Several of these have been found in scattered places in Kentucky.
From — The Jewish Encyclopedia (1905).

Coin of Bar Kokba Bearing a Lulab.

In response to McCulloch's work, in a 1993 article Mainfort and Kwas used the term "cult archaeologist" or "cult archaeology" *14 times* in an attempt to rebut McCulloch. Mainfort and Kwas also wrote, apparently for the first time ever, that the tablet was "allegedly" found. They declared the tablet to be a hoax perpetrated by the head of the excavation so he could maintain his job and funding. This flimsy "psychological analysis" by archaeologists of the discovery of the tablet in 1889 seems baseless and may actually provide more insight into them than the 1889 excavators.

The Los Lunas Decalogue Stone. In 1850 or so, settlers were shown an inscribed rock on the side of Hidden Mountain near Los Lunas, New Mexico. The site is 35 miles south of Albuquerque. The rock is actually a huge boulder weighing about 80 tons. (See figure 128.) The first translation was made in 1949, when Robert H. Pfeiffer of Harvard University stated it was a copy of the Ten Commandments. Most scholars agree and believe it is written in Old Hebrew with some Greek. On the top of Hidden Mountain is an inscribed star map indicating a celestial event in 107 B.C. and other scattered inscriptions are found in the area. All of these sites are, to say the least, controversial.

Figure 128
The Los Lunas Decalogue in New Mexico. *Photo — Courtesy of United Israel.*

Possible Frauds — Or Genuine Artifacts? During the 1800s and early 1900s, over 10,000 stone and clay tablets were excavated from mounds in Michigan. All have been declared fakes. But the sheer number and variety of these is overwhelming. Many of the tablets are now in the archives of the Church of Latter Day Saints in Salt Lake City after they sought to preserve some. The majority of them were destroyed or "lost." They depict Biblical scenes and are similar to finds currently coming from the mysterious Burrows Cave supposedly 50 miles from Olney, Illinois. *Ancient American* magazine has featured these finds for several years. Another set of

---

Figures 129 (left, front) & 130 (right, reverse side)
The most important "Newark Holy Stone" shown at about 60% size. *Photos — G. Little.*

artifacts, certainly *visually interesting*, is the "Newark Holy Stones." (See figures 129 & 130.) A county surveyor named David Wyrick found a series of five inscribed artifacts in the Newark Earthworks between 1860 and 1867. One of the stones depicts Moses and is believed to have the Ten Commandments engraved on it. Some people believe Wyrick was duped; the artifacts are on display at the Johnson-Humrickhouse Museum in Coshocton, Ohio.

Cayce & Lost Tribes

Cayce stated that "remnants of the Lost Tribes" came to southern America in about 3,000 B.C. They then went to the area around Mexico City and returned to America with refugees fleeing the Yucatan. They eventually found their way to Ohio and were part of the culture that started the mound building eras. As we have seen in prior chapters, the chronology of the Watson Brake Mounds, the establishment of Poverty Point, and the beginning of the mound building period in Ohio all fit Cayce's chronology. So too does the mtDNA evidence. The presence of a "Star of David" artifact at Uxmal in the Yucatan seems to confirm an ancient Hebrew presence there. But most of the evidence cited in *this* chapter involves Hebrews in America around 165 B.C. The obviously genuine Hebrew evidence (the Bat Creek Stone and the Milford menorah earthworks) dates to that general time frame. The Los Lunas Decalogue, if authentic, could date far earlier (to 2000 B.C. perhaps), but it still doesn't fit the 3000 B.C. date given by Cayce. Yet the Watson Brake Mounds do fit Cayce's Lost Tribes chronology as does the later Poverty Point Culture. But it should be recalled that the Cayce readings appear to tell of several different migrations to ancient America by "Lost Tribes" or their predecessors.

As stated before, Cayce's chronology for the Lost Tribes certainly doesn't match the traditional dating for them in history. But it could be that Cayce was referring to another event where the "chosen people" were scattered. The Mormons base many of their beliefs on several migrations to the Americas by Semitic people and pre-Hebrews. Could these ideas be linked to Cayce's mysterious claim about the Lost Tribes?

Chapter 12

Who Were The Lost Tribes? Hebrew History and the Mormon Connection

It must be evident to the Bible reader that the writer of the book of Genesis appears to be in a hurry to reach the story of Abraham. After only ten chapters of very condensed history we already find ourselves reading the story of Abraham.
J.A. Thompson (1957) *Archaeology*

One of the most controversial and puzzling aspects of Cayce's history of the Americas is the coming of the "Lost Tribes." In a reading on the origin of the Mayan culture, Cayce stated that, "those peoples who were of the lost tribes" traveled by boat to the American continent in 3000 B.C.[1]

This poses a major timeline problem. The 3000 B.C. date does not coincide with the known history of the Hebrew people as passed down through the *Torah* and the Old Testament. According to Hebrew tradition, the term "lost tribes" refers to the 10 tribes of Israel that were scattered during the Assyrian conquest of the Northern Kingdom of Israel in 722 B.C.[2]

Over the years, Biblical scholars and historians have posed many theories as to the ultimate fate of these groups. According to the *Jewish Encyclopedia*, some scholars believe they remained in the Middle East and were absorbed into existing cultures. Others have theorized that they migrated to the Americas, England, India, Ethiopia, China, Japan and Afghanistan.[3]

Cayce does refer to the Assyrian period specifically in several life readings indicating that some of the "ten tribes who were carried away" escaped into the southwestern portion of North America.[4] He also describes migrations to England by individuals he refers to as "daughters of Hezekiah" who was King of Judah during the Assyrian conquest. He does not, however, provide any dates in these readings.[5]

To further complicate the issue, in other life readings Cayce refers to "daughters of Zedekiah" as Hebrew immigrants escaping to America, England, Ireland, India and elsewhere during the time of the Babylonian captivity.[6] This period in Jewish history refers to the conquering of the last remaining Hebrew kingdom and tribe (Judah) and is believed to have occurred around 586 B.C.[7]

In Cayce's version of the Assyrian/Babylonian story, migrations occurred over a period of several hundred years as the Northern (Israel) and Southern (Judah) Hebrew kingdoms were conquered and broken up. Again, Cayce does not give specific time references in these life readings so he may have been saying that these migrations occurred during the 722-586 B.C. timeframe as per conventional Biblical chronology.[8] If so, this does not explain the 3000 B.C. date Cayce gave for the "lost tribes" migration to the Americas in the Maya origins reading.

Cayce was a Sunday school teacher for several decades. It is a near certainty that he knew the traditional dating of the "lost tribes" and realized his 3000 B.C. date was far too early for that well-known event. Thus, it seems likely that the 3000 B.C. date refers to an earlier migration unrelated to the known, historical events that occurred far later.

It is possible that the "Lost Tribes" group in 3000 B.C. was a Semitic group descended from Adam, Seth, and Noah who dispersed *prior* to God's covenant with Abraham. This covenant is the moment in history that is identified as the beginning of the Hebrews as a specific group. Since Cayce did not call the 3000 B.C. Lost Tribes "Hebrews" or "Israelites," this seems to be a plausible explanation.

Conventional dating of biblical events would require a 3000 B.C. group to have migrated near the time of Noah's Flood. The Masoretic Hebrew text of the Old Testament gives 2239 B.C. (292 years before the birth of Abraham) as the date of Noah's Flood while the Greek and Samaritan versions give a 3119 B.C. date.[9] It is interesting to note the Maya date marking the creation of the current World era was 3114 B.C.

Also in support of Cayce are the claims of the *Book of Mormon*, which details three ancient migrations to the Americas. Two of these migrations were groups from the ancient Hebrew lands from the time of the traditional lost tribes. The other was *an earlier, pre-Abraham Semitic group* that was Hebrew-like in their worship of the one God. This latter group left shortly after the Flood. Descendants of all three groups were said to have mixed with the natives already living in the land becoming part of the Native American population. These groups were part of not only the Maya civilization, but, in Mormon belief, were thought to be responsible for the unusual mounds and earthworks found in North America. Mormon researchers have studied the archaeological findings throughout Central and North America and have identified what they believe to be proof of this version of ancient American history.[10] We shall address some of this evidence shortly.

An alternative explanation of Cayce's 3000 B.C. date is simply that his historical timeline for Biblical events does not correlate with the conventional chronologies. That is, Cayce may be asserting that the traditional dates are wrong. In fact, Cayce gives several specific dates for the Flood, the Exodus and the Chaldean (ancestors of the Babylonians) civilization that are many *thousands* of years earlier than conventional dates. He also tells us that the Egyptian civilization is thousands of years older than commonly believed.

Lost Tribes Before Abraham?

In Cayce's Maya origins reading, which contains the 3000 B.C. date, he does not clearly identify the lost tribes as Hebrew or "Israelite" using the post-Abraham definition. Most researchers, however, do assume that this reading refers to groups of people from the Hebrew kingdoms of Judah and Israel who migrated to the Americas during the Assyrian and Babylonian conquests. One reason for this is that several paragraphs earlier in the same reading Cayce refers to altars that were used for human sacrifice due to "the injection of the Mosaic."

It is possible that the "Mosaic" reference could be describing a different event than the 3000 B.C./lost tribes. The paragraph which contains the term "lost tribes" occurs later in the reading. If this is the case then it is certainly possible that Cayce was referring to two different groups or "injections" as he describes both of them. One of these was pre-Abraham (3000 B.C.) and one post-Abraham. This is further supported by the fact that the life readings which relate to the Assyrian/Babylonian period contain much more specific Hebrew identifiers with references to the "peoples of Promise," " the ten tribes who were carried away," "the carrying away of the children of promise into captivity," as well as to daughters of both Hezekiah and Zedekiah who were among the final Kings of Judah.

In fact, Cayce does not connect the term "lost tribes" with specific Hebrew identifiers in *any* of the seven additional readings in which it appears. And even more importantly, these readings do not contain dates. In four of them, lost tribes is used to describe a particular group or culture which was the result of a mixture of ancestors including lost tribes, people from Mu, Atlanteans, Incas, and Yucatan natives.[11] This would seem to be consistent with the way the term "lost tribes" is used in the 3000 B.C./ Maya origins reading. The fifth reading indicates that a "lost or strayed tribe" settled in the Samoan islands.[12] The sixth refers to "tribes that were lost or journeyed to...settled in the Aleutian Islands."[13] And the seventh mentioned a "lost or strayed tribe that came across (to America) from Lemuria" in addition to a group that "came from the lands of bondage by the Persians" as if these were two separate groups.[14]

If the term "lost tribes" is a pre-Abraham reference, doesn't it move us away from any Hebrew or Semitic connection? Not really, since Cayce did not draw a strict line between pre- and post-Abraham peoples. *As Cayce pointed out in several readings, the Hebrews were God's Chosen People because they were directly descended from the most spiritually pure Atlantean Sons of the Law of One through Amilius, Adam, Seth and Noah.* The Old Testament also makes a point of emphasizing that Noah was of the line of Seth. Abraham, in turn, was descended from Noah and thus the Hebrew people were part of an important group or "tribe" long before Abraham. Therefore it seems possible that Cayce may have used "lost tribes" to describe a pre-Abraham Semitic group or groups. Certainly his time frame would make more sense if this is the case.

Were there Semitic migrations prior to the time of Abraham?

Actually, the Bible mentions several dispersions of Semitic peoples prior to the Abraham period. First, is the period after Cain slays Abel when Cain "went out from the presence of the Lord, and dwelt in the land of Nod, on the east of Eden...and he builded a city" (Gen. 4: 16-17). The next is after the Flood when Noah's sons are cited: "from them the whole earth was peopled" (Gen. 9:19). Another is after the destruction of the Tower of Babel at which time God "scattered them all over the earth" (Gen. 11:9).

According to conventional Bible chronology (based on the Greek and Samaritan versions), the dispersion after the Flood would be closest to Cayce's 3000 B.C. date, although recent archaeological evidence involving the Tower of Babel story now shows that Noah's flood was probably even earlier. According to the Old Testament, the Tower of Babel event occurred among a new civilization that developed several generations after the Flood. (See figure 131.) And yet the construction of the first known Babylonian towers, called ziggurats, which are the best candidates for the Tower, have now been dated to as early as 3300 B.C. and no later than 2800 B.C.[15] A connection between Babel and Cayce's 3000 B.C. lost tribes is especially significant since the *Book of Mormon* describes a dispersion of pre-Abraham Semitic peoples by boat to the Americas from exactly that Biblical event.

Interestingly, considering all of the varied questions Cayce received while giving readings, there is no evidence that Cayce was ever asked about the Mormon story while in a trance state. He did comment about it in a letter to a friend written in 1938 (five years after the 3000 B.C.—Maya origins reading). In the letter he stated that he was very familiar with the

Figure 131
The Tower of Babel
depicted by
Gus*tave Doré*
(1866).

Mormon literature and had read many of their books and had heard them preach. He became interested while a child when one of his teachers was made to leave because her husband was an Elder in the Mormon Church and apparently was practicing "bigamy" as Cayce termed it. But the most significant comment he made in the letter was that he thought the Mormons "...have a great deal of truth - possibly have to many of us a peculiar way of application - but feel sure the founders were a part of the lost tribes - when some of those tribes went to England - others came here to America."[16]

The *Book of Mormon* and the Lost Tribes

"While I was thus in the act of calling upon God, I discovered a light appearing in my room, which continued to increase until the room was lighter than at noonday, when immediately a personage appeared at my bedside, standing in the air, for his feet did not touch the floor...He said there was a book deposited, written upon gold plates, giving an account of the former inhabitants of this continent and the source from whence they sprang. He also said that the fullness of the everlasting Gospel was contained in it, as delivered by the Savior to the ancient inhabitants." [17]

So wrote Joseph Smith of a visit he received from the angel Moroni while in prayer on the night of September 21, 1823 at the tender age of seventeen. He continued to receive visits from the angel, who in 1827, instructed Smith to dig up a large number of inscribed gold plates from a mound located in a place called Hill Cumorah in western New York State. According to Smith the plates were in a stone and concrete box, which had been hidden there under a very large stone around 400 A.D. by Moroni himself. They had been inscribed by the descendants of ancient Hebrew immigrants and contained an overview of the history of this group beginning with their first migration immediately after the destruction of the Tower of Babel and ending in 400 A.D. when their civilization was destroyed by a series of civil wars. The plates told the story of three different migrations to the Americas by both pre- and post-Abraham Hebrews and of the appearance to these peoples of the resurrected Christ.

Needless to say, after revealing this discovery to his friends and family, the young Joseph Smith became a very controversial figure in his community and eventually a much hated and feared person throughout the country. His translation of the contents of the plates was published in 1830 as the 500 plus page *Book of Mormon* and remains the seminal document for the Church of Jesus Christ of Latter-Day Saints (also known as the Mormons). After the translation was completed, Joseph Smith was instructed to return the plates to Moroni — no one knows where the plates are now.

The golden plates were inscribed in an altered style of Hebrew, which the translated plates themselves referred to as "Reformed Egyptian." (See figure 132.) Only a few witnesses ever viewed the plates, but Smith sent a handwritten copy of the script to a Charles Anthon of Columbia University who claimed they were an unintelligible combination of several different languages. He later wrote to colleagues suggesting that the samples he had seen looked like they had been "copied after the Mexican zodiac (meaning the Mesoamerican codices which are books written by the ancient Aztec and Maya peoples)."[18]

Moroni instructed Smith to translate the strange writing by using two "seer stones" contained in the box with the plates and an ancient breastplate. He was told these stones were the Urim and Thummim as used in Old Testament times. Eyewitnesses told of Smith putting the stones into a hat and then placing his face into the hat. Without even having to look at the plates Smith could dictate their contents to a person helping him who would then write it down. It appeared to these witnesses that Smith was able to actually visualize each line of the completed interpretations through some sort of mental imagery. Smith himself claimed that the power to translate the ancient texts was given to him by God.[19]

In many ways this mirrors the descriptions of the Urim and Thummim that appear in the Old Testament and in documents of Hebrew tradition.

Figure 132
Fragment of copy of script on plates sent to Anthon for evaluation.
Preserved by a supporter of Joseph Smith in 1828.

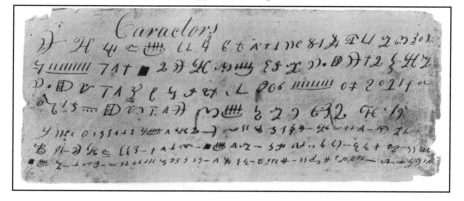

The words Urim and Thummim have been translated to mean "the Light (or revelation) and the Truth (or perfection)." They were given by Moses to Aaron to be worn on a special breastplate as a part of the priestly garments and to be used as an oracle to receive divine guidance. Some sources speculate that the stones were made of sapphire (lapis lazuli). Similar oracle stones have been identified from the Babylonian history of their ancient patriarchal times, which predate Abraham. The use of the Urim and Thumin appears to have stopped around the time of the Babylonian captivity. They do not appear in the New Testament, which seems to have replaced this tool with the gifts of the Holy Spirit available to all through the Death and Resurrection of the Christ.[20, 21]

Cayce also addressed the Urim and Thumin in several readings pertaining to Biblical times and described them as simply tools used by the ancient priests to attune their consciousness to the Divine. He further emphasized that the stones themselves do not contain the force, but rather that the power comes from the Creative Forces of the Divine. He put the use of these stones on the same level as obtaining guidance and attunement through dreams, meditation and intuition or psychic perception.[22]

The Story of the Dispersions to America as Given by the *Book of Mormon*

The *Book of Mormon* tells of three migrations of Middle Eastern groups to the Americas. The first was a people the book calls the Jaredites who traveled across the Pacific Ocean from Mesopotamia during the Early Dynastic period of the Sumerians (i.e. after the fall of the Tower of Babel). Their name comes from Jared who was their leader during the original migration. The actual location of their landing place is unknown, but, due to the large number of geographical descriptions in the Book, Mormon scholars currently believe they landed on the Pacific side of the Isthmus of Tehuantepec. This area in South Central Mexico is the location of the Olmec and Zapotec cultures which archaeologists believe began as early as 2000 B.C. (See figure 133.) Previous Mormon studies had concluded that the Jaredites landed in Panama or the Yucatan or even South America, but the more recent discoveries in Olmec, Maya, Toltec and Aztec archaeology have provided much support for a Central American location. Cayce seems to agree with contemporary Mormon scholars since he also identifies Central Mexico as one of the places settled by the 3000 B.C. lost tribes. He differs, however, in the landing site which he said was in the southern

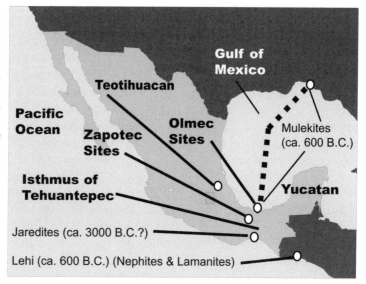

Figures 133
Map of Mexico showing the locations where some Mormon scholars believe the Jaredites, Mulekites, and Lehi landed.

Gulf of Mexico

Teotihuacan

Pacific Ocean

Zapotec Sites

Olmec Sites

Mulekites (ca. 600 B.C.)

Isthmus of Tehuantepec

Yucatan

Jaredites (ca. 3000 B.C.?)

Lehi (ca. 600 B.C.) (Nephites & Lamanites)

United States.[23] However, as mentioned in earlier chapters, Cayce also stated that at least one group (described as a strayed or lost tribe) came across the Pacific.

The Jaredites were described as being skilled in implement and pottery making, metallurgy, temple building and the pre-cuneiform semipictographic writing of the Sumerians. They were also said to have worshipped "a great anthropomorphic god of life and the rains (referred to simply as 'the Lord')." Mormon scholars have noted that the Jaredite religious practices were similar to those of the Mesoamericans. Their highly developed civilization of many large cities was destroyed by a great civil war in 600 B.C. A few remnants are believed to have survived to around 34 A.D. where they were among witnesses to an event in which Christ appeared in the Americas.[24]

The second and third migrations are interpreted by Mormon scholars to have occurred shortly after the Assyrian/Babylonian conflicts around 600 B.C. One of these, the Mulekites was a very small group that is not mentioned in much detail in the narratives. This group was led by Mulek, said to be a son of King Zedekiah of Judah. They traveled east from the Mediteranean first landing in "the land northward" which is believed to be the southern coast of the United States. After staying an unknown period of time they then traveled by boat landing and settling in "the land southward" which is believed to be in or near the Olmec city of La Venta. *This description, of course, closely resembles Cayce's story discussed ear-*

lier and may relate to the site of Watson Brake. The only difference between the two stories is the assumed time frame.

The other group, also made up of Hebrews escaping from the period of the Babylonian captivity, was led by a patriarch named Lehi. Lehi and his family left by boat from the western Arabian peninsula and landed in an area said to be "southward" of the Jaredite lands. Some Mormon scholars believe this to be the Pacific coast near the southern highlands of Guatemala. Two groups, the Nephites and the Lamanites, descended from Lehi and went through alternating periods of war and peace until such time as they caused the demise of both their civilizations around 400 A.D.

Approximately 33-34 A.D. a great catastrophe consisting of earthquakes, thunder, lightening, and "mountains that tumbled into pieces" changed the surface of the land and destroyed several of the Nephite cities. This natural disaster was said in the narrative to have occurred at the crucifixion of Christ as described in the New Testament (Mat. 27:45-54). Shortly thereafter, the Nephites witnessed an appearance by the Resurrected Christ who spoke to them from the top of a temple. Christ then spent time in the Americas preaching to the inhabitants, baptizing them, and selecting 12 disciples. When he had completed instructing them, he ascended into heaven and, as in the New Testament, sent the Holy Spirit to descend upon them.[25]

In general the Nephites were considered to be the people who most correctly retained their connection with God and more readily accepted the teachings of Christ. However, there were both "good" and "bad" Lamanites. The "bad" Lamanites were believed to have intermixed with the native peoples of Central and North America.[26] If true, this would parallel Cayce's idea of the chosen people as descending from the spiritually pure Sons of the Law of One who had not mixed with the impure and rebellious peoples of Atlantis called the Sons of Belial. According to Cayce both groups migrated to Central and North America. Perhaps the Mormon narrative is telling of Lamanites intermixing with descendants of the Sons of Belial group.

The location of the final religious battle of the "bad" Lamanites versus the "good" Nephites around 400 A.D. is a source of controversy among Mormon researchers. Brigham Young University anthropologist, John Sorenson, believes that all of the events in the Book took place within Central America. He speculates that Moroni traveled to New York several years after the final battle to hide the plates. (The angel Moroni, before his appearance to Joseph Smith, was the son of a the last Nephite King.) Other factions believe that this final battle occurred near Hill Cumorah in western New York State. They interpret the Book as describing large-scale migrations to North America where the groups "spread forth into all parts of the land" around 55 B.C. After the final battle the victorious Lamanites continued to persecute the few remaining Christian Nephites and scattered them throughout North America.[27]

Those who support the North American battle site theory also believe that the mounds and earthworks of the Hopewell and Adena eras in the Ohio Valley were the work of the ancient Nephites and Lamanites. In the 1830s Joseph Smith and his followers claimed to have found the bones of these people while digging into the mounds as they traveled across Ohio and Illinois to their promise land in Missouri. Witnesses claimed that Joseph Smith received a vision from God in which he identified a set of bones from an Illinois mound as belonging to a particular white Lamanite who was a Chief during the final Nephite battles. Despite the vision, Joseph Smith later changed his opinion to support Central America as the location for the last battle. However, the debate continues and is unresolved to the point that the Church itself has chosen not to speculate about the geography of the *Book of Mormon*. [28]

Archaeological Evidence for the Book of Mormon and the Lost Tribes

In the 1800s the belief that lost Israelite tribes were responsible for the many mounds and earthworks east of the Mississippi River and the ancient civilizations of Mesoamerica was common. By the 1900s, as archaeology grew into a more scientific and some would say close-minded profession, this theory was considered totally ridiculous. Also, a growing bias against the Mormon religion helped to shut the door to consideration of ancient Hebrew migrations. And yet, well-documented and not-so-well documented discoveries of Hebrew style artifacts kept popping up in North America. As discussed in the prior chapter, the best scientific evidence is the Bat Creek Stone and the artifacts found with it[29] and the "Hanukkiah" Earthworks. [30, 31]

Evidence in support of Hebrew migrations has also been found in Central America. In the 1920s and 30s, sculpted stones discovered at the Olmec site of La Venta in Mexico depict bearded persons dressed in Middle Eastern style clothing. (See figure 134.) One example is La Venta Stela 3 which seems to reflect a meeting between the leaders of two different groups. The person shown has several characteristics of Hebrews of that time frame

- 1500 -1000 B.C. Bearded figures were also found on sculptures from the Zapotec civilization at the site of Monte Alban. (See figure 135.) Beards are especially significant since Native American groups from that period are not known to have been able to grow much facial hair. The Olmec and the Zapotec civilizations were located in the south central area of Mexico near where both Cayce and the Book of Mormon indicate ancient Hebrew groups migrated.[32] Also mentioned previously was the "Star of David" sunstone found at Uxmal.

As mentioned in Chapter 4, the discovery of a European/Middle Eastern genetic marker (Haplotype X) among the ancient North American Indians provides another connection to the theory of lost Israelite tribes in America. The marker particularly seems to mirror Cayce's story of the dis-

Figure 134
Bearded man with Middle Eastern features depicted on relief at La Venta. *From — The Lost Hall of Records.*

person of Atlanteans near the period of their final destruction beginning around 10,700 B.C. At first glance this would seem to contradict the 3000 B.C. migration. However, the important point is that this marker shows up in both the Middle East and America. Therefore the X type could represent not only the Atlanteans, but specifically the more spiritually pure of that civilization who, per Cayce, were the ancestors of the Chosen People, the Israelites. If the Hebrew lost tribes did travel to the Americas then this would have given the gene another opportunity to be spread throughout that continent. The fact that Haplotype X has not been found among the Maya, as would be expected per Cayce's story, may simply be due to the minimal sampling of both contemporary and ancient members of this group. As the genetic studies continue, it will be interesting to see if more than one wave of Haplotype X will be found in the Americas as well as in the Yucatan.

Figure 135
Bearded man on
stela at Monte
Alban.
*From — The Lost
Hall of Records.*

With regards to the Mormon story, John Sorenson has provided a very detailed comparison of the latest archaeological findings regarding the known ancient civilizations in Central America with the *Book of Mormon*. He makes a number of very reasonable correlations. First, he notes that the language inscribed on the golden plates, as Charles Anthon pointed out in the 1800s, does have much in common with ancient Maya documents. Although the small Anthon sample is the only remaining example of script from the plates, it appears to have several features that resemble the typical Maya format such as the arrangement of script in columns of two. Also, the plates, like many of the Maya documents from sculpted stone, contained specific types of content. Both groups recorded in great detail their political and military struggles as well as the lineage history of kings and their right to rule. Both groups recorded ancestry from a distant past and stories of the Creation including a worldwide flood. Both tell of worshipping a main God and a god of rain. Both Aztec and Maya traditions also refer to a god-like character (Quetzalcoatl/Itzamna) that some Mormons believe may be a record of the appearance of Christ in the Americas.[33]

The Mormon plates were said to be written sometime after 600 B.C. using a language of altered Hebrew the plates call Reformed Egyptian. This language was used instead of Hebrew, according to the angel Moroni, in order that the history would fit on the plates. Mormon researchers note that in many countries today it is not unusual to find that one language has been written using the script of another language. For example, Yiddish, which is a form of German, is normally written in Hebrew letters. In addition, an example of a type of Reformed Egyptian script has been discovered which is very similar to the writing on the plates. A papyrus scroll which contains Aramaic script (the language spoken by Jesus) written in Egyptian by ancient Hebrews, has been translated as a version of Psalm 20:2-6.[34]

Even more interesting given the possible Central American location for the *Book of Mormon*, a non-Mormon researcher has pointed out that Maya and Egyptian hieroglyphs are actually quite similar and share six highly significant linguistic characteristics. Maya glyphs are now thought to be equally as sophisticated as Egyptian in their ability to communicate. In addition, both civilizations developed a more cursive style in writing the hieroglyphs over time and when painting as opposed to carving.[35] Given Cayce's story of Atlantean migrations to both the Yucatan and Egypt, this connection becomes especially meaningful.

Also in support of the plates' authenticity is the discovery that metal plates were a commonly used means of recording significant historical events among Israelites in 600 B.C. and, like the Mormon plates, the title page was normally recorded at the end of the document. Many of the names of individuals in the Mormon narrative, which had previously been criticized as non-Israelite, have now been discovered in other Middle Eastern writing of the same period. Another interesting point is that the plates contain a common Hebrew style of composition called "chiasmus" which is an inverted parallel pattern widely known among Bible scholars for its use in the Old Testament.[36]

A second type of research that supports the *Book of Mormon* are the many geographical descriptions in the book that seem to correlate to the weather, terrain and distances within the southern Mexico/Guatemala area.[37] Related to this is the discovery by geologists that a massive volcanic incident occurred around the time of Christ in El Salvador. This catastrophic event buried many settlements and is believed to have impacted a 3,000 square mile area. As mentioned earlier, the occurrence of a similar natural disaster during this very time frame is described in the *Book of Mormon*. In addition, the probable location of Lehi's 600 B.C. Arabian place of departure has been discovered. This is significant since it was described as a green garden spot and thus ridiculed by skeptics as not fitting into the known geography in that part of the world.

The Book of Mormon also describes ancient American civilizations that had urban gardens, multiple markets, highways, towers, and understood the use of cement. Again skeptics found these laughable until the last several decades when archaeological exploration determined that all of these are known to have existed among Central American civilizations. Mormon researchers also see reflections of the lost tribes' religious beliefs and practices in the artwork of these civilizations and are especially interested in the Christian cross-like depiction of the Maya World Tree that occurs in a temple in Palenque, Mexico.

And finally, with the discovery of the Dead Sea Scrolls even non-supporters of the *Book of Mormon* find in the Essenes an example of a pre-Christian Judaic group very much like the Mormon Nephites. Like their *Book of Mormon* counterparts, the Essenes "wrote important information on metal, believed in baptism, were led by a council of twelve with three governing priests, they had sacred meals of bread and wine administered by priests, and they believed in continuing revelation through a prophetic leader." Evangelical Christian writers Carol Mosser and Paul Owen were the ones who actually picked up on these similarities and presented them in a paper as a warning to their colleagues at the 1997 Evangelical Theological Society Far West Annual Meeting. In their paper they noted that, "All of this leads us to the conclusion that in many ways the Essenes may have been closer to the (Mormon) gospel than (they were to) other Jewish sects."[38]

Cayce's Bible Chronology

As mentioned earlier, there is another possible explanation for Cayce's 3000 B.C. date for the migration of the Israelite lost tribes to the Americas. This explanation revolves around Cayce's sometimes unbelievable time-table for the events in the Bible. For example, he gives two different dates for a major worldwide flood - 28,000 B.C. and 10,700 B.C.[39] Both of these are Atlantean destruction dates. When asked specifically for the date of Noah's flood Cayce states that it was during the second destruction of Atlantis and gives two dates 22,006 B.C. and 28,000 B.C.![40] However, he also indicates that the fourth root race and thus the fourth and last (so far) Adam and Eve lived around 12,000 B.C.[41]

Regarding the Tower of Babel, Cayce did not give a date but stated that it was built by the Chaldeans. It was constructed just before the world was broken up into nations.[42] He notes in another reading that the Chaldeans were at the peak of their civilization and able to do psychic readings like Cayce around 4000 B.C. He does not say that this was the time frame in which they built the Tower.[43] Cayce, however, seems to push the Tower date back considerably by giving 5500 B.C. as the date of "the periods of the Egyptian activity covered by the Exodus...."[44] This most likely refers to the entire Book of Exodus in the Old Testament which begins with the death of Joseph. Considering this dating, the 3000 B.C. lost tribes *could* be from the Assyrian/Babylonian captivity phase since in this "expanded" chronology the captivity could have occurred in 3000 B.C.

Cayce also mentioned in several of the life readings that Israelites from the Assyrian/Babylonian era migrated to England gathering together in the area of Somerset near the site of the ancient megalithic structure Stonehenge. He indicated that they were responsible for the building of altars in that area. Radiocarbon dating of material in the parking lot imme-diately northwest of Stonehenge shows occupation as early as 8500 B.C. However, the small amount of organic samples found so far within the monument area itself, including a human burial, have been dated to 3020-2910 B.C.[45] Both dates are supportive of not only Cayce's 3000 B.C. date, but also the dispersion at the time of the final destruction of Atlantis (10,000 B.C.). Perhaps the lost tribes picked this part of England because it had previously been settled by their Atlantean Children of the Law of One an-cestors.

Although Cayce's chronology for some Biblical events supports the 3000 B.C. lost tribes date, it does not explain the problem with his dating of the Flood. If Noah was around during the middle Atlantean times, how could he be descended from Adam and Seth? B. Ernest Frejer, longtime Cayce researcher and author of *The Edgar Cayce Companion*, recommends caution in trying to give literal interpretations to Cayce's Biblical dates. Especially to those which use the term "before the Prince of Peace came" since he believes that in some instances Cayce was actually referring to the Christ Soul at an incarnation other than as Jesus.[46]

Robert Krajenke in his series *Edgar Cayce's Story of the Old Testament* explains that some of the events Cayce describes took place in the Spiritual Realm prior to the full descent of man into flesh. The Israelite Bible as we know it contains stories that are true, but more in terms of representing a spiritual truth. They cannot actually be placed in a reliable chronological order. As Krajenke puts it, "Moses (in writing the first five books of the Old Testament) was recounting the evolution of God's Spirit in the earth, telling the story in a highly condensed, symbolic language through which the finite mind of the Israelites could grasp an understanding of infinite happenings."[47]

Another way to look at it is to suspend the concepts of time and space and view the events of the Bible as occurring in simultaneously repeating cycles. There may have been several Noah's — one for each of the major eras in the history of mankind — performing the same spiritual discipline of preparation for catastrophe in order to preserve the purified lineage. Perhaps the 10,700 B.C. flood had a Noah also. If so, then the Tower of Babel, as Krajenke suggests, may have actually been a story about the Atlantean Sons of Belial causing a destruction that dispersed people all over the world. Perhaps then, the Jaredites of the *Book of Mormon* were actually migrating Atlanteans. The *Book of Mormon* does not date their migration, but only states that it occurred after the Tower of Babel. This would again allow for Cayce's 5500 B.C. Exodus period and, more importantly, for the Assyrian/Babylonian period "lost tribes" to have occurred in 3000 B.C.

So, did a "Lost Tribe" come to America in 3000 B.C.?

As we have shown, there is ample evidence for a literal interpretation of Cayce's 3000 B.C. lost tribes' story. There may have been two different migrations as the Mormon book tells us; one in 3000 B.C. by pre-Abraham Semites and one around 700-600 B.C. during the traditional lost tribes' period. The Cayce readings imply more than one ancient migration from the Holy Lands. Genetic evidence and several archaeological finds show that ancient America did have migrations from "Hebrew" lands. The chronology of mound building in America also fits Cayce's idea.

Academic archaeology will likely continue to snicker at the possibility that ancient Israelites or pre-Hebrew Semites came to America by boat. But now their snickers and derisive tactics stem from anxiety. Their long-maintained dogmas have collapsed. How much more "wrong" can they be? The genetic evidence — hard science at its best — has shown how people coming to ancient America came from places archaeologists have told us they couldn't have.

Cayce's endorsement of the Mormon story gives both his story and theirs greater credibility. It also means that many of the details he failed to provide may be available. From a scientific standpoint it seems that such a detailed account of ancient America as is contained in the *Book of Mormon* cannot and should not be totally discounted. Especially since it appears that even some of its most outlandish claims are now being verified through ongoing research in the field of archaeology. One thing is for certain. The more we learn through the continuing work of truly objective scientists, the more we realize that we have understood almost nothing about our past. As this new evidence emerges, Cayce's history of the Americas is becoming more and more credible. And even one of Cayce's most outlandish claims — the 3000 B.C. migration to America by "Lost Tribes — appears to be true.

Chapter 13

Evaluating Cayce's History of Ancient America

All the wrong notes are right!
Composer Charles Ives commenting to his copyist
after realizing that the "mistakes" weren't.

In Chapter 2 an overview of Cayce's history of ancient America was presented. The chapter ended with a list of 30 specific claims Cayce made that could be compared to the available evidence. In subsequent chapters, we reviewed the archaeological record and the emerging evidence especially focusing on post-1997 findings. Our findings on these 30 verifiable claims follow.

1. Parts of Utah, New Mexico, and Arizona were occupied 10 million years ago.

Cayce told us that these early people were more mental in nature than physical. Yet, he says, they could produce cave drawings. While the "age" of man is constantly being pushed back, *at present, no evidence exists that supports this idea. At the same time, we cannot say that it is untrue.*

2. Cave drawings in northwestern New Mexico remain from these very early people.

There are countless cave drawings in New Mexico. However it is highly unlikely that any that have been found date to 10 million years of age. ***Presently, no evidence supports this idea. At the same time, we cannot say that it is untrue.***

3. People were present in the Americas prior to 50,000 B.C. in the southwest and California.

Evidence clearly shows that the Americas were occupied far earlier than archaeologists ever suspected — especially in the very areas Cayce mentioned. ***Cayce was correct.***

4. Large, dangerous animals freely roamed the Americas prior to 50,000 B.C.

Some detractors have interpreted this idea as meaning Cayce said dinosaurs were present in 50,000 B.C. America. Cayce didn't say that. But ancient America was overrun with huge, very dangerous animals as clearly indicated in the archaeological record. ***Cayce was correct.***

5. A temple dedicated to the sun and moon was established near present-day Santa Barbara, California prior to 50,700 B.C.

Archaeological evidence shows that the area around Santa Barbara was probably occupied by 50,000 B.C. Indications are that these people were sun worshippers and we know that lunar alignments were important to them. Cayce did not claim that this temple would be found, only that it was built. ***The evidence shows that Cayce's statement was probably correct.***

6. People from Mu (and Atlantis) migrated to America at the time of the first disturbances in Mu and Atlantis (50,000 B.C.).

The evidence from mtDNA analyses and new carbon dating shows that America had migrations into it during this time frame. These people came from the west and probably also from the east. Cayce called the homelands of these people Mu and Atlantis. Despite claims to the contrary, there is an ancient historical record of both Mu and Atlantis. In fact, there is more evidence for the past existence of ancient civilizations that called themselves Mu and Atlantis than there is for the terms "Adena," "Hopewell," or "Mississippian." ***Cayce's claim appears to be correct.***

7. These people migrated to areas of Pennsylvania around 50,000 B.C.

Pennsylvania sites are among those that have shattered the Clovis barrier. Archaeologists have not yet dug to the 50,000 B.C. levels, but it appears that sites at least 30,000 years old are present. ***Cayce's claim is probably correct.***

8. They also migrated to areas of Ohio around 50,000 B.C.

As yet, there is no archaeological evidence to support this claim. It may be that, in order to find this evidence, mounds will have to be destroyed and, it seems logical that, if people were in Pennsylvania at this time, they were also in Ohio. ***At present, no evidence exists that supports this idea. But future evidence may well emerge that does support it.***

9. People from Mu established the custom of totem, or family trees, in Oregon prior to 50,000 B.C.

The ancient people that came to Oregon certainly came from the west. And totem poles were used in this area of America. But no evidence has emerged that Oregon was occupied this early. ***At present, no evidence exists that supports this idea.*** However, it must be recalled that, during the Ice Ages, the sea levels were at least 300 feet lower. Archaeologists are now examining the underwater areas of the continental shelf for evidence of early "Clovis" people moving down the coast on boats. These investigations could well turn up evidence of a much earlier occupation.

10. Women ruled during the time of the great Mu migration (50,000 B.C.).

While it has not been discussed previously, during the most remote times archaeology has investigated, throughout the world, women were revered. Hundreds of statues and figurines of a "Great Mother" or "Fertility Goddess" have been recovered worldwide — including in America. These date back to as far as 33,000 B.C. A comparable form of artifact showing men has never been found. The evidence is that, for whatever the reason, women in ancient times were held in reverence and probably made the most important decisions. ***Cayce's claim is probably correct.***

11. People from the South Seas came to the four corners area and began the "cliff dweller," or pueblo culture, about 50,000 B.C.

Despite the long-held belief that no one from the South Pacific ever migrated to ancient America, mtDNA evidence has shown that this did, in fact, probably occur. The probable dates of this migration extend back into Cayce's suggested timeframe. *Cayce's claim appears to be correct.*

12. In 28,000 B.C. some people from Atlantis migrated to Nevada and Colorado.

MtDNA analysis on the Navaho tribe has shown that the X type, which we have hypothesized to be "Atlantean," is present in some living tribal members. In addition, evidence shows that, the geographical area indicated by Cayce, was occupied by 28,000 B.C. *Cayce's claim is probably correct.*

13. People coming "across the Pacific" entered ancient America in 28,000 B.C.

The mtDNA analyses on Native Americans definitely show migrations from the other side of the Pacific to America in 28,000 B.C. This could well be the "horde" of nomads crossing Beringia that archaeologists, prior to 1997, believed came in 9500 B.C. Cayce didn't mention Beringia, nor did he state that these people came by boat. He simply stated that they came from "across the Pacific." *Cayce's claim is correct.*

14. People coming from China entered ancient America in 28,000 B.C.

Once again, mtDNA analyses on Native Americans indicate that migrations of people carrying the "Chinese" haplotype came to America probably around 28,000 B.C. This haplotype (the B type) may well be the genetic heritage of people from the first occupied place on Earth — Mu. *Cayce's claim is correct.*

15. The Iroquois, especially those of noble blood, were pure Atlantean.

The mtDNA analyses on Native Americans who are Iroquois in origin as well as on ancient remains found in the traditional Iroquois land show the X type. We hypothesize that the X haplogroup originated in Atlantis. *Cayce's claim is probably correct.*

16. Pure Atlanteans also migrated to Iberia, especially to the Pyrenees Mountains.

The X type has been found in Iberia as well as in the areas surrounding the Pyrenees. In fact, it has been found everywhere Cayce predicted including the Gobi and the Middle East. *Cayce's claim appears to be correct.*

17. An Atlantean priestess who had moved to Egypt visited southwestern America sometime around 10,000 B.C.

As mentioned previously, the X type has been found in the southwest. A remarkable underground shrine containing Egyptian religious artifacts was reportedly found and "looted" in 1909 near the Grand Canyon— in the area Cayce stated a temple was built. A 1991 find by professional archaeologists in that area appears to describe the identical underground site, emptied of its treasures. ***Cayce's statement appears to be correct.***

18. Descendants of Atlanteans and others who had originally moved to the Yucatan in about 10,000 B.C., migrated north to begin the Mound Builder culture. This occurred sometime after 3,000 B.C.

The evidence is overwhelming for this part of Cayce's story. ***Cayce was correct.***

19. The mounds were replicas of the Yucatan, Atlantis, and Gobi experiences.

American mounds were built to represent the Yucatan alignments to stars and solar events. The Belt of Orion pattern and the triangular "Cosmic Hearth" are both found in numerous mound sites. In addition, American mounds are identical to those found near the Gobi. The presence of the X haplotype in the Gobi also strengthens this connection. Finally, several American mounds and earthworks appear to accurately reflect ancient Atlantis. ***Cayce was correct.***

20. Remnants of the "Lost Tribes" came to ancient America in 3000 B.C. in boats. They went first to the southernmost US.

The evidence at Watson Brake in Louisiana appears to indicate an intrusion of an ancient pre-Hebrew group entering ancient America via the water in 3000 B.C. Not long after this incursion, sacrificial altars began to be used in Central America and later in the heart of mound builder areas. ***Cayce's statement appears to be correct.***

21. After staying for a brief time in the southern part of America, the Lost Tribes moved to the area around Mexico City where they impacted the pyramid-building culture already present.

The appearance of the Star of David at Uxmal, Hebrew-like features at other sites, carvings depicting "bearded Middle Eastern men," and the gradual establishment of altar sacrifices appear to show an ancient pre-Hebrew influence near Mexico City. The sudden disappearance of the Watson Brake people just prior to these events also supports the idea. *Cayce's statement appears to be correct.*

22. Portions of the Lost Tribes then migrated north merging with other groups to become the Mound Builders in Ohio.

The sudden appearance of Poverty Point prior to the Ohio mound builder culture, with the known "Mexican" influence at Poverty Point, shows that groups migrating from the Mexico area played a pivotal role in development of the mound builder culture. Since there is evidence that "Lost Tribes" played a role in Mexican pyramid-builder culture, this claim is probably valid. *Cayce's statement appears to be correct.*

23. Some Israelites escaped the captivity by fleeing to southwestern America from the West across the Pacific. They crossed through areas (perhaps utilizing islands) that were once a part of Mu. They established temples in the southwest. They are referred to as a "lost" or "strayed tribe."

The existence of Zodiac Ridge and the Los Lunas Decalogue Stone show that this claim has validity. The research by the Mormon scholars also suggests this is true. *Cayce's statement is probably correct.*

24. The mound builders were a mixture of influences from Atlantis, Mu, Lost Tribes, and others.

The shape of the mounds, the reflection of Atlantis in their construction, the appearance of sacrificial altars in them, the burials and the artifacts discovered in them points to this as genuine. *Cayce's statement appears to be correct.*

25. The Norse made many trips to ancient America and actually settled here.

Despite the long-time claims of archaeology that the Norse sagas were fictional, evidence shows this happened just as written. *Cayce was correct.*

26. Some of the Norse merged with the mound builders.

There are a number of tantalizing clues on this assertion. The presence of iron in some mounds, the genuine claims that some natives were white with red hair, and the discovery of Norse artifacts shows that it was true. *Cayce was correct.*

27. The location of the Norse settlement in America, Vinland, was placed in Rhode Island, Massachusetts, and Connecticut by Cayce.

While Leif Ericson's settlement was probably in Newfoundland, the land of Vinland is not reflected in the surroundings of this settlement. The Norse sagas tell us that Vinland was a far larger territory. Descriptions in the sagas relate that the land of Vinland was similar to the areas Cayce described. In addition, the discovery of Norse artifacts (coins) in these areas shows that Vinland extended at least to the U.S. Atlantic seaboard. *Cayce was correct.*

28. Providence, Salem, and Newport are specifically named as modern cities where Vinland was located.

The Newport Tower is a possible Norse settlement, however, it is quite uncertain when this structure was built. Coins and a few artifacts found in nearby areas are tantalizing clues. However, this remains an unsettled issue. *At present, there is no convincing evidence that this statement is true.*

29. The Norse reached Montana in the 1500s via the Great Lakes. An artifact, a knife supposedly belonging to Eric the Red, was recovered in Wisconsin around 1940 that would prove this excursion. In addition, a Norse excursion reached Minnesota.

The presence of Norse mooring stones extending into the west suggests deep Norse excursions into America. The many runestones also suggest a series of Norse explorations into the heart of ancient America including into Minnesota and Wisconsin. The genuine Norse swords that have been recovered come from questionable sources. The statement of Eric the Red's knife being found appears to have come from a prank played by archaeologists. *Portions of this statement appear to be valid, but other parts are incorrect.*

30. Cayce mentions the Five Great Nations, Chief Powhatan, and a meeting in the "Octagon" by the Ohio River.

This statement has not been previously discussed. Powhatan was a chief of the Virginia-area tribe that later took on his name. A great meeting was held prior to the arrival of the white settlers, but the location and date of this meeting is not known. There was, at one time, an "octagon" earthwork by the Ohio River at Grave Creek, West Virginia. This earthwork was very obscure and few people knew about it. Whether this is the site Cayce was referring to is unknown. *However, there is no evidence showing that Cayce was correct.*

Summary

Of Cayce's 30 specific statements, 23 (or seventy-seven percent) of them have enough support to be considered accurate. Another six statements are, as yet, not supportable by evidence, but could be verified in the future. Only one statement, the discovery of the knife of Eric the Red in Wisconsin, appears to be wrong. Thus, of all of Cayce's seemingly impossible statements about ancient America, only 3% are definitely wrong. Of the remainder, 77% have been supported by scientific research, and the 20% that remain could be verified in the future.

It's remarkable indeed to comprehend the astonishing accuracy of this humble man, Edgar Cayce. Had Cayce's history been shown to be predominantly inaccurate, we could probably dismiss many of his other claims. Not necessarily all claims, for it must be recalled that his health readings have been shown to be over 80% accurate. But some of his claims about the history of humanity, as well as our connection to the spiritual world, are just as astonishing as the ancient history he related.

Since we have now shown that Cayce's history of America is substantially supported, it's appropriate to go one more step. We want to briefly explore another area of scientific investigation that has been making inroads into understanding Cayce's deep ideas. This relates to humankind's connection to the spiritual world, and how the mounds and sacred sites were utilized in the pursuit of the spiritual world. First we will briefly look at the use of sacred sites and mound rituals.

Chapter 14

Magic Machines of Earth

Who shall ascend into the hill of the Lord? Or who shall stand in his holy place?
He that hath clean hands, and a pure heart; who hath not lifted
up his soul unto vanity, nor sworn deceitfully.
Psalms 24: 3-4

The secret of magic — that is, its real essence — is in the manipulation of symbols.
William R. Romain (2000) *Mysteries of the Hopewell*

The mounds and marvelous earthworks scattered across ancient America were constructed and used over a vast time period of nearly 5,500 years. As we have seen, the early mound eras (Poverty Point, Adena, and Hopewell) certainly represented an effort to do more than make a resting place for the dead. The complex walkways built over many miles were intended to channel and control the movements of people from one sacred area to another. The circular, square, octagonal, and horseshoe earthworks served as key areas for rituals. And the high mounds were places where one could commune with God.

The ancients duplicated the specific shapes of mounds and earthworks at one site after another. These shapes were important symbols representing something far deeper in meaning than modern-day archaeology has understood. The creation of these symbols in physically real earth-formed images permitted a controlled ritual to be performed. This ritual involved a process of mental preparation followed by actions involving the earthen symbols. This ritualistic manipulation of symbols was, in essence, a magical process. The mounds and earthworks were magic machines of earth. They were places where one could seek God.

Seeking God in High Places

Mountaintops, hilltops, mesas, or simply an area of raised land in an open plain were favored locations upon which ancient people constructed their sacred sites. The Incas of the Andes believed that the higher the site, the more intense was its quality of sacredness (*huaca*). The Choctaw traditional name for ancient mounds is *Nanne-yah*, literally the "hills or mounts of God." Usually, the ancient people built an additional structure on these high places, from simple piles of rocks (reminiscent of the Tibetan *obo* heaps and Inca *apoceta* piles) to elaborate terraced altars and temples (such as the temple of Natchez on a truncated mound with elaborate steps of gradual ascent).

These high sites were used for festivals, ceremonies, and initiations. Individual and clan offerings, libations, sacrifices, and tithes were brought to these sites. These were offered to the forces of Nature, or to their gods, or to the Supreme God, or in many cases, to one's ancestors. Usually, these offerings were intended to give praise and honor as a form of worship and devotion. (See figure 136.)

Figure 136
The "Green Corn" ceremony, thanking the Great Spirit with an offering of the first harvest.
From Schoolcraft (1851).

In some cases, there were much more profound purposes underlying the rituals. A sacred ritual could be a way to gain guidance for individuals and entire tribes. Some rituals allowed participants to move back and forth between this world and the realm of spirits. And some rituals led to deeper experiences; perhaps even communication with God. The final chapter in this book explores this aspect of rituals.

Sacred Sites As Special Places

A high place often became sacred by some event or sign that the people or their ancestors associated with the site. For example, the Cherokee tell an amazing story about a sacred mound at the head of the Little Tennessee River at Nikwasi in North Carolina (see figure 137). In the 1800s, they related that long ago a powerful tribe from the south invaded their lands and defeated Cherokee warriors at several sites before reaching Nikwasi. An attack was made on the defending Nikwasi warriors, which resulted in another Cherokee defeat and a hasty retreat. When the Cherokee were running by the mound, a stranger suddenly appeared in their midst. He stopped them in their tracks, staring at them and yelling to the Chief to pull his men back so he could defeat the attackers. The Cherokee assumed that the stranger was the Chief of a northern Cherokee town coming to their aid. As the Cherokee warriors reached the mound, **a doorway sud-**

Figure 137
The Nikwasi Mound in Franklin, North Carolina. Photo by H. Trotter 1890.
From — Bureau of American Ethnology (1897).

**denly opened on its side and hundreds of armed and painted warriors
rushed out.** They were recognized as the *Immortals* — powerful spirits. As
soon as the Immortals reached the edge of the settlement and faced the
enemy, they became nearly invisible. But their weapons were apparently
physically real as the arrows and tomahawks they flung at the attacking
force hit their mark. The attackers fell back and hid behind rocks and trees,
but the arrows of the Immortals *went around* the trees and rocks. When only
five attackers were alive, they began crying for mercy and the attack ceased.
Today the Cherokee call this site, *"Where they cried."* The Immortals were
watched as they silently reentered the mound and the doorway disappeared.
The Cherokee tell this as a genuine historical story, not as a myth.[1] A similar
mound builder myth relates to a mound in Mississippi. (See figure 138.)
The Choctaw believe that their ancestors *emerged* from the *Nanih Waiya*
mound in the remote past at a time the world was covered with water.

Some places become sacred because of significant events that happened
there. For example, Jacob's vision of a ladder to heaven occurred at what is
now the sacred site of Bethel. Most of the Native American sacred sites
have a long-term verbal history associated with them. They are places where
their ancestors had one profound experience after another. In modern times,
sites where verifiable religious apparitions occur continue to be deemed
as sacred. These include Fatima, Guadalupe, Lourdes, Medjugorje, and
Zeitoun (Egypt).

Sacred sites often have ongoing reports of unusual happenings. A phenomenon of nature, a star alignment, or a specific planetary movement
could have been observed at a key time from a specific location. When

---

Figure 138
The *Nanih Waiya* mound in Mississippi, place of the Choctaw emergence.
Photo — University of Mississippi (1914).

these phenomena occurred in combination with a profound human experience, the site was said to have "power." For example, the Big Horn Medicine Wheel was used to observe specific pre-dawn star risings. These risings were deemed as signals from God that announced the beginning of ceremonies. In the case of the prehistoric Cheyenne, the signals from God seen at the Big Horn Medicine Wheel were messages to their priests to begin the Massum Ceremony — an extended ritual of communion with God.[2, 3] In another well-known report, the famous Chief Red Plume spent four days and nights at the Medicine Wheel during a vision quest. He was taken *inside* the mountain by spiritual beings who imparted a special wisdom to him.[3] In brief, some locations became sacred because odd mental states developed when one lingered in the area or because extremely unusual events seemed to regularly occur there.[2, 3]

Some high places were erected to be ideal locations for observing cyclical events like the solstices or the equinox. The timing of rituals was often determined by these cycles. The Mississippian Era mounds were especially erected for this purpose.

Smoke was often an important element in the rituals conducted at sacred sites. Many ancient people considered rising smoke to be a means for carrying their offerings to the unseen heavens above. Thus, altars and sacred fires were typically used in high places. Large quantities of incense could be used in altar fires, perhaps because the scent raised the people's consciousness and touched the gods or ancestors' senses. An alternative explanation relates that smoke gives spirits an actual physical medium into which they can manifest.[2]

The mound builders employed fire and smoke in their ceremonies. The smoking of tobacco was, of course, an important personal ritual. But the use of altars was also widespread. Not only were these altar ceremonies conducted on these sites, but also *within* them. As the Egyptian and Central American pyramids have inner chambers, so, too, did many of the North American mounds. For example, in the King Mounds at Wickliffe, Kentucky, three rectangular altars were found in chambers inside the mounds.

Connecting The Upper, Middle, And Under Worlds

Mounds were a means of rising above the physical world. They were used to connect the physical realm to the spiritual. They reflect a common sense belief that God, heaven, and the forces for good are above us; and conversely, evil, the underworld, and the forces of darkness are below us. We live in between these two worlds. Some rituals, of course, were conducted *within* the earth. The Kivas of the southwest, used in the traditional ways of the Ancient Ones, served a similar function. In the Kivas, a "spirit tunnel," called *sipapu*, was bored into the earth. This small tunnel was a representation of the place of emergence of the Ancient Ones into the physical world. During the ritual, one's consciousness could move through the *sipapu* and temporarily enter the spiritual world from which life emerged.[3]

Not only were the high mounds and earthworks sacred, but *the journey to the mound* was an important part of the ritual. The journey could symbolically foreshadow the impending connection with the unseen forces. At the Portsmouth Earthworks, for example, there were long, embanked walkways connecting the various ritual complexes. These crossed the Ohio River, which probably involved a cleansing process. Rituals at the complex site of Newark, with its circles, squares, octagon, and parallel walls, certainly involved controlled movements between various areas. The movement from one complex to another through these walled walkways was a literal journey and mental preparation and attitude were important components.

The mound builder rituals obviously involved a complex mental and physical preparation. It is known that stressing the body through extended periods utilizing fasting, sweating, dancing, chanting, and meditating was an integral part of the preparation process. Only the mind could take a physical being to the realms of the non-physical, and the rituals that took the physical body to its limits allowed a release of consciousness.[2, 3] Science has uncovered a great deal of information about these changes in consciousness. In the final chapter we'll explore what has been found and the implications.

When truly released from the physical body, an individual's consciousness could move into the spiritual world where one's ancestors, the unseen spiritual forces working in the universe, and perhaps even God could be accessed. Creating this "mental bridge" required that the seeker shift from normal consciousness to one more capable of perceiving non-physical realms. In addition to the physical rituals that were used, special drinks, herbs, and foods were employed. These substances loosened normal consciousness, sometimes creating a death-like experience that allowed the seeker to temporarily leave physical reality and reach into the other realms. Edgar Cayce's readings tell us that the ancient Egyptians designed and used "potions" to assist them in achieving their altered states of consciousness. So, too, did the mound builders.

The most common substance used by the mound builders was a harsh and potent tobacco. As discussed earlier, the high nicotine content in it could produce a stupor. Another well-known "food" used by both Central and North American Indians to induce an altered state of consciousness was peyote (*peyotl* in Aztec). It is a cactus species (*Lophophora williamsii*) growing mostly along the Rio Grande River (which flows from Colorado, through New Mexico, along the border between Texas and Mexico, and empties into the Gulf of Mexico). Peyote contains the hallucinogen mescaline. Ingestion of mescaline produces vivid, colorful hallucinations— often involving "spiritual" components. Other hallucinogenic substances frequently used in the spiritual rituals of the mound builders included various mushrooms (containing psilocybin or bufotenin), Morning Glory seeds (containing an LSD-amide), and a host of other plants.[4]

Elaborate rituals were developed around the ingestion of hallucinogenics. Many of these rituals took entire nights to complete. The shaman guiding the rituals took care to produce altered states influenced by beneficial forces. Since the mind of a participant was vulnerable to both good and evil spirits (once freed from its bodily home) careful preparation of the individual was important.

How shaman came to understand which plants produced the desired effect is not completely understood. In many of the indigenous tribes along the Amazon River, shamans achieved altered states of consciousness using various plant extracts found in the jungle. In these states they say that they can "see" beyond the normal physical world into the essence behind manifested life. For example, in his book *Cosmic Serpent*, Jeremy Narby explains: "Amazonian shamans have been preparing *ayahuasca* for millennia. The brew is a necessary combination of two plants, which must be boiled together for hours. The first contains a hallucinogenic substance, dimethyltryptamine, which also seems to be secreted by the human brain; but this hallucinogen has no effect when swallowed, because a stomach enzyme called monoamine oxidase blocks it. The second plant, however, contains several substances that inactivate this precise stomach enzyme, allowing the hallucinogen to reach the brain. So here are people without electron microscopes who choose, among some 80,000 Amazonian plant species, the leaves of a bush containing a hallucinogenic brain hormone, which they combine with a vine containing substances that inactivate an enzyme of the digestive tract, which would otherwise block the hallucinogenic effect. And they do this to modify their consciousness."[5] When asked how they know which plants to select, they simply reply, " The plants tell us." Perhaps this statement refers to knowledge acquired in a psychic state.

In addition to drug-induced altered states, many cultures created deathlike experiences that allowed the participants to escape physical consciousness for a time, yet return relatively sane and with profound insights from the unseen worlds. Many of these rituals would be considered today as torture, such as the Sioux Sun Dance, and the Mandan hangings. But other groups, such as the Algonquians, used mandalas and a series of symbols to aid initiates. Almost all American natives used chanting and whirling movements, much like the whirling Sufi mystics of Islam.

The Secret Purpose of Mound Rituals

Mounds and their associated earthworks were shaped into sacred, interconnected symbols. The rituals that were enacted utilizing these earthen representations were a means of interacting with the true essence underlying the symbols. For example, if a mound had been built to represent the spiritual realm of the ancestors, a proper ritual would propel the consciousness of the participants into that realm. The ritual would also "energize" the ancestors themselves and make them receptive.

Rituals literally manipulate symbols. This is, according to ancient sources, the very essence of magic. *The magic, if it can really be called that, is the opening of passageways between the physical world and the spiritual world.* When used in the appropriate way, mounds and earthworks could be used to open the portals between different realms of reality. Most people view this process as essentially a completely mental one. It is an expansion of consciousness that comes from practice, motivations, and specific changes in brain chemistry caused by repetitive body movements, chanting, or sometimes the ingestion of hallucinogens. However, shaman assert that the portals opened through rituals and the spiritual energies they release are very, very real.[6]

In the world of the ancient Hopewell mound builders, mirrors, specific mushrooms, smoke, and animal costumes were utilized in rituals. In addition, it was extremely important that the ritual be conducted at the exact time it was most effective. This moment in time was often at night, and the movements of the moon were a critical factor. In addition, there was an exact place that had to be utilized. The Circle and Octagon at Newark demonstrates this. From inside the gigantic, connected Circle and Octagon, there is no direct path out — nor one that leads inside. The Octagon's 8 sides are not connected, but rectangular mounds block the line of sight at each opening. To enter or leave the earthwork, one has to go *around* these "gatekeeper" mounds. In the Hopewell belief system, spirits can only travel in straight lines. Therefore, whatever spiritual forces were temporarily unleashed inside the Circle and Octagon during rituals remained there.[7]

Portsmouth

The Portsmouth complex of Hopewell earthworks (see figure 139) is one that may demonstrate how rituals were conducted — and perhaps a bit of the meaning underlying them. As related in an earlier chapter, the circular earthworks in Kentucky across the Ohio River from Portsmouth appear to be a remarkably accurate representation of Atlantis. According to Cayce, Atlantis was destroyed, in part, because of conflicts between a group of people who tried to maintain a connection to their ultimate spiritual source with an opposing group who embraced pleasure and desires in the physical world. Prior to the final destruction of Atlantis, many groups fled to various parts of the world. The Children of the Law of One, those who sought to maintain a spiritual life, went to the Middle East, Africa, parts of Europe, and the Americas. Some of these people in the Middle East became part of the "chosen ones" and later migrated to the British Isles and America (becoming known as the Lost Tribes). The mound builder cultures resulted from a combination of Atlanteans, the "Lost Tribes" (some of whom were descended from the Children of the Law of One who escaped Atlantis before 10,000 B.C.), and people who were already present in the land. And, as related by Cayce, the mounds were built as representations of the Atlantean, the Yucatan, and Gobi experiences. This could be the exact story symbolized at Portsmouth.

The ritual utilizing the Portsmouth complex may have begun at the Atlantis-like earthworks atop the central mound (A). The probable day and time the ritual was begun was at the Winter Solstice sunrise. (From the main complex in Portsmouth, the Winter Solstice sunrise would occur directly over the circular Atlantis earthworks.) Modern man's ancient appearance in Atlantis would be acknowledged there with an understanding that it occurred when spiritual consciousness forced its way into physical matter. The ongoing conflict each human faces in life — the struggle between "good" and "evil" — would be demonstrated prior to leaving this circular earthwork. A procession would be led *down* the embanked walkway to the river almost 2 miles in distance (B). This would symbolize the spiritual descent many souls experienced in Atlantis prior to the sinking of the homeland. As represented by the Winter Solstice, this would also symbolize the lowest point in humanity's spiritual decline. The river itself represents the deluge of Atlantis, the cleansing of souls, and the actual physical migration of survivors prior to the final destruction (C). One wonders exactly how the river was physically crossed, but perhaps every individual participating in the ritual had to swim the river at least once. Reaching the other side of the river, the procession would now move uphill through the embanked walkway (D). This 3-mile *ascent* was steep in places and may have symbolized mankind's spiritual and physical climb after the deluge of Atlantis. Reaching the main complex in Portsmouth, a series of rituals would be performed. As the procession moved out of the embanked walkway toward the circular earthwork containing the two horseshoe-shaped formations, they first moved by and under a natural mound oriented toward the Winter Solstice sunset (E). From this station, a ritual that prepared participants for entry into the sacred circle was performed. This ritual would serve as a reminder of their ultimate source and ultimate destiny. The sacred circle (F) contains several elements highly similar to Stonehenge. These include the "U" or horseshoe shaped embankments, an outer circle, and "causeways." This area of the complex could well represent several events from the Cayce story. Cayce stated that Atlantean descendants — the Lost Tribes — went to Avebury and Stonehenge as well as to the Americas. Cayce also stated that some of the Lost Tribes entered America from the west, as did several other groups. The parallel walls that enter the site from the west (G) may symbolize this event. Within the sacred center of the main complex (F), rituals that deal with the present world were conducted. These may have been highly individualized and were based on the personal needs and developmental level of each individual.

At sunset on the Winter Solstice, the ceremony would continue by moving toward the sunset through the walled embankment oriented to the southwest (H). This aspect of the ceremony symbolized the inevitable movement back to the original source of life. It was a gradual descent toward the river representing the physical decline and death of the physical

Figure 139
Portsmouth map labeled according to possible ritual chronology. *From — Squier & Davis.*

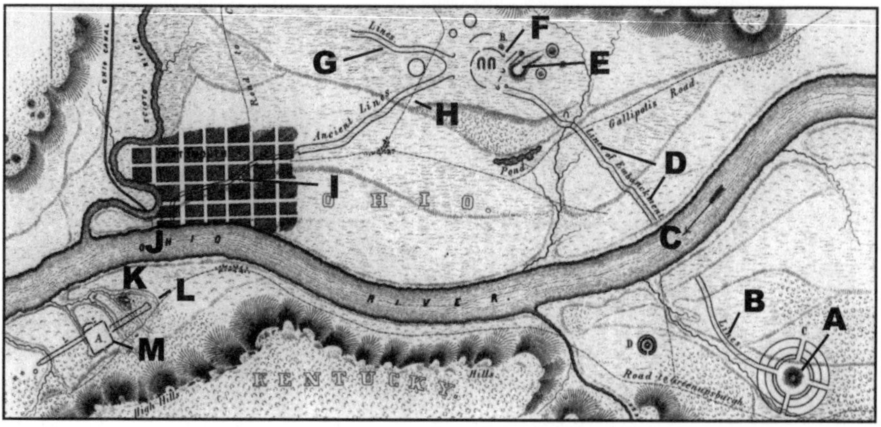

body (I). The crossing of the river, probably well after darkness descended, (J) represented the crossing of the spirit back to the spiritual world. This crossing must have been disturbing and perhaps frightening to some individuals. It is likely that some form of hallucinogenic substance was taken prior to reaching the river.

Since each soul must find its own way after death, there was no walled embankment leading the procession from the other side of the river (K). Each individual had to find his or her way to the small opening (L) leading to the square representing the spiritual world (M). (See figure 140.)

Inside the squared embankment, the "Cosmic Hearth," the portal through which souls enter the earth plane, was shown (N). This was formed by three mounds arranged in a triangular formation to represent the Belt of Orion. They were placed at an opening of the square oriented to the Summer Solstice sunset. One additional "extension" of the spiritual world was experienced (O). The exact meaning of this extension is unclear, but once it is exited through several small openings (P), there is "nowhere" else to go. That is, there are no other earthworks and it points toward the setting sun of the Winter Solstice. Interestingly, a deep ravine (Q) was located just before the small exit openings. Thus, this could represent a "death" or journey from which there was no return.

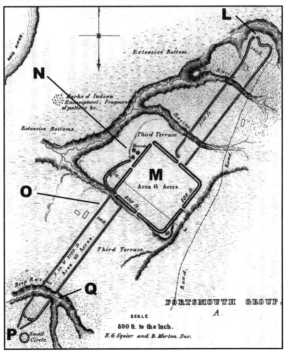

Figure 140
Large survey of the square earthworks in Kentucky where the parallel embankments from the main complex at Portsmouth lead. In figure 139, these earthworks are labelled "M" and are found in the lower left corner. *From Squier & Davis (1848).*

The Body as the Temple
& the Head as the High Place

Achieving God-consciousness through rituals and the "manipulation of symbols" was a means of "going within" oneself to move consciousness beyond self. From his trance state Cayce stated, "For the body is indeed the temple of the living God, and He has promised to meet you

Figure 141
Mounds as "high places." *From Southeastern Archaeology Center, Natl. Park Service.*

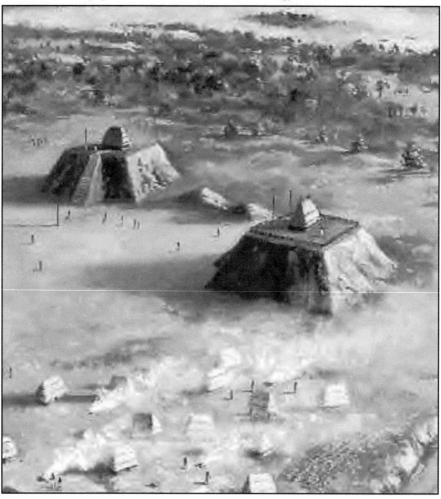

there, in the holy of holies, in the Mount within (reading 1152-2)." In 882-1 Cayce said, "'There I shall meet you, in the Mount of yourself.' For your body indeed is the temple of the living God; there He may meet you as you turn within." In reading 707-6 we have, "Remember all that has been given as to the manner in which the individual finds self? Did Moses receive direction other than by the period in the Mount? Did Samuel receive other than by meditating within his own closet? Did David not find more in meditating within the valley and the cave? Did not the Master in the Mount and in the garden receive the answers of those directing forces?" "Why, you may ask, did the Master love to be in Galilee when the house of the Lord His God was in Jerusalem? Why did He love to be alone in the Mount?" [3357-2]

Going to the Mount of God, a realm that lies within all of us, is the ritual by which we find God-consciousness. It is an *ascending* attunement, as going *up* on the Mount implies. It requires that we raise ourselves out of finite, individual consciousness into infinite, universal consciousness. The mounds and their incredible earthworks were utilized as a means of attaining a "God-consciousness."

From Mysterious Electromagnetic Forces To The Cutting Edge of Science

In Cayce's reading 440-16, a fascinating vision is given about Moses' and Joshua's original experience on the Holy Mount: "They had seen the Lord Jehovah descend into the Mount, they had seen the Mount so electrified by the presence of the **od** of the people and **ohm** of the Omnipotent to such an extent that no living thing could remain on the Mount, save those two [Moses & Joshua] who had been cleansed by their pouring out of themselves to God, in the cleansing of their bodies, in the cleansing of their minds."

Cayce's reference to the "od of the people" refers to a term coined by Reichenbach (1788-1869) to explain an unseen force in nature that manifests itself in magnetism, hypnotism, and light, called the "odic force." *Od*, most likely derived from the Greek word *hodos* means path or way, and is used in such modern electrical words as *anode* and *cathode*. (indicating poles of an electromagnetic field or ray as seen in a cathode ray tube). Cayce's use of the word "Ohm" is most probably referring to the term coined by one of Reichenbach's contemporaries, Georg Simon Ohm (1789-1854). This term is used today as a measurement of electrical resistance. However, the way Cayce uses the term seems to equate ohm directly with electricity.

Therefore, we could translate this Mount experience as, "the magnetism of the people's hearts and minds seeking God so long and so hard had attracted the Omnipotent to descend upon the Mount. The nature of the Omnipotent is best equated to the powers of electricity, powers which may destroy or enlighten, depending on how pure the conductor (Moses)." In short, as the biblical adage relates, "seek, and ye shall find." But the effect of what is "found" in seeking rituals is largely dependent on the motivations of the seeker. This is an old idea that appears to have been well understood by the mound builders.

Cayce's idea of electromagnetic forces being involved in seeking God has also been proposed by many others. But this idea is currently receiving an important modern slant — substantial research has nearly confirmed it. This area of investigation is so far on the cutting edge of science, that few people are even aware of its existence. Even fewer people are aware of its significance. As the ending chapter in this book, it is to this amazing body of research that we turn.

Figure 142
Illustration of how Emerald Mound was utilized.
From Southeastern Archaeology Center, Natl. Park Service.

Chapter 15

Neuroscience & Cayce
Incredible Confirmations
With Profound Implications

Sedlak describes "Life" as a process, quantum in nature,
expressing an electromagnetic coupling of chemical reactions
with electronic processes on a protein-nucleic semi-conducting substrate.
Nancy Kolenda (2001) Editor, *Frontier Perspectives*

I f after reading the above quote, you completely understand it and have no questions, you don't need to finish reading this chapter. You may revel in your deep level of scientific knowledge and relax. For those of you who continue to the end of this chapter, don't be concerned. We aren't going to go into a complicated explanation of it. We are, however, going to discuss Cayce's ideas of life and tie them to an understanding of the mounds and their "secret purpose" as mentioned in the prior chapter.

In the previous chapter, a Cayce reading was presented that described how the Holy Mount was "electrified" by the presence of God and how Moses and Joshua had "cleansed" themselves. This cleansing, it was said, magnetically "attracted" God to them. The reading also stated that the Holy Temple where we can meet God was located "inside" us. This statement is similar to the famous statement of Jesus, "the kingdom of heaven is within you." We believe that many mound sites and earthworks served as a means of accessing this "kingdom."

Brain Science & Rituals

Science has learned a great deal about the chemical and electrical changes that occur in the body and brain during certain rituals and "consciousness altering" practices. These research findings have essentially verified that an individual's brain chemistry changes substantially as awareness — consciousness — moves into what are sometimes described as "altered states." Several specific areas in the brain are implicated with a host of unusual experiences including out-of-body episodes, near-death experiences, visions, ecstatic raptures, sightings of ghosts and apparitions, god-consciousness, and even religious conviction.

While the brain is essentially a biological organ, it produces both an electrical field and an electromagnetic field. Today, neuroscientists can record the electrical activity of even a small part of a single brain cell. When one realizes that the average human has 100 *billion* brain cells each averaging less than 1/10,000th of an inch in diameter, this should be seen as quite a feat. Even more astonishing is the recent development of technology that can "read" the electromagnetic field of an individual. Each of us produces a unique electromagnetic field that changes as we develop different moods or enter different mental states. It is believed that some time in the near future, the equipment that reads the human electromagnetic field (called an magnetoencephalograph) will be able to produce a compete personality profile and perhaps uncover one's basic character in just seconds.[1]

Most people have a poor understanding of electromagnetic energy. This isn't surprising since science doesn't really understand it, either. One way to think of it is that it is the "glue" that holds the physical world together and enables us to see it. The Electromagnetic Energy Spectrum is how science typically describes the vast range of this force. (See figure 143.)

Electromagnetic energy (EM) vibrates at rates called "frequencies" and different frequencies have different characteristics. At one extreme, the frequencies vibrate quickly, while on the other extreme, the frequencies are slower. The human visual system is tuned to "pick up" the vibrations of EM energy in a very narrow range. This range, making up less than 5% of the entire EM spectrum, is called the "Visible Light Spectrum."

In actuality, we exist in a literal sea of EM energy. Most of the "substance" in this sea is invisible to us. But it is there nonetheless. For example, some animals can see infrared heat because their visual system is tuned to pick up those frequencies from the EM spectrum.

Electromagnetic Effects on the Brain

For at least 300 years, scientists have called the idea that magnetic fields can influence human behavior, thoughts, and emotions sheer "quackery."[1] In the 1970s and 1980s, a great deal of research was conducted that contradicted this prevailing belief. But scientists continued to insist that magnetic fields could not produce effects on the brain. Then, in 1992, the mineral magnetite was discovered in the human brain. Magnetite is also found in the brains of homing pigeons and is known to serve as the "compass" that they use for navigation.[2] Quite simply, magnetite aligns itself to whatever magnetic or electromagnetic field is present. When it "aligns" it begins vibrating in accordance with the frequency of the prevailing field. This is a physical process operating much like a magnet can move iron filings on a sheet of paper. In brain cells, magnetite crystals are suspended in fluid. Research now shows that the vibration of magnetite within specific brain cells causes electrical changes in areas of the brain — and thereby changes mood and produces experiences. There have been nearly 4,000 scientific articles published on the effects of electromagnetic fields on humans and animal behavior.[1, 2]

Figure 143

The Electromagnetic Energy Spectrum as it is typically depicted in textbooks in Introductory Physics and Psychology. We perceive only a very narrow portion of this reality. If the EM Spectrum represents the spiritual world, the realm of "Heaven" and God would be on the far right hand side. Cosmic rays were produced in the original act of creation — The "Big Bang." They are continually produced by stars. Humankind lives in the "middle world" of this spectrum— between the Upper World (heaven) and the Lower World. *From Grand Illusions (1994).*

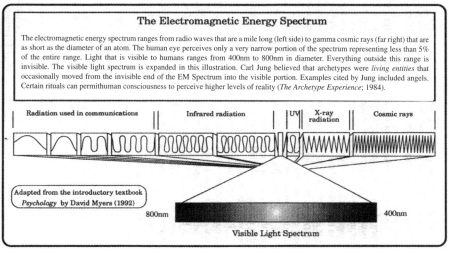

The Electromagnetic Energy Spectrum

The electromagnetic energy spectrum ranges from radio waves that are a mile long (left side) to gamma cosmic rays (far right) that are as short as the diameter of an atom. The human eye perceives only a very narrow portion of the spectrum representing less than 5% of the entire range. Light that is visible to humans ranges from 400nm to 800nm in diameter. Everything outside this range is invisible. The visible light spectrum is expanded in this illustration. Carl Jung believed that archetypes were *living entities* that occasionally moved from the invisible end of the EM Spectrum into the visible portion. Examples cited by Jung included angels. Certain rituals can permit human consciousness to perceive higher levels of reality (*The Archetype Experience*; 1984).

Radiation used in communications | Infrared radiation | UV | X-ray radiation | Cosmic rays

Adapted from the introductory textbook *Psychology* by David Myers (1992)

800nm   400nm

Visible Light Spectrum

It has long been recognized that sacred sites were often found in areas where strong magnetic anomalies occurred.[1, 2, 3] In recent years, researchers have found that many sacred mound sites are located on top of powerful magnetic anomalies.[4] Another recent finding is that, during an eclipse, gravity actually changes (although no one understands why). This is referred to as the Allais Effect.[1] This could be an explanation for why charting the moon's movements over 18.61 years was important to the mound builders.[2] Rituals performed during eclipses could potentially take advantage of gravity changes.

The earth's magnetic field constantly swirls and changes as it is affected by the sun. But the side of the earth facing away from the sun has a fairly stable field. Researchers have shown that a stable background of electromagnetic energy is essential for producing certain experiences. In the midst of this stable background, a sudden shift in magnetic fields can lead to profound changes in consciousness. This is something the ancients appeared to know.

Michael Persinger in Canada has done some of the most important research that has shown how magnetic fields can influence behavior. The implications of this research are more profound than most people understand. Persinger has applied small, weak magnetic fields to different brain areas in hundreds of college students. He has been able to produce visionary experiences, religious ecstasy, fear, apprehension, feelings of oneness with God, as well as a host of other important experiences. In another study, he demonstrated how pulsed, weak magnetic fields could essentially put thoughts into his subjects' minds.[3] Persinger believes that virtually all mystical and spiritual experiences are a by-product of electromagnetic fields which produce changes in brain processes.

A fact about the ancient world that is seldom considered relates to electromagnetic pollution. The ancients lived their entire lives in touch with a fairly stable background of electromagnetic energy. Rituals that physically moved an individual from a magnetically stable area to an area with anomalies produced profound effects. Today, however, we exist in what has been termed an *electromagnetic cesspool*.[1] Power lines, phone lines, cell phone towers, computers, electric lights, and televisions all constantly pulse electromagnetic waves. Virtually every electrical device creates EM waves. We live in a swirling ocean of EM energy created by all of these devices, and, to top it off, radio stations and television stations are continuously bombarding us with varying frequencies of EM energy in the hopes we'll turn on an electrical receiving device and listen to their commercials. In short, no longer does a stable background of electromagnetic energy exist. If a correct utilization of these energies is the pathway to communication with God, what can this manmade electronic swirl of energy mean to us? Interestingly, when Persinger conducts his experiments on humans, he has to use a specially shielded copper room to block out the EM pollution.

In telling the story of the conflicts between the Atlantean Children of the Law of One with the Sons of Belial, Cayce stated that the Belial group lost their contact with God and the spiritual world from whence they came. They had embraced technology and tried to take control of the forces of nature. Is it possible we have done the same thing? Is it possible that the technology to which we have so quickly adapted could somehow block our connection to the spiritual world?

The Essential Question

Many scientists have asserted that God-consciousness is simply a change in brain chemistry. And some people, they assert, are more prone to these experiences because they are more "magnetically sensitive." In truth, research does show that some people are more sensitive to electromagnetic fields than others. The amount of magnetite present in one's brain may account for this. And the idea of "chosen ones" may relate to how much magnetite is present in the brain. Perhaps those who are "chosen" are more able to respond to magnetic fields because they have more magnetite. The implications of electromagnetic pollution for such people aren't pleasant. In short, research verifies that our consciousness does move through one "doorway" to another. A host of spiritual and religious experiences confirm this, as do hundreds of experiments showing how the brain changes as consciousness changes. But all this leads to a crucial question: Where, exactly, do these doorways in our mind lead?

Some scientists assert that the research outcomes lead to the conclusion that everything we experience is in our own mind. There is no spiritual world, no God, no afterlife. No matter how deep a spiritual experience is, this view asserts that it is simply a by-product of chemical processes in brain cells.

On the other hand, there is recognition that the brain chemical model fails to account for several other bodies of research. This point of view asserts that the chemical and electrical changes that occur in the brain during spiritual and religious experiences do open doorways. But these doorways allow consciousness to escape the confines of the physical body into another realm.

The Spiritual World

In *Grand Illusions*[2], the idea was put forth that the Electromagnetic Energy Spectrum *is* the spiritual world. We humans exist in the middle of this spectrum normally perceiving only the light we can see in a narrow range. We are affected by the unseen EM energy swirling around us, but we don't usually perceive the effects. Under some circumstances, we can alter our perceptions by changing our vibrational rates. This is not meant in an esoteric sense, but in a very real way. Recall that the electromagnetic field produced by the human brain can be measured and analyzed. We can change our electromagnetic frequencies intentionally. By altering our thoughts, focusing our attention, and through willful behavior, our electromagnetic field changes. Thinking about our electromagnetic "aura" in this way leads to another profound realization. Our moods, thoughts, and behavior influence others in a subtle but quite real way — we affect others by sending out electromagnetic waves tuned to match our moods. This idea is far deeper than we wish to pursue in this book, but the Cayce readings say something very similar. The readings also relate that reaching and maintaining the correct attitude is essential when seeking God.

In numerous readings, Cayce spoke about the electrical and electromagnetic nature of both the physical world — and God. Here are a few examples:

"For Life is, and its manifestations in matter ARE of an ELECTRONIC energy." (440-20)

"Electricity or vibration is that same energy, same power, ye call God. Not that God is an electric light or an electric machine, but that vibration that is creative is of that same energy as life itself. (2828-4)

"…materiality IS - or matter IS - that demonstration and manifestation of the units of positive and negative energy, or electricity, or God." (412-9)

"… materially, whatever electricity is to man, that's what the power of God is." (3618-1)

There is much research that argues for the position that a realm of reality truly exists outside of the biochemical processes of the brain. Perhaps the best body of evidence for this idea comes from research on Near-Death Experiences (NDE). While scientists can produce some aspects of the NDE in laboratory settings, there is one crucial aspect they have not been able to duplicate. The consciousness of people experiencing a genuine NDE can leave the body and move around under its own will. In dozens of cases, the individual's consciousness has gone to areas outside the room housing his or her body. When the person returns to life, they can recall specific happenings, events, and descriptions of the areas they visited. Medical researchers who were initially skeptical about such reports have rigorously verified these. And a great many of these findings were derived from children who underwent the experience.[5] This is a truly fascinating phenomenon made all the more interesting by the fact that this was exactly what Edgar Cayce appeared to do while in his trance states.

Spiritual Breakthrough in the Search For God

The story of humanity as told through the Cayce readings is both incredible and filled with lessons for living. The fact that Cayce's health readings were fundamentally accurate lends credence to his overall story. The fact that his preposterous and seemingly impossible history of ancient America is now largely verified, only increases his validity that much more. Perhaps the most important lesson in this book is expressed in the deep spiritual beliefs and practices of the ancient Americans. These were people who understood that it was essential to maintain ongoing contact with the Creator — the ultimate spiritual source. They apparently realized the trap that the physical world became for their ancestors and what was required for a spiritual breakthrough. According to this view, the "kingdom of heaven" is real and is found by looking inside oneself. It is accessed by a turning inward and a tuning of heart, mind, spirit, and day-to-day actions to the will of God. The physical world and human desire can impede this process of searching for God, but the outcome is worth the effort. The ancient Native Americans sought to maintain a simple way of life to maintain their connection with God.

The essence of the human condition as Cayce relates it can be expressed simply: "We are spiritual beings manifesting temporarily in a physical dimension...the physical body is a bio-spiritual instrument, containing both the physical and spiritual elements of the whole being."[6] Understanding this simple truth is one step toward making a spiritual breakthrough and finding God.

Figure 144
From Southeastern Archaeology Center, Natl. Park Service.

Rererences & Notes

Chapter 1

1. Folsom, Franklin, & Folsom, Mary. (1983) *America's Ancient Treasures*. Albuquerque: University of New Mexico Press.

2. Time-Life. *The American Indians: Tribes of the Southern Woodlands* (1994) Alexandria, VA: Time-Life.

3. McMillin, David. (1995) *Case Studies in Depression*. Virginia Beach, VA: A.R.E. Press.

4. McMillan, David. (1991) *A Holistic Approach The Treatment of Depression*. Virginia Beach, VA: A.R.E. Press.

5. Kirkpatrick, Sidney D. (2000) *Edgar Cayce: An American Prophet*. New York: Riverhead Books.

6. Lou Whitworth. www.leaderu.com/orgs/probe/docs/cayce

7. Cayce, Edgar Evans, Schwartzer, Gail Cayce, & Richards, Douglas G. (1997) *Mysteries of Atlantis Revisited*. New York: St. Martins Paperback.

8. Bernal, Martin. (1987) *Black Athena. The Afroasiatic Roots of Classical Civilization. V. I. The Fabrication of Ancient Greece 1785-1985*. New Brunswick, NJ: Rutgers Univ. Press.

9. Cole, John R. (1980) Cult archaeology and unscientific method and theory. In: *Advances in Archaeological Methods and Theory*, Vol. 3. Michael B. Schiffer (Ed.) New York: Academic Press.

10. Van Auken, John, & Little, Lora. (2000) *The Lost Hall of Records*. Memphis: Eagle Wing Books, Inc.

Chapter 2

1. Wilford, John Noble. (April 8, 2001) Fossil discovery in Kenya sparks new debate about human origins. *The New York Times News Service*.

Chapter 3

1. Snow, Dean (1976) *The Archaeology of North America: American Indians and their Origins*. London: Thames & Hudson.

2. Kopper, Philip (1986) *The Smithsonian Book of North American Indians Before the Coming of the Europeans*. Washington: Smithsonian Books.

3. *The First Americans*. (1992) Time-Life Books.

4. George F. Carter (1998) The diffusion controversy. In: (D. Gilmore & L. McElroy, Eds.) *Across Before Columbus?* Edgecomb, MA: The New England Antiquities Research Association.

5. Folsom, Franklin, & Folsom, Mary. (1993) *America's Ancient Treasures*. Albuquerque: University of New Mexico Press.

6. Michael Woods (October 30, 1999) Who got here first? Debate is rekindled. *Post-Gazette*.

7. Stuart Fiedel (2000) The peopling of the New World: Present evidence, new theories, and future directions. *Journal of Archaeological Research*, 8, 39-103.

8. Richard S. MacNeish, G. Cunnar, G. Jessop, & P. Wilner (1993) *1993 Fort Bliss Archaeological Project Annual report: A summary of the Paleo-Indian discoveries in Pendejo Cave near Orogrande, New Mexico.* Andover, MA: Andover Foundation Archaeological Research.

9. Fred Budinger (1999) Pleistocene Archaeology of the Manix Basin, Central Mojave Desert, California. *Clovis & Beyond Conference*, October 1999, Santa Fe, NM.

10. Center for the Study of the First Americans. (2000) A personal view: Older than we think. *Mammoth Trumpet*, March 29, 2000.

Chapter 4

1. Sharon Begley & Andrew Murr (1999) The First Americans. *Newsweek*, April 26, 50-57.

2. Li, H.-G., Fujiyoshi, T., Lou, H., Yahiki, S., Sonoda, S., Cartier, L., Nunez, L., Munoz, I., Horai, S. & Tajima, K. (1999) The presence of ancient human T-cell lymphotrophic virus type I provirus DNA in an Andean mummy. *Nature Medicine* 5, 1428.

3. Hansjürgen T. Agostini, Richard Yanagihara, Victor Davis, Caroline F. Ryschkewitsch, & Gerald L. Stoner (1997) Asian genotypes of JC virus in Native Americans and in a Pacific Island population: Markers of viral evolution and human migration. *Proceedings of the National Academy of Science*, 94, 14542-14546.

4. Franz Parsche, Svetlana Balabanova, & Wolfgang Pirsig. (1993) Drugs in ancient populations. *The Lancet*, 341, 503.

5. Carl L. Johannessen (1998) Maize diffused to India before Columbus came to America. In: D. Gilmore & L. McElroy (Eds.) *Across Before Columbus?* Edgecomb, ME: The New England Antiquities Research Association.

6. Dennis Kawaharada, (1996) "The Settlement of Polynesia," *The Polynesian Voyaging Society*, 29 January 29, 1996.

7. Douglas C. Wallace, Michael D. Brown, Theodore G. Schurr, Estella Chen, Yu-Sheng Chen, Yelena B. Starikovskaya and Rem I. Sukernik (1998) Global Mitochondrial DNA Variation and the Origin of Native Americans. *Science*, 279, February 27, 1998, 1306-1307.

8. Brown MD, Hosseini SH, Torroni A, Bandelt HJ, Allen JC, Schurr TG, Scozzari R, Cruciani F, Wallace DC. (1998) mtDNA haplogroup X: An ancient link between Europe/Western Asia and North America? *American Journal of Human Genetics*, 63, 1852-1861.

9. Ann Gibbons (1996) The Peopling of the Americas. (1996) *Science Magazine*, 274, 31-33.

10. Torroni A, Chen YS, Semino O, Santachiara-Beneceretti AS, Scott CR, Lott MT, Winter M, Wallace DC. (1995) mtDNA and Y-chromosome polymorphisms in four Native American populations from southern Mexico. *American Journal of Human Genetics*, 54, 303-18.

11. Torroni A, Neel JV, Barrantes R, Schurr TG, Wallace DC. (1994) Mitochondrial DNA "clock" for the Amerinds and its implications for timing their entry into North America. *Proceedings of the National Academy of Science*, 91, 1158-1162.

12. Torroni A, Sukernik RI, Schurr TG, Starikorskaya YB, Cabell MF, Crawford MH, Comuzzie AG, Wallace DC. (1993) mtDNA variation of aboriginal Siberians reveals distinct genetic affinities with Native Americans. *American Journal of Human Genetics*, 53, 591-608.

13. Ann Gibbons (1996) Mother Tongues Trace Steps of Earliest Americans. *Science Magazine*, 274 (5292), 1447-1451.

14. Miroslava V. Derenko, Tomasz Grzybowski, Boris A. Malyarchuk, Jakub Czarny, Danuta Micicka-liwka, and Ilia A. Zakharov (2001) The Presence of Mitochondrial Haplogroup X in Altaians from South Siberia. *The American Journal of Human Genetics*, 69 (1), 237.

15. John U. Terrell. (1971) *American Indian Almanac*. New York: Barnes & Noble.

16. Snow, Dean (1976) *The Archaeology of North America: American Indians and their Origins*. London: Thames & Hudson.

17. Powell, J. W. (1900) *Nineteenth Annual Report of the Bureau of American Ethnology to the Secretary of the Smithsonian Institution — 1897-98*. Washington: U.S. Government Printing Office.

18. Van Auken, John, & Little, Lora (2000) *The Lost Hall of Records*. Memphis: Eagle Wing Books, Inc.

Chapter 5

1. Snow, D. (1976) *The Archaeology of North America*. London: Thames & Hudson.

2. Corliss, W.F. (1999) *Ancient Infrastructure: Remarkable roads, mines, walls, mounds, stone circles*. Glen Arm, MD: The Sourcebook Project.

3. Folsom, F. and Folsom, M.E. (1993) *America's Ancient Treasures*. Albuquerque: University of New Mexico Press.

4. DuTemple, O. J. (2000) Prehistory's greatest mystery: copper mines of ancient Michigan. *Ancient American*, 35, 8-13.

5. Gibson, J. L. (1983) *Poverty Point. Baton Rouge: Louisiana Archaeological Survey and Antiquities Commission Anthropological Study No. 7.*

6. Saunders, J., (et. al. – 14 others) (1997) A mound complex in Louisiana at 5400-5000 years before present. *Science*, 277, 1796.

7. Frink, D. S. (1999) OCR Carbon Dating of the Watson Brake Mound Complex. Presented at the symposium "An Overview of Research at Watson Brake: A Middle Archaic Mound Complex in Northeast Louisiana" during the *53rd Annual Meeting of the Southeastern Archaeological Conference*, Birmingham, Alabama.

8. Saunders, J. W., Jones, R., Moorhead, K., and Davis, B. (1998) Watson Brake objects: An unusual archaic artifact type from Northeast Louisiana and Southwest Mississippi. *Southeastern Archaeology*, 17, 72-79.

9. *The Jewish Encyclopedia*. (1902) London: Funk & Wagnalls.

Chapter 6

1. Dragoo, D. W. (1963) *Mounds for the Dead*. Pittsburgh: The Carnegie Institution.

2. Silverberg, R. (1968) *The Mound Builders*. Athens, Ohio: Ohio University Press.

3. Fell, B. (1976) *America B.C.* NY: Simon & Schuster.

4. Woodward, S. L., & McDonald, J. N. (1986) *Indian Mounds of the Middle Ohio Valley*. Newark, Ohio: McDonald & Woodward Publ. Co.

Chapter 7

1. Silverberg, Robert (1968) *The Mound Builders*. Ohio University Press.

2. Little, Gregory L. (1987/1988) Unearthing Pinson Mounds — Parts 1 and 2. *Fate Magazine*, Vol. 40 & 41, pgs. 32-41; 84-91.

3. Little, Gregory L. (1990) *People of the Web*. Memphis, TN: White Buffalo Books.

4. Mainfort, R. C. (1986) *Pinson Mounds*. Tennessee Department of Conservation.

5. Marshall, James A. (1996) Towards a definition of the Ohio Hopewell core and periphery utilizing the geometric earthworks. In: Paul J. Pacheco (Ed.) *A View from the Core: A Synthesis of Ohio Hopewell Archaeology*. Columbus: The Ohio Archaeological Council.

6. Mayell, Hillary (1999) Secrets of North American Mound Builders Unearthed. *National Geographic News*, September 9, 1999.

7. Romain, William (2000) *Mysteries of the Hopewell*. Akron: University of Akron Press.

8. Offering of a Mound. *TriWeekly Intelligencer*, October 25, 1851.

9. Little, Gregory (1997) *Psychopharmacology*. Memphis: Advanced Training Associates.

10. Lepper, Bradley (1996) The Newark Earthworks and the geometric enclosures of the Scioto Valley: connections and conjectures. In: Paul J. Pacheco (Ed.) *A View from the Core: A Synthesis of Ohio Hopewell Archaeology*. Columbus: The Ohio Archaeological Council.

11. Lepper, Bradley (1998) The archaeology of the Newark earthworks. In: R. Mainfort, & L. Sullivan (Eds.) *Ancient Earthen Enclosures*. Gainesville: Univ. Press of Florida.

12. Mallam, R. Clark (no date cited) *Effigy mounds in Iowa*. U.S. National Park Service.

13. Hopkins, Bruce (2000) *Effigy Mounds*. Fort Washington, PA: Eastern National.

14. Material from Dr. Scherz as well as other effigy mound information was furnished to the authors by Neal & Aileen Weber of Richland Center, Wisconsin.

15. Knapp, Joseph M. (1998) *Hopewell Lunar Astronomy: The Octagon Earthworks*. http://www.geocities.com/~ss245/octagon/lunar.html

16. Bauer, Ted (April 11, 1987) Moundbuilders seem influenced by sun, moon. *The Marietta Times*.

17. Bauer, Ted (May 2, 1987) Search continues for evidence about mounds' purpose. *The Marietta Times*.

Chapter 8

1. Little, Greg (1999) Cahokia: Ancient fortress city with 120 mounds. *Alternate Perceptions*, Issue #47, 12-16.

2. Little, Greg (1999) What is under Monk's Mound? *Alternate Perceptions*, Issue #47,16.

3. Little, Greg (1999) Monk's Mound Update: the mystery deepens. *Alternate Perceptions*, Issue #48, 9.

4. Little, Greg (2000) Moundville. *Alternate Perceptions*, Issue #49, 10.

5. Little, Greg (1996) Etowah mounds. *Alternate Perceptions*, Issue #36, 6-8.

6. Little, Greg (1996) The Etowah statues. *Alternate Perceptions*, Issue #36, 9.

7. Little, Greg (1996) Aztalan: Wisconsin's northern outpost of the mound builders. *Alternate Perceptions*, Issue #33, 8-9.

8. Korp, Maureen (1990) *The sacred geography of the American mound builders*. Lewiston, NY: Edwin Mellen Press.

9. Sherrod, P. Clay, & Rolingson, Martha A. (1987) *Surveyors of the ancient Mississippi Valley*. Fayetteville: Arkansas Archaeological Survey.

10. Schafer, Edward H. (1967) *Ancient China*. New York: Time-Life Books.

11. Parada, Carlos. From: *Genealogical Guide to Greek Mythology*. Greek Mythology Link: www.hsa.brown.edu

12. Reading 5748-6.

13. Hancock, Graham (1995) *Fingerprints of the Gods*. NY: Crown.

14. Hancock, Graham (1993) *The Sign and the Seal*. London: Mandarin.

Chapter 9

1. Zangger, Eberhard (1992) *The flood from heaven.* NY: William Morrow Co.

2. *Associated Press* (Lancaster, California) Kite lifts 3.4-ton obelisk; is this how Egyptians did it? Sunday, June 24, 2001.

3. Romain, William (2000) *Mysteries of the Hopewell.* Akron: University of Akron Press.

4. Hudson, Charles (1976) *The Southeastern Indians.* Knoxville: University of Tennessee Press.

5. Willoughby, Charles (1932) Notes on the history and symbolism of the Mushogeans and the people of Etowah. In: (W. K. Moorehead, Ed.) *Etowah Papers – I.* New Haven: Yale University Press.

Chapter 10

1. Waters, Frank (1977) *Book of the Hopi.* New York: Penguin Books.

2. As in the first chapter of the Gospel of John, which begins: "In the beginning was the Word..." In the original Greek manuscript, the word for Word is "Logos," which in Greek means much more than the English "Word".

3. Waters, p. 17.

4. Waters, p. 17.

5. Waters, p. 20.

6. www.sacred-texts.com

Chapter 11

1. Carter, George F. (1998) Introduction: The Diffusion controversy. In: D. Gilmore, & L. McElroy (Eds.) *Across before Columbus?* Edgecomb, Maine: The New England Antiquities Research Association.

2. There were many references to the Norse utilized in this section. The most important ones we used are listed below:

Blegen, Theodore (1968) *The Kensington Rune-stone; New Light on an Old Riddle.* St Paul: Minnesota Historical Society.

Hall, Robert Anderson (1982) *The Kensington Rune-stone is Genuine: Linguistic, Practical Methodological Considerations.* Columbia: Hornbeam Press.

Holand, Hjalmar R. (1940) *Norse Discoveries and Explorations in America*, 982-1362. New York: Dover Publications.

Ingstad, Helge (1969) *Westward to Vinland.* New York: St Martin's Press.

Jones, Gwyn (1984) *A History of the Vikings.* Oxford: Oxford University Press.

Landsverk, Ole Godfred (1961) *The Kensington Rune-stone: A Reappraisal of the Circumstances under which the Stone was Discovered.* Glendale: Church Press.

Magnusson, Magnus (1980) *Vikings!* NY: E P Dutton.

Magnusson, M, & Paulsson, H. (1965) *The Vinland Sagas.* NY: Penguin.

McGhee, Robert (1988) The Vikings: They Got Here First but Why Didn't They Stay? *Canadian Geographic*, 108 (4) August/September.

Redmond, Jeffery R. (1979) *Viking Hoaxes in North America.* New York: Carlton Press.

Wahlgren, Erik (1958) *The Kensington Rune-stone: A Mystery Solved.* Madison: University of Wisconson Press.

3. Newport Historical Society. (1997) The History and Mystery of the Old Stone Mill. *Journal of the Newport Historical Society*, 68, Part 2.

4. Williams, Stephen (1991) *Fantastic Archaeology*. Philadelphia: Univ. of Pennsylvania Press.

5. Wyckoff, Don (1973) No stones unturned: Differing views of Oklahoma's runestones. *Popular Archaeology*, 2 (12), 16-31.

6. Verwyst, J. (1887) Mound containing wrought iron and brass buckle. *American Antiquarian*, 9, 39-40.

7. Olson, John J.; *'Mooring Stones': An Enigma Deserving More Attention*, Epigraphic Society, Occasional Publications, 18:253, 1989

8. Autrey, N. E., & Autrey, W. (1981) Zodiac Ridge. In: R. A. Williamson (Ed.) *Archaeoastronomy in the Americas*. College Park, MD: Center for the Study of Archaeoastronomy.

9. Cyrus Thomas (1894) *Report on the Mound Explorations of the Bureau of Ethnology*. Washington, DC: Smithsonian.

10. J. Huston McCulloch (1996) Ohio's 'Hanukkiah Mound.' *Ancient American*, 3 (14), 28-37.

Chapter 12

1. Reading 5750-1

2. "Lost Tribes," *Microsoft Encarta Online Encyclopedia* 2000.

3. Singer, Isidore (Ed.) (1905) *The Jewish Encyclopedia, Vol. XII*. New York: Funk and Wagnalls Company, pp. 249-252.

4. Reading 3513-1.

5. Readings 5384-1, 3590-1, 2109-2.

6. Readings 1598-1, 1580-1, 1856-1, 2005-1.

7. D. Adams, J. McKee (1934) *Biblical Backgrounds*. Nashville, TN: Broadman Press. p. 281.

8. Readings 2540-1, 5259-1, 3581-1.

9. Jakeman, M. Wells (1963) The Flood Story of Genesis. In Ross T. Christensen (Ed.) *Progress in Archaeology: An Anthology*. (Ed.) Provo, Utah: Brigham Young University, pp.11-16.

10. Sorenson, John (1985) *An Ancient American Setting for the Book of Mormon*. Salt Lake City, Utah: Deseret Book Company.

11. Readings 1159-1, 1286-1, 1391-1, 2822-1.

12. Reading 1258-1.

13 Reading 620-1.

14. Reading 1434-1.

15. Mellaart, Melvin (1979) Egyptian and Near Eastern Chronology: A Dilemma? *Antiquity*, 53, 6-18 and 54, 225-227.

16. Edgar Cayce CD Rom Letter to Mrs. (1319).

17. *The Book of Mormon*. Salt Lake City, Utah: The Church of Jesus Christ of the Latter Day Saints.

18. (1930) *A Comprehensive History of the Church of Jesus Christ of the Latter-Day Saints. Century 1, Vol. 1* , Salt Lake City : The Church of Jesus Christ of Latter-Day Saints, pp. 100-107.

19. Reynolds, Noel (1997) *Book of Mormon Authorship Revisited: The evidence for ancient origins*. Provo Utah: Foundation for Ancient Research and Mormon Studies. pp. 62-63.

20. F. C. Cook (Ed.)1905) *The Bible Commentary, Vol. 1*, pp. 390-393.

21. Singer, Isidore (Ed.) (1905) *The Jewish Encyclopedia, Vol. XII*. New York: Funk and Wagnalls Company, pp. 384-386.

22. Readings 707-2, 355-1, 261-15, 987-2.

23. Reading 5750-1.

24. The Chronology of the Book of Mormon. In Ross T. Christensen (Ed.) *Progress in Archaeology: An Anthology*. (Ed.) Provo, Utah: Brigham Young University, pp. 85-88.

25. Lindsay, Jeffrey (2000) Evidence for the Book of Mormon: Another Testament of Jesus Christ. Internet site: www.Jefflindsay.com/BMEvidences.shtml

26. Sorenson, John (1985) *An Ancient American Setting for the Book of Mormon*. Salt Lake City, Utah: Deseret Book Company.

27. The Chronology of the Book of Mormon. In Ross T. Christensen (Ed.) *Progress in Archaeology: An Anthology*. (Ed.) Provo, Utah: Brigham Young University, pp. 196-197

28. Godfrey, Kenneth W. (1999) What is the Significance of the Zelph in the Study of the Book of Mormon Geography? *Journal of the Book of Mormon Studies*, Internet site www.farmsresearch.com/member/jbms.

29. McCulloch, J. Huston (1988) The Bat Creek Inscription: Judeans in Tennessee? *Tennessee Anthropologist*, 16, 1-19.

30. Thomas, Cyrus (1894) *Report on the Mound Explorations of the Bureau of Ethnology*, Washington, D.C.: Smithsonian.

31. McCulloch, J. Huston (1996) Ohio's 'Hanukkiah Mound.' *Ancient American*, 3, (14), 28-37.

32. Sorenson, John (1985) *An Ancient American Setting for the Book of Mormon*. Salt Lake City, Utah: Deseret Book Company.

33. Sorenson, John (1997) The Book of Mormon as a Mesoamerican Record. In Noel Reynolds (Ed.) *Book of Mormon Authorship Revisited: The evidence for ancient origins*. Provo Utah: Foundation for Ancient Research and Mormon Studies. pp. 391-522.

34. Peterson, Daniel (1993) *Review of Books on the Book of Mormon*, Vol. 5, pp. 43-45.

35. Miller Van Blerkom, Linda (1979) A Comparison of Maya and Egyptian Hieroglyphics. *Katunob*, 11, pp. 1-8.

36. Welch, John (1997) What Does Chiasmus in the Book of Mormon Prove? In Noel Reynolds (Ed.) *Book of Mormon Authorship Revisited: The evidence for ancient origins*. Provo Utah: Foundation for Ancient Research and Mormon Studies. pp. 199-224.

37. Sorenson, John (1985) *An Ancient American Setting for the Book of Mormon*. Salt Lake City, Utah: Deseret Book Company.

38. Lindsay, Jeffrey (2000) *Evidence for the Book of Mormon: Another Testament of Jesus Christ*. Internet site: www.Jefflindsay.com/BMEvidences.shtm

39. Reading 364-4.

40. Reading 364-6 and 257-201.

41. Van Auken, John, & Little, Lora (2000) *The Lost Hall of Records*. Memphis: Eagle Wing Books.

42. Reading 2888-2 and 3976-29.

43. Reading 3744-1.

44. Reading 470-22.

45. English Heritage Scientific Dating Services "Dating Stonehenge" Internet site http://ww.eng-h.govuk/stoneh/start.htm

46. Frejer, B. Ernest (1995) *The Edgar Cayce Companion: A Comprehensive Treatise of the Edgar Cayce Readings*. Virginia Beach, VA: ARE Press.

47. Krajenke, Robert (1994) *Edgar Cayce's Story of the Old Testament: From the Birth of Souls to the Death of Moses*. Virginia Beach, VA: ARE Press, p. xix.

Chapter 14

1. Powell, J. W. (1900) *Annual Report of the Bureau of American Ethnology.*

2. Little, G. (1994) *Grand Illusions.* Memphis: White Buffalo Books.

3. Little, G. (1990) *People of the Web.* Memphis: White Buffalo Books.

4. Little, G. (1997) *Psychopharmacology.* Memphis: ATA. (This college text discusses the use of about a dozen hallucinogenic substances by ancient Americans. Virtually all of these substances are toxic unless taken in exacting dosages. Even then, the dangers are great. No one should experiment with these substances nor are we in any way advocating their use. The inclusion of this information is simply a necessary acknowledgement that hallucinogenics were utilized in many rituals.)

5. Narby, J. (1998) *The Cosmic Serpent.* NY: Tarcher.

6. Lyon, W. (1998) *Encyclopedia of Native American Shamanism.* Santa Barbara: ABC-CLIO.

7. Romain, William F. (2000) *Mysteries of the Hopewell.* Akron: University of Akron Press.

Chapter 15

1. Little, G. (2001) Science at the frontier: a merging of ancient and modern science. *The Journal of Religion and Psychical Research,* 24, 2-25.

2. Little, G. (1994) *Grand Illusions.* Memphis: White Buffalo Books.

3. Little, G. (1990) *People of the Web.* Memphis: White Buffalo Books.

4. Apostal, A. (1995) North American effigy mounds: an enigma at the frontier of archaeology and geology. *Journal of Scientific Exploration,* 9, 549-563.

5. Morse, D. (2000) *Searching for Eternity.* Memphis: Eagle Wing Books.

6. Van Auken, J. (1992) *Spiritual Breakthrough.* Virginia Beach: Inner Vision.

Appendix A
Cayce's Readings on Ancient America

In preparation for this book, a comprehensive search of the Cayce readings was performed utilizing *The Complete Edgar Cayce Readings* CD ROM (1995). The terms mound, mounds, moundbuilders, Indian, Indians, Norse, Mu, Lemuria, Atlantis, Lost Tribes, Vinland, and medicine man provided the most relevant readings. Some terms (e.g., Indians) had more than one meaning and had to be carefully interpreted to determine the intent. In addition, approximately 1000 index terms from the *American Indian Almanac* (1971) were searched on the Cayce Readings CD ROM to identify possible references to tribal names, locations, and other terms. This search yielded a few additional relevant readings. Finally, all of the previously published books discussing Cayce's statements about ancient America mentioned in Chapter one were carefully examined for any readings our search had missed. Despite our efforts with the previous searches, two additional relevant readings were found.

A total of 68 readings were found that provided information on ancient America. These readings were given between April 4, 1925 and April 14, 1944. An effort was made to categorize them based on their content and subject. Table 1 shows the number of readings discussing various subjects. Most readings discussed more than one subject area. For example, a few readings gave an overall view of how ancient people from Mu mixed with Atlanteans, remnants of the Lost Tribes, and natives already present in the land to form the mound builder culture.

Finding Specific, Testable Statements in the Readings

Identifying the specific date of particular events described in the readings is difficult for those unfamiliar with Cayce. This fact may explain why some scholars have avoided investigating the historical outline the readings have provided. For example, a 1936 life reading (1211-1) indicated that the individual was a leader in the region of the 4-Corners (Arizona, New Mexico, Colorado, Utah). This person was then responsible for alleviating a serious problem affecting all of earth. Enormous animals were producing havoc, as uncontrolled herds were not only competing with man but also often killing him. A meeting was held to discuss ways of dealing with the animals. The reading does not give the date, however, other readings do provide it. It was in 50,722 B.C. (reading 262-039).

The bulk of the readings involving ancient America are much like the example above. Many of these readings date the happenings they describe as at "the time of the first break-up," "the second destruction," or the "final destruction." These are references to the three destructions of Atlantis, with each being more severe than the prior one. They took place, according to Cayce, in 50,700 B.C., 28,000 B.C., and 10,014 B.C.

Further complicating the problem, but also making it very intriguing, is the fact that Cayce's timetable for all ancient history varies from the history given in accepted sources. This is especially true of events and history recounted in the Bible. For example, while authoritative sources like *The Jewish Encyclopedia* dates "The Lost Tribes" to events in 734 B.C., the Cayce readings state some "Lost Tribes" left in 3,000 B.C.

Table 1
Subject Areas of the Cayce Readings On Ancient America

Subject	Number of Readings Discussing
Atlantean migration to America	21
Norse settlements in America/Vinland	16
Mound builder culture	14
Early historical contact between Indians/settlers	14
Mu/Lemurian migration/settlements in America	10
Lost Tribes in America	5
Medicine men in America	5
Rituals, visions, nature/sun worship in America	4
Incals' influence in America	3
Migration from the "west" or China to America	2
Early occupation (50,000 B.C.) of America	2
Man in southwest America in 10 million B.C.	2
Migrations from "south seas" islands	1
Southwestern "cliff dwellers"	1

Problems Interpreting the Cayce Readings

It is easy to become frustrated when first trying to comprehend Cayce's readings. The overall style of the readings presents some difficulties in interpretation and understanding. First, they are somewhat difficult to read, mostly due to their syntax and the presence of archaic or biblical terms and phrases. For example, modern readers can be perplexed by terms such as "children of promise."

Some people become frustrated because of the grammar utilized in the readings. However, what was produced during the readings was not a reflection of how Edgar normally spoke. The readings resulted from how the Source of the material chose to provide the information. And they reflect the entire, relevant history of each person — from ancient time to the present. Thus, why should modern terms and modern grammar be expected?

In addition, the readings, as we see them today, are *written* records of a *verbal* presentation. This process occasionally did not carry the full intent that was expressed, and punctuation can significantly change the meaning or intent of the voiced statement. Also, most of the readings were given to specific people with uniquely personal perspectives and prejudices on the topics being discussed. Therefore, the responses were slanted to fit the seeker's perspective.

Finally, because some of Cayce's readings cover so many points or issues within the text, it can be difficult to determine which one he is referring to when the paragraphs are so complex. Despite all of this, with sufficient practice, one can become familiar enough with the syntax, archaic terms ("thys," "thees," and "thous"), a repetitive use of the word "that"; and the complex thought pattern, so that one can learn to read and understand the Cayce readings fairly easily.

Cayce's Statements & Relevant Reading Portions

1. Parts of Utah, New Mexico, and Arizona were occupied 10 million years ago.

2. Cave drawings in northwestern New Mexico remain from these very early people.

2665-2
10. In the one before this we find in the land of now the Utah and Nevada forces, when the first peoples were separated into groups as families. The entity then in the name of Ulda, and gave then much to the people in the manner of the way to prepare the dwellings for the mates, as the entity one among the few who were successful in holding same to that view; that is, her

own mate, see? In this we find the entity developed much and gave much to the peoples who were to succeed in this land, and in the ruins as are found that have arisen, in the mounds and caves in the northwestern portion of New Mexico, may be seen some of the drawings the entity then made. Some ten million years ago. [See 2665-2, Par. R6, R8.]

195-14
20. Before that we find the entity during the first of the appearances of man in the earth's plane, during that period when the five [nations] appeared. The entity then was in that now of the Nevada and Utah territory in America, then in the name Udulj.

---

3. **People were present in the Americas prior to 50,000 B.C. in the southwest and California.**

4. **Large, dangerous animals freely roamed the Americas prior to 50,000 B.C.**

1211-1
37. Before that, then, we find the entity was in the land of the present nativity, during those periods when there were the first of the activities of those peoples in the lands which now represent a portion of Arizona, New Mexico, Colorado, Utah.

38. There the entity was among those who made for the associations with those activities when the great powers or nations - through those influences as brought by the activities in Egypt, India, the Gobi, the Og - cooperated in one great cause. (Note: The great cause was ridding the planet of the huge animals roaming freely. The year was 50, 722 B.C.)

1473-1
46. There the entity was a priestess; and the entity's experience there overshadows ALL ...

47. For the entity was of the peoples of the Law of One, and with the breaking up of the land itself and the beginning of the exodus of those peoples, the entity was among those that journeyed to what is now called the Yucatan land - or the Ithmus land.

48. And with the building up of those activities, the establishing of the temple service, the applications of the temple's activity to the commercialization - or those activities in which discoveries, these were but a portion of the entity's associate's activities during that experience.

49. And when there became the heresaying, yea in those periods when there became an activity in which those portions of the land were discovered from what was left of Lemuria, or Mu - in what is now lower California, portions of the valleys of death, the entity journeyed there to see, to know.

50. And during those experiences much was set up that may be of interest to the entity, that will be a part of the discoveries of natures or natural formations in what is now the Canyon Island.

51. For THIS was the entity's place of the temple.

52. Is there any wonder that new expeditions to ANY land become fraught with interest to the entity?

53. For the entity then was a priestess that made for the correlating of tenets of all portions of the earth, for the unifying of the activities of spiritual understanding, and the application of spiritual laws - not as for material but for the harmonious and the peace of the peoples. And such longings were then, are now, the desire of the inmost self.

54. The entity was named the Princess Shu-Tu.

55. Also in those periods, the entity journed to what was later known as the meeting of the seven nations for the protection from the common foe of man during the experience. (Note: The great cause was ridding the planet of the huge animals roaming freely. The year was 50, 722 B.C.)

---

5. A temple dedicated to the sun and moon was established near present-day Santa Barbara, California prior to 50,700 B.C.

509-1
28. Before this we find the entity in that land now known as the American, during the periods when the Lemurian or the lands of Mu or Zu were being in their turmoils for destruction. (Note: Zu was a portion of Mu; the continent experienced its greatest destruction in 50,700 B.C.)

29. And the entity was among those that - in what is now not far from that land in which the entity in this sojourn first saw the light - (that must in the near future fade again into those joinings with the land of Mu) - established a temple of worship for those that escaped from the turmoils of the shifting of the earth at that particular period.

30. The entity, in the name Oeueou, established near what is now Santa Bar-

bara the temple to the sun and the moon; for the satellite of the moon had not faded then, and there was enjoined as to the entity in the worship as the goddess to the moon and the sun.

---

6. People from Mu (and Atlantis) migrated to America at the time of the first disturbances in Mu and Atlantis (50,000 B.C.).

3188-1

... the entity was in the land of the present sojourn [America] when there was the breaking up following the first destruction of Mu and Atlantis.

328-1

32. In the one before this we find the entity was in that called the Lemurian land, during those periods when the people were leaving - through the conditions that were arising in that land.

33. The entity then was among those that first came to that portion of the present sojourn that would now be called Ohio, or western Pennsylvania.

34. For, the entity then set up in this new land the first of the temples from the Lemurian land; that has since been termed the Mound Builders' land. Not the present as seen, but that from which same arose.

3188-1

40. Before that the entity was in the land of the present sojourn [America] when there was the breaking up following the first destruction of Mu and Atlantis.

691-1

27. Before that we find the entity was in that land now known as the American, during the periods when there were the sojourning of those from the land of Mu, or Lemuria.

28. The entity was then among the first of those that were born in what is now portions of Arizona and of Utah, and among those that established the lands there for the building up or growing up of that civilization in those experiences; and was in the name Uuluoou.

816-3

26. Before that (among those that influence the entity in the present) we find the entity was in that land now known as the land of the entity's nativity, in those portions that were the place of refuge from Mu and the upper or first activities of the Atlantean land - and in that now known as Arizona and Utah did the entity then become the first of those that established the cave dwellers

7. These people migrated to areas of Pennsylvania around 50,000 B.C

8. They also migrated to areas of Ohio around 50,000 B.C.

328-1

32. In the one before this we find the entity was in that called the Lemurian land, during those periods when the people were leaving - through the conditions that were arising in that land.

33. The entity then was among those that first came to that portion of the present sojourn that would now be called Ohio, or western Pennsylvania.

34. For, the entity then set up in this new land the first of the temples from the Lemurian land; that has since been termed the Mound Builders' land. Not the present as seen, but that from which same arose.

---

9. People from Mu established the custom of totem, or family trees, in Oregon prior to 50,000 B.C.

10. Women ruled during the time of the great Mu migration (50,000 B.C.).

630-2

24. Before that we find the entity was in that land now known as Mu, or the vanished land of the Pacific, the Peaceful; during those periods when many of those had risen to power when there were being those banishments and preparations for the preserving; for they had known that the land must be soon broken up.

25. The entity was among those that journeyed from Mu to what is NOW Oregon; and there STILL may be seen SOMETHING of the worship as set up, in what was the development FROM that set up by the entity's associates, as the totem or the family tree.

26. In that experience the entity was in the same sex as at present, but among those that were the leaders; for THEN the women RULED - rather than men.

---

11. People from the South Seas came to the four corners area and began the "cliff dweller," or pueblo culture, about 50,000 B.C.

1252-1

19. Before that we find the entity was in the land of the present nativity during those periods when there was the breaking up of the islands in now the South Seas, and the combinations of those that made for the changes in those environments of those peoples.

20. The entity then was among those first that have become known as the cave or cliff dwellers, in that portion now known as Utah, Arizona, Colorado, New Mexico.

---

12. In 28,000 B.C. some people from Atlantis migrated to Nevada and Colorado.

13. People coming "across the Pacific" entered ancient America in 28,000 B.C.

14. People coming from China entered ancient America in 28,000 B.C.

497-1
22. Before this we find in the Atlantean sojourn when there were those turmoils from the second period of the separations in the land, and there began the first of the leavings of the peoples to other lands that were being prepared or were arising in their activities. And the entity was among those that were persuaded, through the relationships and the activities, to leave the law of One to join rather in the mysteries of that as might be accomplished among a strange people. And hence came into the land of Mayra (?) [Maya?], or that now called - in America Nevada and Colorado.

1434-1
32. Before that we find the entity was in the lands of the present nativity or sojourn in the present, during those periods when there were those peoples entering into the land now called the Yucatan - after leaving the Atlantean and Poseidon land.

33. The entity was among those peoples who journeyed to the farther West or North and West from the Yucatan land; and the entity there was a priestess, and of the children of the Law of One.

34. The joinings in activities there were for the attempts to establish with those peoples that had been a portion of the lost or strayed tribe, that came across from Lemuria; as well as with those that came from the lands of bondage by the Persians and those that later were called the Indo-Chinans - or those peoples from the mountain who raided the Indian land.

35. There the entity aided in establishing a new unison of activity, in what would now be called the Arizona land.

500-1
13. ... especially where the sons of the Atlanteans had settled and later become the Mound Builders, when joined with the peoples that had crossed the Pacific...

1434-1

32. Before that we find the entity was in the lands of the present nativity or sojourn in the present, during those periods when there were those peoples entering into the land now called the Yucatan - after leaving the Atlantean and Poseidon land.

33. The entity was among those peoples who journeyed to the farther West or North and West from the Yucatan land; and the entity there was a priestess, and of the children of the Law of One.

34. The joinings in activities there were for the attempts to establish with those peoples that had been a portion of the lost or strayed tribe, that came across from Lemuria; as well as with those that came from the lands of bondage by the Persians and those that later were called the Indo-Chinans - or those peoples from the mountain who raided the Indian land.

35. There the entity aided in establishing a new unison of activity, in what would now be called the Arizona land.

---

15. The Iroquois, especially those of noble blood, were pure Atlantean.
16. Pure Atlanteans also migrated to Iberia, especially to the Pyrenees Mountains. (This is found in numerous other readings.)

1219-1

23. The entity then was among the people, the Indians, of the Iroquois; those of noble birth, those that were of the pure descendants of the Atlanteans, those that held to the ritualistic influences from nature itself.

---

17. An Atlantean priestess who had moved to Egypt visited southwestern America sometime around 10,000 B.C.

1144-2

26. Before that we find the entity was in the land now know as or called Egypt, yet the entity was a native of the Atlantean land - and one that made a visit and became active in many of the lands to which the Atlanteans went and made THEIR various settlements in that period.

27. Hence the entity was among the daughters of the Law of One, being a priestess of the temple in the Poseidian land; among those that went to the Egyptian land with those peoples for the establishing of the associations; also visiting those established themselves in now the Pyrenees - or the eastern portion of the continental Europe, and those that themselves in what is now known as a portion of America - in Arizona, New Mexico, Colorado, and those portions of the land.

18. A group of 2nd generation Atlanteans and others who moved to the Yucatan about 10,000 B.C. migrated north to begin the Mound Builder culture. This occurred sometime after 3,000 B.C.

5750-1
18. Those in Yucatan, those in the adjoining lands as begun by Iltar, gradually lost in their activities; and came to be that people termed, in other portions of America, the Mound Builders.

3528-1
21. Before that the entity was in the land of the present sojourn, during the early activities of a peoples that had been banished from Atlantis.

22. The entity was among those of the second generation of Atlanteans who struggled northward from Yucatan, settling in what is now a portion of Kentucky, Indiana, Ohio; being among those of the earlier period known as Mound Builders.

19. The mounds were a replica of the Yucatan (and Atlantis & Gobi) experiences.

3004-1
14. Before this the entity was in the land of the present nativity, especially in that period of the Mound Builders - a little farther to the west; when there was the laying out of the plans for those interpretations that had been a consciousness in another organization or group to which the entity had previously belong or been a part.

15. There the entity was the priestess. And there may be seen some of those activities that are a part of the awareness to some in that land of Ohio, where there were those plans for such, in the mounds that were called the replica or representative of the Yucatan experiences, as well as the Atlantean and in Gobi land. All of these are as one consciousness in the entity's activity.

20. Remnants of the "Lost Tribes" of Israel came to ancient America in 3000 B.C. in boats. They went first to the southernmost US.
21. After staying for a brief time in the southern part of America, the Lost Tribes moved to the area around Mexico City where they impacted the pyramid-building culture already present.
22. Portions of the Lost Tribes then migrated north merging with other groups to become the Mound Builders in Ohio.

5750-1

17. With the injection of those of greater power in their activity in the land, during that period as would be called 3,000 years before the Prince of Peace came, those peoples that were of the Lost Tribes, a portion came into the land; infusing their activities upon the peoples from Mu in the southernmost portion of that called America or United States, and then moved on to the activities in Mexico, Yucatan, centralizing that now about the spots where the central of Mexico now stands, or Mexico City. Hence there arose through the age a different civilization, a MIXTURE again.

...

19. Ready for questions.

20. (Q) How did the Lost Tribe reach this country?
   (A) In boats.

---

23. Some Israelites escaped the captivity by fleeing to southwestern America from the West across the Pacific. They crossed through areas (perhaps utilizing islands) that were once a part of Mu. They established temples in the southwest. They are referred to as a "lost" or "strayed tribe."

2540-1

... the entity was in the own land of nativity during the early settlings; not America as known in history; but when there were the activities of these peoples that were dispersed by the carrying away of the children of promise into captivity.

The entity was among those born to those who escaped across the waters into what is now the southwestern portion of the entity's present land (America).

1434-1

32. Before that we find the entity was in the lands of the present nativity or sojourn in the present, during those periods when there were those peoples entering into the land now called the Yucatan - after leaving the Atlantean and Poseidon land.

33. The entity was among those peoples who journeyed to the farther West or North and West from the Yucatan land; and the entity there was a priestess, and of the children of the Law of One.

34. The joinings in activities there were for the attempts to establish with those peoples that had been a portion of the lost or strayed tribe, that came across from Lemuria; as well as with those that came from the lands of bondage by the Persians and those that later were called the Indo-Chinans - or those peoples from the mountain who raided the Indian land.

35. There the entity aided in establishing a new unison of activity, in what would now be called the Arizona land.

2540-1
44. Before that the entity was in the own land of nativity during the early settlings; not America as known in history, but when there were the activities of those peoples that were dispersed by the carrying away of the children of promise into captivity.

45. The entity was among those born to those who escaped across the waters into what is now the southwestern portion of the entity's present native land (America).

46. There the entity came in contact with those who were a part of the Atlantean civilization before it was broken up, and the entity was made a priestess - as in keeping with a combination of the old Mosaic teachings and those of Ax-Tell and the children of the Law of One.

---

24. The mound builders were a mixture of influences from Atlantis, Mu, Lost Tribes, and others.

1286-1
27. Before that we find the entity was in the land of the present nativity, during those periods when there were the spreadings of those teachings that had come from the lands from which those peoples came that were known as the Lost Tribes, as well as from Atlantis, Yucatan, the Inca, and the land of On [?]. [Og?]

28. They were portions of the entity's people then, in that part of the land now known as the central portion of Ohio, during the early portion of the Mound Builders.

---

25. The Norse made many trips to ancient America and actually settled here.
26. Some of the Norse merged with the mound builders.

583-3
10. .. for the entity, then, as we see, came into this country from the descendants of the Norse peoples who first landed and settled the Northeastern coast of this country, during that time. The entity then of strong physical forces and giving much to the aid of the peoples in establishing forts and the outposts of the peoples who joined later with that peoples in the country South of there, known as Mound Builders...

27. The location of the Norse settlement in America, Vinland, was placed in Rhode Island, Massachusetts, and Connecticut by Cayce.

28. Providence, Salem, and Newport are specifically named as modern cities where Vinland was located.

1450-1

21. Before this, then, we find there was the activity of the entity in the earth during those periods when there had been the many that had given their activity in the discovery of the lands to the west of the entity's land of nativity.

22. For the entity then was a Norseman, in those activities then known as Olson; and made the journeys with Eric and those who came to the Vinland or those portions now known as Connecticut, Massachusetts, Rhode Island

261-21

28. (Q) In Life Readings [566-1 and 628-1] of each of my two children it gives the previous appearances before this as having been in Vinland, in Providence or old Providence Town. Will you give the present name and location of this town?

(A) That which has been now incorporated into Salem and those surrounding territories is that of OLD Providence Town, while Providence and Provincetown are two separate or two others - yet all of this was once known as Vinland. For all those portions of the Cape Cod area, called now Providence and Newport and the Rhode Island area, area covered with vines - in Eric's time. While those activities as indicated are in the records there, in a portion of now Salem, Mass.

2377-1

26. Before that the entity was in the land of the present sojourn, during the early settlings in the land; during those periods of the activities in what is now known as Vinland, or the Rhode Island and Connecticut land.

2502-1

10. In the one before this we find among those peoples who first settled in the land then called Vineland, and now the coast now known as Connecticut. The entity then among the first as were born of those peoples settling there; came to an EARLY demise through the hardships suffered, yet GAINED in that experience, and in the name Olaief.

2124-3

9. In the one then before this we find in that period when there were the

journeyings of peoples in that of the spirit of adventure, when those peoples in the Norse land journeyed into those of the westward land. The entity then among those that came into the land in that portion of same now known as the Vinland, or about that place now known as Rhode Island, Connecticut ...

---

29. The Norse reached Montana in the 1500s via the Great Lakes. An artifact, a knife supposedly belonging to Eric the Red, was recovered in Wisconsin around 1940 that would prove this excursion. In addition, a Norse excursion reached Minnesota.

2157-1
16. Before this the entity was in the Norse land, and among those who were the daring, as the sailors; and the entity was Eric [See 2157-1, Par. R13 giving Norse incarnations for entire family.], as called through that experience; journeying to or settling in the land of its present nativity.

39. (Q) In the Norse land experiences, how often and in what years did I cross the ocean?
A) In 1552, 1509 and 1502.

40. (Q) What was accomplished in that life, either for my own country or for this country?
(A) In this country there were the settlements in the northwestern lands; portions even of Montana were reached by the entity, - because the entrance then was through the St. Lawrence, through the Lakes.

41. (Q) Are there any proofs to be found now in this country, that might prove it?
A) They have just been uncovered by a recent expedition there in Wisconsin!

42. (Q) What would I find there that belongs to me personally?
(A) Among the knives and stones that were found, one of those was Eric's!

3651-1
13. Before this the entity was in the Norse land, among those who journeyed into the greater western portion or near to the central portion of Minnesota in the present land of nativity, when Eric the Red was among those active there.

---

30. Cayce mentions the Five Great Nations and Chief Powhatan and the meeting in the "Octagon" by the Ohio River.

500-1

12. Before this we find the entity in the present land and among the peoples that were called natives of the land... The entity then was named Virginia, yet - in those associations - the name was changed to Alahoi (A-O-I) (?) by the chief Powhatan. And in those environs the entity grew to become chief among those that aided in the application of the surrounding environs to aid in the ills... The entity brought ease to many, aid to those that suffered with all characters of disorder or disturbance... And when there had been the activities in and among the chiefs of the five great nations, as they met in their pow wow within the Octagon (?), what is now known as the bank of the Ohio, the entity then acted as the counsel to those peoples as to how they might better themselves, even with their relationships to those peoples that later entered in to become the settlers of the land.

Appendix B
Press Release on the Collapse
of the Clovis Barrier

CHILEAN SITE VERIFIED
AS EARLIEST HABITATION OF AMERICAS;
FINDINGS SHOW MONTE VERDE DATES BACK 12,500 YEARS

Site May Fuel New Debate on the Peopling of the Americas

DALLAS — Human beings migrated to the Americas 1,300 years earlier than previously thought, pushing human habitation of the New World back to some 12,500 years ago, according to a team of eminent archaeologists who verified the antiquity of the Monte Verde archaeological site in Chile.

The Chilean site was excavated by a team led by Tom Dillehay of the University of Kentucky and the Universidad Austral de Chile from 1977 to 1985. The site was investigated Jan. 3-13, 1997 by a team of archaeologists sponsored by The Dallas Museum of Natural History, Susan and Claude Albritton, Lamar Norsworthy, the Holly Corporation and the National Geographic Society, which will feature the findings in an upcoming issue of its magazine. The archaeologists reported their unanimous conclusions today in Dallas.

"It's hard to overstate the importance of the team's consensus," said Alex Barker, Dallas Museum of Natural History curator of archaeology. "For 60 years, the Clovis-period entry of humans into the New World has withstood all challenges. Now the Monte Verde site establishes that humans arrived earlier."

The Clovis horizon, named after a distinctive fluted projectile point styling, was thought to mark the earliest spread of hunter-gatherers into North America at about 11,200 years ago, coinciding with the opening of an ice-free corridor from Asia to America.

Monte Verde, located 500 miles south of Santiago, has human artifacts as well as material never seen at early American sites: remnants of hide-covered huts; a chunk of animal meat, which DNA analyses indicate is mastodon; digging sticks, finely crafted tools of bone and tusk, and more than 700 stone tools; and, a child's footprint.

"I am fully convinced that both Monte Verde 1 (MV1) and MV2 (MV2 is the layer dating to at least 12,500 years ago; MV1 is a deeper and older layer) are cultural manifestations and push the time limit back further than previously thought," said Dennis Stanford, curator of North American Archaeology, Smithsonian Institution. "I suspect we'll start finding earlier sites coming out of the woodwork."

"The implications of Monte Verde are profound," said David Meltzer, professor of anthropology at Southern Methodist University. "While it's only a thousand years older than the previously accepted dates, its location 10,000 miles south of the Bering land bridge route that the first Americans took into the New World implies a fundamentally different history of human colonization of the Americas."

George Stuart, National Geographic's chief archaeologist and chairman of the Society's Committee for Research and Exploration, said, "All of the numerous pre-Clovis sites proposed through the decades have had a shadow over them. The Monte Verde conclusion is as definitive as archaeology gets."

The Dallas Museum of Natural History, located in Dallas' historic Fair Park, receives a third of a million visitors each year. In addition to the Monte Verde project, museum curators also are currently conducting archaeological projects in Texas and Louisiana, and paleontological projects in Texas, Wyoming and Colorado.

In addition to Dillehay and Barker, the team included:

- Jim Adovasio, Professor of Anthropology, Mercyhurst College;
- Robson Bonnichsen, Director, Center for The Study of the First American, Oregon State University;
- Dena Dincauze, Professor of Anthropology, University of Massachusetts;
- Donald Grayson, Professor of Anthropology, University of Washington;
- Vance Haynes, Professor of Anthropology, University of Arizona;
- David Meltzer, Professor of Anthropology, Southern Methodist University;
- Francisco Mena, Curator, Museo Chileno de Arte Precolombino;
- Lautaro Nunez, Research Associate, Smithsonian Institution; and,
- Dennis Stanford, Curator of North American Archaeology, Smithsonian Institution.

Index

About The Authors

Dr. Greg Little has a master's degree in psychology and doctorate in counseling from Memphis State University. He is a Nationally Certified Psychologist (NAMP) and has worked over 25 years in criminal justice agencies for dozens of states. He is author or co-author of 8 books and 17 workbooks dealing with the subject of moral behavior and substance abuse. He has also published several hundred articles in professional journals, newspapers, and magazines. He is an expert in brain processes and is author of a popular college textbook, *Psychopharmacology*. His interest in Native Americans began in the 1980s while considering the effects of rituals on brain processes.

John Van Auken is a former director of the Edgar Cayce organization (A.R.E). He is Editor of the monthly newsletter Living in the Light and author of many books, audiotapes, and videos, and is a columnist for *Alternate Perceptions Magazine*. He is author of many books on Cayce including *The Lost Hall of Records*. He's considered an expert in Egyptian, Maya, Hindu, Hebrew, and Christian mysticism, and is a skillful teacher of meditation — from kundalini to his unique "passage in consciousness." He is a popular speaker and leader of retreats, workshops, and tours to Egypt, Israel, and the Maya lands in Yucatan.

Dr. Lora Hunter Little, a long time member of ARE, has been a student of the Cayce readings and ancient American archaeology for over 20 years. Her interest in archaeology has led her to travel extensively to ancient sites throughout North and Central America. She writes a regular column on Cayce for the magazine *Alternate Perceptions* and coauthored the book *The Lost Hall of Records* with John Van Auken. She has had careers both as a psychological counselor and as a health care administrator in a large urban public health department. She is a qualified Fellow in the Bonny Method of Music Centered Psychotherapy and volunteers in a music services program she helped to found at a hospice in Memphis. Dr. Little, who has participated in a Search for God study group for over 10 years, is also codirector of music ministry and coordinator of scriptural study groups for her multicultural parish church.